Inspiration from the Garden

SUNFLOWER HOUSES

A Book for Children and Their Grown-Ups

by SHARON LOVEJOY

WORKMAN PUBLISHING · NEW YORK

I owe my publisher, Peter Workman, and my editor, Ruth Sullivan, a debt of gratitude for keeping the spirit of my first book, SUNFLOWER HOUSES, alive. Thank you just doesn't seem like enough to say to you both, but for what it is worth . . . THANK YOU!

My love and thanks always to my son, Noah W[III] Arnold, and my patient husband, Jeffrey Prostovich, for believing in me and providing unflagging love, loyalty, and devotion.

Heartfelt thanks to Virginia "Skippy" Shoemaker, the creator of the first sunflower house and one of the most delightful ladies I've ever known. Skippy and I would never have met had it not been for her daughter, Ginny Kirschenman, who shared the story of the sunflower house with me.

Finally, bouquets of thanks to all of you who contributed stories, games, and gardens to this book. Your floral traditions will continue to grow and flourish through the years.

DEDICATED TO

MY SON, NOAH

W[M.] ARNOLD,

WHO

REAWAKENED

IN ME THE JOY

AND PROMISE

OF LIFE

Foreword to the New Sunflower Houses

In 1991, when this book was released, I never anticipated that it would be received so lovingly. Like windborne seeds, the ideas from its pages traveled throughout the world, germinated, rooted deeply, and flourished. Now, in this new edition, the spirit lives—and the floral traditions and garden play of our ancestors will reach new generations of readers and nature lovers.

I first thought of this as a collection just for children, but the letters soon proved me wrong. An 80-year-old gardener from Kentucky wrote, "If it is indeed true that it is never too late to be a child at heart, this will be my best spring ever. I am going to plant my first sunflower house." Letters came from kids as young as three to grown-ups 96 years young. Educators, camp counselors, church groups, horticultural therapists, and 4-H leaders shared the joy of newfound or rediscovered gardening pleasures. I want to thank the thousands of readers who wrote such inspiring letters. I always expected the tide of correspondence to stop, but with the publication of my newest book, *Roots, Shoots, Buckets & Boots*, the letters and requests for copies of *Sunflower Houses* increased. Because of your interest, *Sunflower Houses* is being reprinted for the tenth time with its new family at Workman Publishing.

My book appeared at a time when people realized that many of our kids are estranged from nature. A movement began in the early 1990s to design and plant community, botanical, and schoolyard gardens specifically for children—our most precious and valuable resource.

Whatever your age, welcome to the pages of *Sunflower Houses*. May you always remember that the most joyous and important experiences in life are not to be bought, but grown and nurtured in our homes and gardens.

I wish you many garden pleasures and magical memories.

Sharon Lovejoy

Table of Contents

A note from the author

My first memories of home are of a tiny redwood cottage tucked into a vale in my Grandmother Lovejoy's garden. The vine-covered house was surrounded on all sides by old apricot and peach trees, and the lawn was carpeted with carnations. Raspberries and boysenberries grew along a wall, providing a secret nesting place for the night-singing mockingbirds.

My favorite haven in the garden was my playhouse—a pair of ancient guava trees that formed a huge, light-pierced tent with branches that swept the ground.

The pathway that led from Grandmother's house to mine was flanked with hollyhocks as tall as trees. Giant bumblebees nestled into the pink recesses of the blooms, while darting hummingbirds danced from petal to petal looking for unoccupied flowers.

The main spirit of our garden was a gigantic, mottled old sycamore tree with limbs so strong and comforting I would often curl up on the lower one to read or to watch for figures in the clouds. Grandmother's swing sat under the sycamore, and on sunny afternoons—with a gentle wind stirring the papery leaves—we would sip cream teas and eat sugar and

GRANDMOTHER

ABIGAIL BAKER

LOVEJOY,

WHO STARTED

IT ALL...

*In Grandmother's garden
the hollyhocks*

---

*Row upon row lifted
wreathed stalks*

---

*With bloom of purple, of
pearly white,*

---

*Of close-frilled yellow, of
crimson bright.*

---

*In Grandmother's garden
the roses red*

---

*Grew in a long, straight
garden bed,*

---

*By yellow roses with small,
close leaves;*

---

*And yuccas—we called
them Adams and Eves!*

Threaded with fringes of
fairy weaves;

———

By marigolds in velvet
browns,

———

And heart's-ease in their
splendid gowns;

———

Primrose, waiting the
twilight hours.

———

Touch-me-nots, and
gilliflowers.

———

Was it October, or June,
or May

———

Grandmother's garden was
always gay.

Sara Andrew Shafer

cinnamon sandwiches, and Grandmother would teach me about the flowers, trees, and animals of her garden.

On the day my Grandmother Lovejoy died, I ran to the shelter of my guava tree playhouse and closed myself inside for hours. I could hear the mockingbird's young in the wall of berries, the wind rustling through our sycamore leaves, and the humming of the bumblebees working in the hollyhocks. I couldn't understand how the person who had given me this life could have gone, leaving these smaller things behind, unchanged.

What I have learned through the ensuing decades is that my Grandmother Lovejoy lives on. Her stories and teachings have enriched my life and the life of my son Noah for years. Now I pass this treasure on to you, and hope that you in turn will share the joys with the children in your life. Gentle lessons are waiting to be taught—and you, my friend, are the one to teach them.

Sharon Lovejoy
Cambria-Pines-by-The-Sea

Introduction

For the past dozen years, I have earned my living by growing, selling, and teaching about herbs and flowers. My passion for plants started when I was a youngster and was lovingly taught about gardens by my Grandmother Lovejoy—a teacher, naturalist, and one of the best gardeners ever.

My earliest and fondest memories are of endless days of summer play: hollyhock dolls under the peach tree, necklaces of rosebuds, wreaths of clover, daisy chains, and other simple pastimes Grandmother shared with me.

As I grew up, I realized that my early garden freedom had somehow given form and meaning to my whole life. My love for plants became the nucleus of my lifestyle, and I chose to devote myself to creating a beautiful community garden and to teaching about gardens and plants to people of all ages. At first I wanted to emphasize classes for children, but found, to my amazement, that adults became as animated and curious as the children. One of my oldest and most delightful students said, "I wanted to come and learn about all this before I got too old. I'm just 96 now."

I started thinking about what a garden had done for me, and to wonder about other's experiences in gardens. And so I began questioning people. "Can you remember any garden games or things you learned about plants and flowers when you were a child?" I would ask. Most times I could immediately tell if the person I was questioning had a memory to share. Generally there would be a start of recognition, a quick smile, and a nod, "Yes, I sure do, let me tell you about making trumpet vine dolls, acorn tops, and walnut sailboats."

All summer long we made belts, crowns, garlands - necklaces of tiny, perfect, pink rosebuds...

From my 7th summer

GENTLE

———

LESSONS

———

ARE

———

WAITING

———

TO BE

———

TAUGHT

In 1983, I ran ads in *The Business of Herbs* and *Pot Pourri from Herbal Acres.* I asked people to share stories with me about their childhood experiences in gardens or with flowers. I received many responses to the ads, and I began interviewing people and collecting historical materials, garden plans, poetry, riddles, garden lore, and flower crafts. A true gleaning from hundreds of childhood memories!

In 1986, I started sketching some ideas for a very personal garden book that would incorporate my drawings of flower and plant projects, poetry, history, and first-person stories. That year my husband Jeff bought me an Apple Computer (which I promptly named Sarah Orne Jewett after one of my favorite authors) and said, "Get on with it, Sharon! Write your book." So I got on with it!

An author's note in an old book I found in Castine, Maine, a few years ago sums it up for me. "I can never repay the hollyhock the debt of gratitude I owe for the happy hours it furnished to me in my childhood." I feel that way, too, but perhaps my book will be a beginning.

Home

I WANT TO HAVE A LITTLE HOUSE
WITH SUNLIGHT ON THE FLOOR,

A CHIMNEY WITH A ROSY HEARTH,
AND LILACS BY THE DOOR;

WITH WINDOWS LOOKING EAST AND WEST,
AND A CROOKED APPLE TREE,

AND ROOM BESIDE THE GARDEN FENCE
FOR HOLLYHOCKS TO BE!

NANCY BIRD TURNER

A Child's Garden

Working and teaching in the gardens at Heart's Ease, I have always tried to note which plants most attract children and why. Some plants act almost as magnets, drawing children back again and again.

What are the secret qualities that make certain plants favorites of children? Well, my friend Georgie (who has been an avid gardener for nearly 80 years!) says, "What children really need is to have a lot of things that grow fast." She's right. Kids want to see some sort of quick response to the work and care they've showered on their piece of land. Also important: Personality (faces in a pansy, sunflower, or snapdragon); fragrance (once thought to be the very soul of the flowers); texture (woolly lamb's ear); and color—riotous, vibrant color.

Here are some of the plants I would choose for a children's garden, but remember not to limit yourself to just this list. The key to keeping children's sense of wonder and enjoyment alive is to let them make choices. Take the children to nurseries and let them search through the seed packets and flats of flowers for ones that twang their heartstrings. Allow them the freedom in their own gardens that they may not yet have in the rest of their lives.

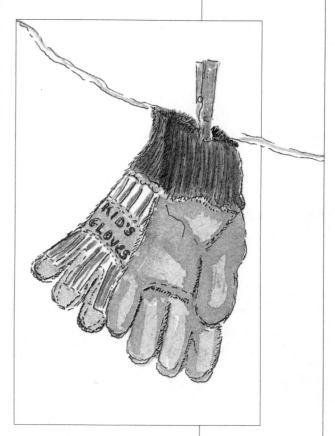

Perennials

BALLOON FLOWER
Platycodon grandiflorus

Just plain fascinating.

BLEEDING HEART
Dicentra spectabilis

For fairy gondolas or earrings; a perfect flower for pressing.

CHINESE LANTERN
Physalis alkekengi

These brilliant orange globes look like real Chinese lanterns—perfect for a doll tea party. Exceptionally easy to grow and will self-sow prolifically.

COLUMBINE
Aquilegia spp.

Also known as Little Doves or Granny's Bonnets, these are the fairy shoes of flower dolls.

DAY LILY
Hemerocallis spp.

These are colorful and easy to grow, provided you have lots of sun. Children can gather the blossoms and buds and cook them. The flower blossoms make skirts for dolls.

**DOLLAR PLANT,
MONEY PLANT,
OR HONESTY**
Lunaria redeviva,
or *L. annua* (a biennial)

This makes play money, play dishes, gypsy jewelry. Easy to grow, and self-sows with abandon.

PLANT RED FLOWERS FOR ME

FALSE DRAGONHEAD *Physostegia virginiana*	Kids can twist this into all sorts of funny positions and it will maintain the pose for hours (it is also referred to as Obedient Plant).
LADY'S MANTLE *Alchemilla spp.*	Children love the dew diamond in the middle of the leaf (a gift from the fairies, no doubt).
PINK *Dianthus spp.*	"Fresh pinks cast incense on the air, In fluttering garments fringed and rare." The scent remains in your memory forever. The petals are edible, and kids love to strew them in salads. Carnations (from the word coronet, and they can be made into coronets) are in this family, too. It's fun to string pinks together to make garlands and jewelry.
POPPY *Papaver orientale*	They make excellent dancing dolls on their stems. Children use them as water ballerinas, and they are fun to watch opening and closing (sometimes we have helped open them). The seed pods are like tiny rattles or pepper shakers.
STOCK *Matthiola incana*	They have a sweet scent and are good in sand castles and in a moonlight or flower-dial garden. There are also annual stocks that are easy to start from seed.

The annuals we plant each Spring—

. . .

They perish in the Fall;

. . .

Biennials die the second year,

. . .

Perennials, not at all!

SUNFLOWER

Helianthus annuus

Sunflowers have true personalities, they attract birds and bees, they are the framework for our sunflower house, and the seeds are yummy. The mature flower heads can be harvested and used as birdfeeders. No children's garden can be considered complete without the whimsical presence of sunflowers.

I Meant To Do My Work Today

I meant to do my work today—
But a brown bird sang in the apple tree,
And a butterfly flitted across the field,
And all the leaves were calling me.
And the wind went sighing over the land,
Tossing the grasses to and fro,
And a rainbow held out its shining hand—
So what could I do but laugh and go?

· · · · · · · · · · · · *Richard Le Gallienne*

Annuals

CORNFLOWER, BACHELOR'S BUTTON
Centaurea cyanus

A good garland flower, and their rich blue and purple colors are jewels.

COSMOS
Cosmos bipinnatus

Brilliant and easy to grow, they attract lots of butterflies. My son Noah chose cosmos out of hundreds of plants in a nursery. They became his flower and were always planted outside our front door.

FOUR O'CLOCK
Mirabilis jalapa

These plants amaze me every day when they open at about 4 p.m., and at night they attract the wonderful, fascinating hummingbird moth.

CALENDULA
Calendula officinalis

The old-fashioned marigold. This is one of the plants that can be held under the chin to see if you like butter. Individual flower petals can be used in salads and in rice dishes. Sit your child down at a table and let him add petals to dishes as you cook. These flowers are easy to grow.

LOVE-IN-A-MIST
Nigella damascena

Its seed pods are wonderful—the tiny seeds shake out like pepper, and the pods can be used as teacups.

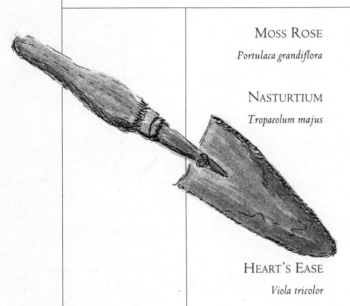

MOSS ROSE
Portulaca grandiflora

Brilliant and easy to grow, they belong in the flower-dial garden.

NASTURTIUM
Tropaeolum majus

The Elizabethans called them yellow lark's heels. These fiery charmers attract hummingbirds and children. With their peppery flavor, they can be used in salads or stuffed with cream cheese; children love to fill up the blooms and giggle as they eat them. The blossoms can be used in flower crowns and in leis and as hats on flower dolls.

HEART'S EASE
Viola tricolor

Also called johnny-jump-ups. Who can resist those faces? Teach the children how to make heart's ease dolls.

SNAPDRAGON
Antirrhinum majus

Along with hollyhocks, pansies, and sunflowers, this is one of the "personality" flowers. Snapdragons are great for hiding secret messages, making clip-on earrings, having snapdragon battles, or using like paper clips on each placecard at a child's birthday party.

SWEET ALYSSUM
Lobularia maritima

It spreads like a delicate carpet of snow, and children love the tiny, almost miniature bouquet blossoms. These flowers, like the tiny blossoms of thyme, fit perfectly into a child's fairy garden.

Sweet Pea
Lathyrus odoratus

A little more difficult to cultivate, but worth the try just for the colors if not for the fantastic scent that children of all ages love!

Verbena
Verbena × hybrida

Colorful and easy to grow, it attracts skippers and other butterflies.

Zinnia
Zinnia elegans

Easy to grow and colorful, they also attract the skippers and other butterflies that bring so much life into a garden. A child-sized variety is fittingly called Thumbelina.

the • perfect • nursery!

Buy your eggs in the old-fashioned egg carton. • Tear off the lid, fill the egg holes with good potting soil. • Plant the seeds in each egg hole. • Water daily. • When the seedlings are about an inch high, gently tear or cut each egg compartment from the carton. • Each seedling may be planted still in its cardboard egg holder. • The cardboard will quickly disintegrate.

Biennials

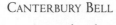

CANTERBURY BELL *Campanula medium*	Whole quadrilles of dolls with canterbury bell skirts can be formed on twigs and lined up for dancing.
ENGLISH DAISY *Bellis perennis*	Easy to grow, can be made into daisy chains, daisy grandmothers, garlands, and 'he-loves-me, he-loves-me-not' charms.
FORGET-ME-NOT *Myosotis sylvatica*	Soft, green, mouse-ear leaves with sky blue eyes. These are grown easily in very shady spots and children love to use them in miniature bouquets.
HOLLYHOCK *Alcea rosea*	The all-purpose flower. They attract hummingbirds and bumblebees, they make great dolls, fairy goblets, and leis, and my favorite, firefly lanterns! The seed pods make good play money, too.
SWEET WILLIAM *Dianthus barbatus*	An old-fashioned flower that is extremely easy to grow and can even take a little neglect; it loves to be picked for bouquets or all kinds of flower projects.

H e r b s

GARDEN CRESS
Lepidium sativum

A fast growing herb that gives children a feeling of instant success. Have the child write his or her name in cress seed, and watch it grow.

FENNEL
Foeniculum vulgare

A must for the back wall in your garden. This hardy plant provides food for the caterpillars of swallowtail butterflies. The caterpillars are incredibly beautiful and fascinating and the kids will watch the brilliantly mosaicked "pillars" eating their way from one branch to another. Fennel is a nibbler plant. Kids love to pick the tender, dark new growth and chew it like gum. It makes a soothing tea for upset stomachs, but best of all, it helps bring more butterflies into our world.

LEMON VERBENA
Aloysia triphylla

When children visit my garden, they always return again and again to the lemon verbena. When they leave, their pockets are usually stuffed full of the aromatic lemon-scented leaves. They know they can dry them for potpourri or use them in tea or just keep them in their pockets and pull them out for sweet smelling during the day.

MINT
Mentha spp.

Easy to propagate from cuttings, its tangy, sweet leaves are great in teas, sachets, potpourris, and dream pillows. Kids just love to chew them. My favorite is the orange-bergamot variety.

SCENTED GERANIUM
Pelargonium spp.

Easy to grow from cuttings and tolerant of drought, they make a good houseplant for children. The leaves, smelling of rose, apple, lemon, mint, nutmeg, or dozens of other scents, are intriguing to kids as they hop from one to another and try to determine what they are smelling. Flowers can be used in cookies, teas, cakes, icings, syrups, fruit sorbets, fruit salads, and vinegars. Leaves are excellent in homemade potpourri mixes.

WOOLLY LAMB'S EAR
Stachys byzantina

A touch-me, rub-me-on-your-cheek, and keep-me plant. Children spend lots of time at our woolly lamb's ear patch. I allow them to pick leaves and save them as bookmarks or to mail them off in letters. They are even more fascinated when I tell them that in olden days they were used as bandages!

MY GRASS IS GREEN

MY SKY IS BLUE—

I SING A SONG

OF SPRING FOR YOU!

Roses

Perfect,

doll-sized

teapots can

be made with

a rosehip,

stuck with a

thorn for

a spout.

Roses are not easy for children to grow or to play around, but they really are a must near a child's garden area. My favorite for ease of care, fragrance, and plump, beautiful rosehips, is the old-fashioned *Rosa rugosa*.

Children love to eat rose petals in rosy-cakes, they rub them on their lips as lipstick, or use them as fragile, tiny note paper for rose-notes to a special friend. Pea pod boats must have sails of rose petals or rose leaves! Perfect, doll-sized teapots can be made with a rosehip, stuck with a thorn for a spout. Necklaces can be strung with rosehips, and rosehip dolls can be made. You can brew up a cup of rosehip or rose petal tea for your tired little ones at the end of a long, hard day of play in the garden.

In California there is an Indian tribe that calls roses "Ska Pash Wee", which means, "Mean old lady, she sticks me!" Remember that rose thorns can be mean, so plant them out of the children's play area; but do plant them.

Vegetables

Carrots
Daucus carota

The minis (called Little Fingers) are the best for children and they can easily be grown in a container. Kids love to pull the little finger-sized carrots and eat them raw. They're a hundred times better than the giant, woody, tasteless ones you get in a market. A swag of carrots can be hung on your door with ribbon to help greet the Easter bunny, or a bunny tussie-mussie can be made with carrots and radishes, surrounded by the herbs of your choice and beribboned like a floral tussie-mussie.

Decorative Gourds of all types
Cucurbita spp.

They can be used as bird houses, dippers, bowls, doll coaches, storage containers, baby rattles, false hen setting eggs, pretend dinosaur eggs, and Christmas tree ornaments. Young, tiny gourds can be made into gourd dolls. A variety called the spaghetti gourd or squash is a delicious, edible oddity as tasty as the pasta for which it was named.

Easter Egg Eggplant
Solanum melongena

An aptly named ornamental edible that can be grown in containers. Fruit is satin-white and egg-shaped.

Fraises des bois, or Alpine Strawberries
Fragaria vesca

Not a vegetable, but these should have a place somewhere in your garden! The kids call them fairy berries at Heart's Ease and they head straight for the berry borders to fill up on the tasty little gems. The love children feel for these berries cannot be equated with their size!

Painted Lady Beans
Phaseolus coccineus var.

Heirloom British pole beans that love to clamber over trellises, arches, and teepees. This bean flowers prolifically and produces beautiful coral and white flowers with a sweet, light bean flavor—yes, the blooms are edible and can be used in salads, sandwiches, and as a great snack.

Pumpkins
Cucurbita pepo

Both the mini and giant varieties are great personality plants to have in a garden. Pumpkins can be scratched with a nail, and as they grow the etched name or message grows.

Radishes
Raphanus sativus

They are so easy to grow that they make children feel like master gardeners. Several seed companies now have a variety of radishes called "Easter Egg". These delicious round radishes are colored lavender, red, pink, and white. What a surprising treat for kids!

TOOLS

OF THE

FARMER'S

TRADE

SCARLET RUNNER BEANS *Phaseolus coccineus* var.	Fast growing, attracts hummingbirds, and makes excellent teepees. The red flowers are edible.
STRAWBERRY POPCORN AND MINIATURE INDIAN CORN *Zea mays* var.	These are kid- sized. The strawberry popcorn produces a truly strawberry looking head of corn that can be popped (if you have the heart). The mini Indian corns are loved by children because of their charm and tiny size; they make wonderful miniature corn husk dolls. 'Pretty Pops' has confetti-colored kernels of red, blue, orange, black, yellow, and purple that show white when popped. The ears are a great Thanksgiving or autumn table decoration.
TOMATOES *Lycopersicum* spp.	These can make children feel as if they are really accomplishing something. 'Currant' tomatoes are pea sized and would be perfect in a miniature vegetable garden. 'Yellow Marble' is, you guessed it, the size of marbles.

Vines

CUP AND SAUCER VINE
Cobaea scandens

A ready-made tea set. Flowers open yellow-green and age to a rich purple.

HONEYSUCKLE
Lonicera japonica

This sometimes pesky vine has the sweet-tasting flower children love to suck. The vine attracts hummingbirds and the long, supple branches are easily woven into baskets and crowns. The flowers can be stuck inside each other, forming a continuous chain of blooms. Children wear the strings of blooms as crowns, belts, and necklaces.

HOPS
Humulus lupulus

Fast growing; so fast, in fact, that people often place bets on how much a vine will grow during the hot summer nights.

MOON FLOWER
Ipomoea alba

Attracts night moths, including the fascinating hummingbird moth; it is fun to watch the flower as it opens at night.

MORNING GLORY
Ipomoea purpurea

Certain varieties attract hummingbirds, and the 'Heavenly Blue' is the roof of the sunflower playhouse (page 61).

TRUMPET VINE
Campsis radicans

Attracts hummingbirds, makes great dolls and bubble blowers.

A Giant Garden

I like to spend my "free" time reading seed catalogues. Some great ones are available, and I think I get them all (my postman knows I do). One of my very favorites is the Seeds Blum catalogue from Jan Blum of Boise, Idaho. It is chock full of information, ideas, and inspiration. Thus sprouted the idea for Jack-In-The-Beanstalk's Giant garden.

If you have a rough-and-tumble child who is easily bored, tantalize him (or her) with a garden that could be the biggest, best, most unique one in town. Remember, this garden needs plenty of space for the plants to roam—and roam they will!

A tomato called 'Delicious' is listed in the Guinness Book of World Records as the largest tomato ever grown—6 pounds and 8 ounces. Wow! A variety of pumpkin called the 'Cinderella' is large

WE'VE LAUGHED round the corn heap
With hearts all in tune,
Our chair a broad pumpkin—
Our lantern the moon.
Telling tales of the fairy who travelled like steam
In a pumpkin shell coach
With two rats for her team.

John Greenleaf Whittier

IMAGINE VEGETABLES LIKE THESE:
• • • • •

*Big Moon pumpkins
(400 pounds)*
• •

*Oxheart tomatoes
(4 pounds each)*
• •

*Scarlet Imperial Long carrots
(3 feet long)*
• •

*Giant Perfection muskmelon
(15-18 pounds)*
• •

*Grey Stripe sunflower
(10 feet tall)*
• •

*Scarlet runner beans
(12" pods on plants that can
be 30 feet tall)*
• •

enough for a person to ride in! The 'Cinderella' has reached nearly 500 pounds, another world's record.

Take a playful approach to designing your giant garden. Don't just plant plain rows—use trellises (how about old ladders?), teepees and arches. Children need to be able to play among the plants and to interact with them. Children need to feel the energy of the plants as they grow—in fact, it's something everybody needs, not just children.

"You can't just plant regular vegetables and expect them to become giants," Jan Blum says. The varieties mentioned here are genetically larger. There are some tricks to growing the biggest, but they are just tricks. Some people pick off all but one ear of corn, or one pumpkin, in order to allow all of the growth to go to one, special vegetable. Some people sow seed on piles of manure and compost and actually milk-feed the plants! But the most important thing for growing any kind of healthy plant is good soil!

Walla Walla onion
(1½ pounds)
••

Italian parsley (3 feet tall)
••

Lagenaria summer squash
(2-3 feet long)
••

Zwaan Jumbo cabbage
(20-35 pounds)
••

Aconcagua pepper
(12 inches)
••

Armenian cucumber
(3 feet long)
••

Crimson Long radish
(1 foot long)
••

THE SOIL

Teach

IS THE

children

PLANT'S

that:

DINNER!

The Girls

At my home I have a 4 feet x 8 feet worm box. Yes, you read it right, a worm box. We fondly refer to our worms as "the girls". I often ask for leftovers from restaurants for my girls, though this is sometimes

puzzling to waitresses who ask, "You mean you are taking your soggy, left-over salad home to your daughters?"

My worm box is very simply constructed of common cinder blocks stacked three high, with one of the tiers of blocks below ground level (we didn't want any runaways). My husband cut two pieces of plywood which sit side by side on top for a lid. I use one side of the box one week and then switch over to the other.

I got my start of red earth worms from my gardening friend George Kryder, who feels that "the girls" really love and thrive on leftover bread and cake and cold pasta. I started with one bucket of girls

"Sunshine and water,

Love and good soil,

Weed it and feed it,

Harvest your toil."

and found that soon I was the mother of millions. The girls feast on my kitchen refuse and shredded clippings and within about a ten-day period, they are able to consume vast quantities of food, pass it through their digestive systems, and produce rich, thick, chocolaty castings, which are like gold for the plants.

My worm box is clean and odorless (I keep it covered because the robins and the raccoons consider it their private dessert tray). I water the girls often (they like their living quarters moist) and feed them daily, and once a week we take a pitchfork and turn them and remove about a wheelbarrow full of "gold" and girls for our garden. Our small box has been the

parent to many other worm boxes in our town, and everyone is happy with this thrifty and organic solution to a sometimes overwhelming garbage problem. Then there is the satisfaction of working with the girls—so quiet and industrious.

A Floral Clock Garden

Years ago, I read a story about a floral "clock", called "The Garden of Hours". It was created by the great botanist Carl Linnaeus at Hammersby in northern Sweden. In trying to find information about the clock, I wrote to the Linnaean Society in London, England.

The society librarian and archivist kindly sent me a photocopy of the clock as given in Linnaeus' *Philosophia Botanica* of 1755. The clock, the archivist said, is only of academic interest to us because it was designed for latitude 60° north. Thus, it would not work accurately in the United States.

Linnaeus was obsessed with the idea of his flower clock, or "Watch of Flora", as he often referred to it. His watch was composed of forty-six flowers that opened and closed at predictable times through the hours of the day.

I kept mulling over the idea of a flower clock in a children's garden. What a great way to teach children about the characteristics of flowers. By observing opening and closing and rain and sleep behavior, a child could learn about the individuality and miracle of each plant.

I began collecting information on the opening and closing times of plants. The following information comes from my own field work and the writings of botanists of the early 1800s. From it, I designed a child's flower dial that grew first in my mind, then on paper. Finally, it flourished in the soil. Choose from among the plants I've listed those that will do best in your climate. Opening and closing times will vary greatly from one locale to another, so observe your plants carefully, and transplant as necessary!

First, pace off a circle, from a few to ten feet across. Outline your clock circle with rocks and then divide it into segments just like the face of a clock. Run a line of rocks through the center of each segment to separate the times into a.m. and p.m. Put a post two to three feet tall in the middle of the circle or a sundial on a pedestal for a nice focal point.

You can outline your clock garden with a suitable edging plant such as box, germander, or a small lavender such as 'Hidcote' or 'Munstead'. Choose something short and compact that will not shade the other plants.

FLORAL SUN DIAL
How well the skilful gardener drew • Of flowers and herbs this dial new... • And as it works, the industrious bee • Computes its time as well as we! • How could such sweet and wholesome hours • Be reckoned but with herbs and flowers!
Andrew Marvell

Twas a lovely thought

2:00 a.m.

The fragile, folded purple Convolvulus shakes out her silky skirts.

3:00 a.m.

The Egyptian Waterlily and Goatsbeard open slowly just as the Campions are calling it a day.

4:00 a.m.

Spiderwort greets the day just as the beautiful, sky-blue Flax opens its twinkling eyes.

5:00 a.m.

Chicory is also an early riser. In olden days, chicory was called Ragged Sailors or Miss-go-to-bed-at-noon. That name makes it easy to remember when it goes to sleep.

6:00 a.m.

Morning Glories and also Day Lily, Iceland Poppy, Hawkweed, and Cape Marigold bloom between 5:00 and 6:00. Dandelions awaken early, too, but you probably won't want to plant them in your garden!

to mark the hours,

7:00 a.m.

Madwort, African Marigold, St. Bernard Lily, White Water Lily (find an old tub and fill it with water for this one), and Fig Marigolds begin to open.

8:00 a.m.

We can look for the friendly greeting of the Scarlet Pimpernel and the Fringed Pinks. If it is a cloudy day, the Scarlet Pimpernel will not open. In olden days, it was called Poor-man's-weatherglass because it always closed before a storm.

9:00 a.m.

Marigolds, Tulips, Ice Plant, Pink Sandwort, Chickweed, Mallow, Moss Roses and Gazanias look sunward. Dandelion closes at 9 a.m., as do the Water Lilies.

10:00 a.m.

California Poppies and Golden Stars are fully open. Evening Primrose has changed from white to rose to bright pink as the limp, silken flowers close.

11:00 a.m.

Star-of-Bethlehem closes, as do the common Sowthistles lurking along the borders of the garden. Passion Flowers awaken and Sweet Peas embrace the day. What sleepyheads!

12:00 noon

The Chicory is already retiring and the Pinks begin dozing off as the Goatsbeard quietly folds away. The wild Daisies (or day's eyes) are opening.

1:00 p.m.

There's a hush over the garden during the hour after midday, while open flowers continue to follow the sun, and later bloomers wait for the heat of noon to pass.

2:00 p.m.

Scarlet Pimpernel is getting sleepy and the weary Moonflower is preparing for bed time. Pinks join the Moonflower in slumber. Tulips and Daisies are at their fullest.

3:00 p.m.

Vesper Iris opens briefly, a lavender haze of small flowers. Field Marigolds, red Sand Spurry, Ice Plant, Hawkbit, Fig Marigold, and Pink Sandwort call it a day.

4:00 p.m.

Four-o'clocks, called the Marvel of Peru, rise at, you guessed it, four o'clock! Cape Marigold, Madwort and St. Bernard's Lily drift off to sleep.

5:00 p.m.

Evening Primrose, and Jimson Weed begin their debut at 5 p.m. I have read stories and poems about the opening of the Evening Primrose, but I have never been able to catch it in action as Keats must have when he wrote that he was "startled by the leap of buds into ripe flowers." I once heard a child refer to the luminous, fragile blooms as "fairy tents". Cat's Ear closes, and all of the Water Lilies are napping. Buttercup's glow is folded away for the evening.

6:00 p.m.

The Evening Primrose is in full glory. One species of Primrose, *Oenothera hookeri*, opens with "patens of bright gold", as Margaret Armstrong said, shining through the deepening shadows. Nottingham Catchfly scatters white stars across the garden floor, as Honeysuckle opens. As the sun sets for the day, the beautiful, fragrant, white Moon Flower with its ghostly bloom opens slowly and scents the garden with a haunting clove-like fragrance. Grow the elegant Moon Flower at the edge of your clock, perhaps on a low fence or trellis. In olden days, it was common for the whole family to sit on the porch waiting for the opening of this striking bloom. Quietly, they watched as the long white buds moved almost imperceptibly and then the great, white, starfaced flower opened slowly to release its fragrance and welcome the visits of the giant hummingbird moth (a favorite of every child!).

7:00 p.m.

The Iceland Poppy closes as the white Evening Campion awakens. This night-bloomer attracts many interesting night-flying moths. Sweet White Tobacco "...wakes and utters her fragrance In a garden sleeping" (Edna St. Vincent Millay).

8:00 p.m.

The tawny Day Lily slumbers as one of my favorites, the night-scented Stock, unfolds its small purple flowers. In olden days this inconspicuous plant was called the Melancholy Gilliflower because it looks so sad during daylight hours.

9:00 p.m.

Moon Flower should be fully opened by now, joined quietly by Sweet Rocket, often called Daughter-of-the-Evening because she only releases her scent after the sun is down. Postage Stamp Plant, so-called because of its fringed flower petals, awakens in the coolness of evening. When the flowers open, the air is permeated with the smell of almonds and vanilla.

10:00 p.m. to Midnight

Between 10 p.m. and midnight the strange pageant of the Night-Blooming Cereus begins and ends. This regal beauty is called Queen-of-the-Night—you'll soon understand why! I remember being allowed to stay up way past bedtime so that I could watch the Queen awakening. Brilliant Moss Rose prepares for sleep.

1:00 a.m.

Just as in the hour after noon, a hush falls over the garden.

*Shall I sing of
happy hours
Numbered by opening
and closing flowers?*

HARTLEY COLERIDGE

Remember that these hours will probably not be just right for your garden. Some of the sleeping and waking will be up to you to watch and record. You may wish to find other plants to tuck into your clock garden and you may need to move some of the suggested plants from one time area to another.

Flowers often take short naps during the day. You must go outside and watch quietly. Sometimes when the sun goes behind a cloud the scarlet pimpernel and poppies may tuck away for a bit. Some flowers close to protect their pollen from being washed off by an unexpected storm, so they may close many times during the day. Take time to really look at how the flowers sleep. Some bend their heads; others, like oxalis, turn into little tent or umbrella shapes. Look at the tight petals of the California poppy. It is called Dormidera, little sleepy head. Can you see why? So much is going on in the quiet, green world of plants!

YOU MUST

Flowers often

GO OUTSIDE

take short naps

AND WATCH

during the day.

QUIETLY.

A Good Word for the Bugs

I think it is about time for someone to speak up for all of the good bugs out there! I am always startled when I have a group of children in our garden and hear one shout with fright at the approach of an innocent insect. I have to laugh and point out the size difference, asking, "How would you feel if some huge, lumbering thing came walking toward you and you were just a tiny spider?"

Children fear what they do not understand. A good case in point was the unreasonable terror I felt as a child in a garden full of dragonflies! As soon as the dragonfly was explained to me, the fear disappeared.

Take the time to introduce your child (and yourself) to the lady bird beetles, praying mantises, and other interesting and beneficial bugs who feed on the larvae and adults of destructive insects. Hosting a healthy population of these friendly critters can help make your garden a thriving, pesticide-free environment. You'll be happy they chose to call your garden home.

Emily's Kinder Garden

I'm always especially happy to receive my mail when I spy the handwriting of my friend Jane Hogue, The Prairie Pedlar, gardener extraordinaire, and mother extraordinaire! Her letters are always beautiful and inspirational and this one about her daughter Emily's kinder-garden was exceptionally so.

Emily's garden was begun the summer before she was old enough to go to school, and before she knew her ABCs. But she learned them quickly and in the most enchanting manner possible—she learned by planting and taking care of her own tiny garden filled with plants from A to Z.

Jane hoped that in caring for the garden Emily would learn not only her ABCs, but that she would learn to identify the flowers by association. "For example," Jane wrote, "C is for cockscomb that looks just like the comb of the rooster; D is for daisy— 'He loves me, he loves me not'; L is for lamb's ear, which feels just like the real thing; R is for rose—we included a ring of mulch around the miniature rose bush, assuming the garden creatures might want to play 'Ring Around the Rosy'; and S is for sunflower— nature's birdfeeder."

A
ASTER

B
BACHELOR'S BUTTON

C
COCKSCOMB

D
DAISY

E
EMILIA

F
FORGET-ME-NOT

G
GLADIOLUS

H
HOLLYHOCK

I
IRIS

J
JOHNNY-JUMP-UP

K
KALE

L
LAMB'S-EAR

M
MARIGOLD

N

NASTURTIUM

O

OBEDIENT PLANT

P

PETUNIA

Q

QUEEN-ANNE'S-LACE

R

ROSE

S

SUNFLOWER

T

TANSY

U

URSINIA

V

VERBENA

W

WORMWOOD

X

XERANTHEMUM

Y

YARROW

Z

ZINNIA

Emily's garden was laid out in two tiers and snuggled up against the side of Jane's flower drying room. Forming a background to the garden was a friendly line of sunflowers. Each flower and letter of the alphabet was marked by a decorated slate displaying both the letter and the flower. What better way to learn your ABCs and flowers?

In Emily's garden, the letter U was represented by "Unions". Yes, you read right, Emily spells onions "unions", and if you say the word aloud, she is pretty close to right.

For U in my kinder-garden, I chose Ursinia, which is a South African plant in the aster family. Ursinia produces a bright orange daisy and blooms profusely from late summer to the first freeze.

Tyler's Barnyard Garden

Tyler Hogue is a true Iowa farm boy. He loves to spend his daylight hours outdoors exploring and working in his own "Barnyard Garden".

Young boys love tools of all kinds, and Tyler is no exception. Fascinated by an old plow sitting out in the garden, he chose to adopt the plow area as his own.

Tucked in and around the plow are the plant denizens of a farmyard. Hens-and-chicks, Lamb's Ear, Cowbells, Horseradish, Horehound, and Goats Beard vie for their share of sunshine. The plot is just the right size for a ten-year-old to tend. His mother, Jane, worries that another barnyard dweller might take over—Pigweed!

Perhaps you can add even more plants to the barnyard list.

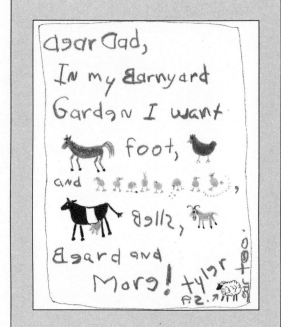

F i s h   i n   a   B o t t l e

How in the world did a huge zucchini get into such a snug place?

A woman visiting Heart's Ease told me that when her children were growing up she liked to surprise them with "different" gifts from her garden. In the spring she would let each child choose a large, empty bottle from her storage pantry. Then they would go out into the

vegetable garden and head for the zucchinis and cucumbers where each child would "catch a fish".

The children would each find a tiny, newly-formed cuke or zucchini and, with a pencil or nail, scratch a fish shape into its side. Gently, slowly, the children slipped each tiny, forming vegetable through the neck of a bottle and into the body.

Every day the children would go outside to check the progress of their fish until finally, before their very eyes, the tiny fish had filled the whole bottle and become a giant whale. Neighborhood children, eyes bulging in wonder, would turn the bottles over and over, trying to figure out how in the world a huge zucchini had gotten into such a snug place.

page 45

Mini Trough Garden

Jan Blum and I were talking about the Jack-in-the-Beanstalk Garden and she said, "If I were a young child, what would really thrill me would be the mini vegetables. In fact, I'm a grown-up and I am thrilled with them—the tiny currant tomatoes just send me over the edge."

In my "Tot's Garden" at Heart's Ease, I have made a miniature vegetable garden in an old English rock trough. The rectangular trough measures 24 inches by 18 inches and is 11 inches deep. It's knee high for the little knee-high gardeners who visit us.

A thick layer of crushed crockery and pebbles lines the bottom of the trough. A good, fast-draining planting soil (enriched with castings from my girls) fills the trough nearly to the top.

And in the trough are lots of wonderful mini-vegetables planted in tiny, symmetrical rows. I have miniature plant markers

SUGGESTED PLANTS

'La Belle'—mini filet bean

'Little Ball'—mini baby beet

'Planet'—a small, ball-shaped carrot

Cornichons—European-style mini cucumbers for pickling

'Little Fingers'—a baby eggplant

'Little Gem Mini Romaine'—lettuce

'Rubens Dwarf Romaine'—lettuce

'Summer Baby Bibb'—lettuce

'Tom Thumb'—lettuce

'Early Aviv'—baby onions

made out of popsicle sticks. The markers are decorated with tiny drawings of the plants in each section.

If your heart runs towards mini-flower gardens, there are many varieties of plants to choose from. 'Little Sweetheart' sweet-peas are a natural for growing in pots or troughs. any of the bulb catalogues now feature miniature daffodils, roses, and irises. My early spring borders are filled with tiny, purple grape hyacinth. Living up to their name, they emit a light, grape scent on a warm day and have a flowery, lemony flavor. My borders host snowdrops, 'Tiny Rubies' dianthus, 'Peter Pan' saxifrage, and innumerable other minis that would be perfect for a pint-sized garden.

Let your children read through your seed catalogues. Take them to local gardens, parks and arboretums. Let your enthusiasm overflow and enjoy your child's awakening awareness of the endless possibilities of gardening—even in the smallest, most unlikely of spaces.

'Barletta'—diminutive onions

'Precovil'—the tiniest of peas

'Cherries Jubilee'—a yummy "new" potato

'Ronde De Nice'—Small, round zucchini (harvest at about 1")

'Peter Pan Green Scallops—1 to 2-inch scallop-edged squashes

'Sweet Dumpling'—mini squash

'Munchkin'—mini pumpkins

'Ruby Pearl'—thumbnail sized tomatoes

Alpine Strawberries—these are the fairy berries

Basil `Fino Verde Compatto'—a charming, compact mini-bush with tiny leaves.

A tussie-mussie of mini carrots from a child's mini garden

A Garden of Greens

When you hear the words vegetable garden, do you conjure up an image of a boring rectangle with straight rows of lettuce and carrots? Unfortunately, that is the image and the reality of most vegetable gardens. No wonder more children aren't thrilled by the prospect of planting vegetables. Let's try to do something just a little different, something that will captivate and personalize a garden for a child.

Find a flat, sunny spot for your child's garden. Turn the soil and add whatever is necessary to make it rich and loose. Trace out a large, plump heart with a stick. Dig a small furrow along the heart shape. The furrow should be about 1/4 to 1/2 inch deep. Inside the heart write your child's name in big letters. Again, dig another furrow of the same depth following your traced letters.

Choose hardy, fast-growing greens such as red and green leaf lettuce, cress, and, of course, the dependable radish, and plant them thickly along the furrows.

Let your child water the garden and watch the delight when the first greens pop through the soil. If you don't think that is exciting for children, you are

"Oh, come, come, come,"

HE SHRIEKED,

"I'm a father to a radish!"

mistaken. My friend Georgie Van de Kamp described the response of a youngster in the Descanso Gardens Children's Garden. "Oh, come, come, come," he shrieked—"I'm a father to a radish!"

As your children harvest the vegetables, sow new seeds to ensure a continuous crop. Allow them to wash and prepare their own salads—they'll love them.

A Child's Own Rainbow

Rainbows are one of the most thrilling sights in nature. One moment a sky is dark with rain and in the next instant a gigantic arch with brilliant bands of color pierces the clouds and touches the earth.

Legends surround rainbows. Some Indian tribes believe that wherever a rainbow touches the ground, the brilliant colors give birth to the flowers of the field. We search for the pot of gold at the end of a rainbow, make a wish on one, watch the angels climbing the rainbow ladder into the sky parade, but most of all, like children everywhere, we stop, look, and feel a sense of wonder.

Help to keep the sense of wonder alive by creating a ground rainbow for your children!

Trace out the pattern of a rainbow arch and prepare the soil. Perhaps you could also trace a pot of gold at the end of your ground rainbow.

Take the children to the nursery and let them choose small plants in the colors of the rainbow: red, orange, yellow, green, blue, purple and violet. (Keep in mind the varying heights of plants and try to guide the children gently. After all, this is their rainbow). The pot of gold could be closely planted with

FIDELITY

Make

me a rainbow

Make it soon!

I've been waiting all afternoon!

The raindrops heard

in their busy dance;

The sun shone out

and gave them a chance;

They seized the rays

with their fingers deft,

and wove the bright-hued

warp and weft.

SUSAN SWOOPE

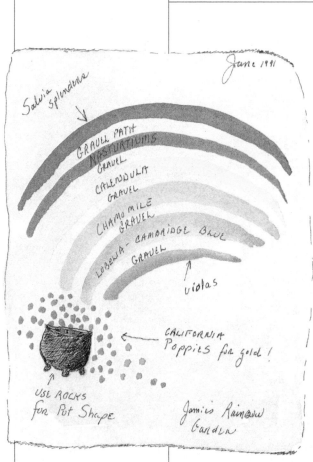

one of the many varieties of tiny marigolds.

Spend a Saturday or Sunday afternoon working with your children in their rainbow garden. The secret word is 'with'. Show them how to gently tap the small plants out of their pots. Help them set their first couple of plants into the ground, firm up the soil around the roots and give the plants a light watering.

Take a "garden walk" every single day—rain or shine. Enjoy the enthusiasm that your children show; it's infectious.

When the rainbow garden is in its glory, take a color photograph of the children tending it. Pin the photo on a bulletin board or put it on your refrigerator and watch the kids smile whenever they look at their very own rainbow.

Longwood Gardens

What a joy to stumble upon the indoor children's garden that Catherine Eberbach and Mary Allinson designed for the conservatory at Longwood Gardens in Kennett Square, Pennsylvania. Crouching under the nasturtium bower and walking through the miniature labyrinth was like entering a different world. Everywhere I looked I found touches that would delight any child. Brilliant splashes of salvia, geranium, and nasturtium spilling over the walls and out of pots. A wayward hummingbird darting from bloom to blossom as a contented butterfly rested at the edge of a child-sized waterfall.

In the corner of a gazebo patterned after a spider's web, I surprised a little girl playing with a nasturtium doll she had dressed. Over her shoulder dangled a spider on a string. When I tugged it, a small bell rang somewhere above us. Around a bend a

ℰVERYWHERE I

LOOKED I FOUND

TOUCHES THAT

WOULD DELIGHT ANY

CHILD.

young boy was sitting on a low, short bench decorated with paintings of Peter Rabbit's favorite carrots. In front of the bench, bricks were etched with the outlines of carrots.

In the place of a traditional wattle fence, the garden was walled with a pastel colored wattle with silhouettes of leaping rabbits leading the way through the maze of ivy hedges.

Huge, friendly topiary rabbits watched over the garden like sentinels as children crouched through hoops and passed through knee-high wooden gates and stopped to rest at a tiny picnic table and bench.

With my friends Louis and Virginia Saso and my husband Jeff, I wandered through the garden and lost myself in its beauty and humor. I could see Virginia posing in the arms of a giant topiary rabbit as Louis snapped her picture. Jeff was sticking his fingers in the bubble fountain (just like all the kids who entered the garden).

We all found it hard to leave the conservatory that day. The children's garden had captured our hearts and our imaginations and helped to awaken the sleeping child inside us.

Precious Water

Every drop counts! Collect precious drips in a bucket or watering can. In my gardens I place terra cotta saucers under faucets—these collect water for my timid, ground-feeding birds.

Mulch! Covering the soil around plants with loose, protective material such as leaves, cottonseed hulls, compost, or straw conserves moisture and helps enrich the soil.

Water early in the morning so that the moisture can soak into the earth instead of evaporating into the hot, sunny air of afternoon.

Buy some rain barrels and catch the rain at each downspout.

Use soaker hoses or drip watering systems.

PLAN,

DREAM, WEED,

PLANT, HOE, WEED,

HOPE.

WATCH AS WATER

WORKS ITS MAGIC.

AND THE MIRACLE

UNFOLDS.

A Butterfly Garden

Noah and I quietly spread the blanket and stretched out on our backs. "Shhhhh," I whispered, "We have to lie still and not talk or the butterflies won't come."

A few minutes passed before the monarch butter-flies began to land on the pineapple sage and sip its nectar. Soon, the sage and hyssop were studded with the brilliant orange of monarchs and one lone swal-lowtail. The butterflies sipped quietly until, dis-turbed by a quick movement, they rose (rustling like the thinnest parchment paper) into the cloudless sky.

"Mom, the butterflies look like letters from the flowers, don't they?" Noah asked. I solemnly agreed.

As the afternoon winged past us, we spent time studying mosaic-bodied anise swallowtail caterpillars gnawing their way through a thick stand of fennel, and "woolly bears" (the mourning cloak caterpillar) feasting on a willow tree.

Late in the day, when the last of the butterflies had left their garden, we began the pleasant chore of watering the two small beds. Working in the dusky light, we noticed that our nicotiana and four-o'clocks, ignored during the day, were hosting half a

dozen hummingbirds. "No, Mom, look, those aren't hummingbirds, they're moths," Noah said.

We paused, still holding our watering cans, and waited patiently. The moonless night settled around us, the darkness studded with the glowing faces of mirabilis, nicotiana, silenes, night-scented stock and moon flowers. Silently, we watched and listened as

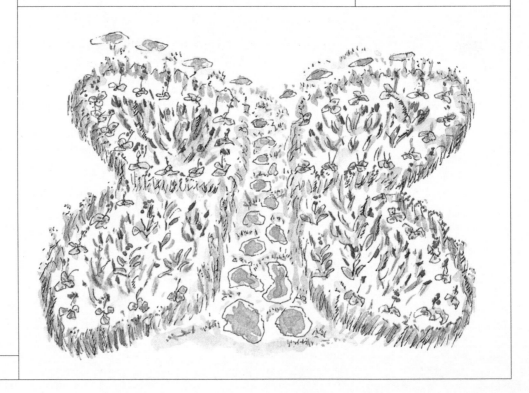

the cricket voices joined in chorus with the frogs and the faerie-like moths hovered (listen closely: you can hear their delicate wings) and fed at the blossom feast.

Noah looked up at me, his nutmeg-brown eyes dancing, "Mom," he said, "this is a miracle! It's like having our very own zoo and it's in our own front yard."

I guess in some ways, the small miracles we can create for our children are the ones most treasured and remembered. My small miracle of a butterfly and moth garden occupied about ten square feet and cost me only time, water and about $25 worth of seed, plant starts, and soil amendments.

The plan for our garden was simple. We chose a sunny site, protected from winds by a high blackberry hedge. We studied the shapes of butterflies wings and scratched the shape into our prepared piece of ground. Next, we outlined the butterfly with small rocks we had collected. We laid flat rocks between the butterfly wings; the rocks were the body.

Inside the butterfly wings we planted starts of perennial pineapple sage, lantana, jupiter's beard, hyssop, lavender, and coral bells. Between the stones of the butterfly body we underplanted with thyme and chamomile.

*Brown and
furry
Caterpillar in a
hurry
Take your walk
To the shady leaf,
or stalk,
Or what not,
Which may be the
chosen spot.
No toad spy you,
Hovering bird of
prey pass by you;
Spin and die,
To live again a
butterfly.*

CHRISTINA
ROSSETTI

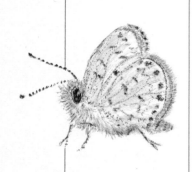

The rest was easy and fun. We went seed shopping, using a list compiled from years of my nature notes. Whenever I noticed a plant that was particularly favored by hummingbirds or butterflies, I would jot down its name and planting requirements.

We bought Nichols' "Border Mix for Bees, Butterflies, and Beneficials," too. This selection was a sure winner, developed by RoseMarie Nichols McGee. And we tried the "Butterfly Garden Seed Collection, Certified Organic" from Seeds of Change. We did test runs with these seed selections in large terra-cotta planters. The seeds germinated quickly, and as soon as the plants started blooming, myriad varieties of butterflies came calling.

So now it is your turn. Buy your family a butterfly book and a magnifying glass. Spend some time outdoors in gardens or along country roads observing butterflies and the kinds of plants they visit for nectar and plants their caterpillars use for food. Plant a pot or plot for the butterflies and moths and wait patiently. You and your child will soon be rewarded by the quiet visits of "flower letters" of the darkness and the day.

In Consideration of Faeries

When you are helping children plan their gardens, remember that the faeries and children must have a swath of low-growing greenery (it could be chamomile, thyme, or grass) on which to dance their dances and hold their faerie meetings.

During the day, the faeries are curled up sleeping in the hearts of the flowers. But at night, when the moon and stars are shining brightly, they troop out onto their green ballroom floor and dance and sing (with tiny cricket voices) in celebration of the children who gave them shelter.

The faeries

•

that live in

•

the hearts

•

of flowers.

Janna of the Sunshine

Jane Hogue says that her 11-year-old daughter Janna is fascinated with the garden. "She explores barns and haymows, along the fence rows and ditches, down garden paths, and among the herb beds," she said. Janna reports home on any beautiful blossoms, unusual spider webs, flowers that are ready for cutting, ripe strawberries, and perfect hiding places.

Janna received a copy of Frances Hodgson Burnett's *Secret Garden* and immediately fell in love. She is busily making plans for her very own secret garden this summer, a place where she can weave dreams, adventures and sunshine into a beautiful tapestry.

Jane and Jack Hogue believe that raising children and growing gardens have many similarities. Both need nurturing and care to grow and blossom. Their children are thriving and blooming under their special care—we could all learn from them!

The Story of the Sunflower House

Working in my garden at Heart's Ease one day, I turned to greet an elderly lady. "Oh," she said, her voice full of nostalgia, "this reminds me of my childhood in Nebraska." I knew she must have some special memories to share. "Can you remember any special garden things you did as a child?" I asked.

She thought a moment then began a wonderful story: "We were poor and didn't have lots of store-bought things. My favorite flower project was our summer playhouse—we didn't have a regular play-house, but one we planted every year.

"In early summer, my mother would wake us up with 'Get up you sleepyheads, today's the day!' and we would get out of bed and pull on our clothes. We didn't even want to eat breakfast, but she would make us sit down and take our time. It all just served to heighten the excitement. We couldn't wait to get outside.

"Chores done, watering can and stick in tow, we would head outside and take time choosing the best, flattest, sunniest spot in our garden. Then the work would begin.

"Mother would use the stick to trace out a large rectangle, usually about 6 by 9 feet, leaving a small

My summer home is the fairest of all With a morning glory roof and sunflower walls!

LOVEJOY

opening for a doorway. She would drag the stick along the ground and gouge out a trench a couple of inches deep. My little sister and brother would trail behind and drop in seeds. John would drop in a big, fat sunflower seed; daintily, my sister would tuck in a 'Heavenly Blue' morning glory seed. I would trudge along behind them lugging the huge tin watering can. I'd use my foot to knock the earth back over the seeds and then I'd give them a small drink of water.

"Every day one of us would have the chore of walking that rectangle of land and giving a drink of water to the sleeping seeds. We all hoped to be the one to discover the first awakening green heads that poked through the soil.

"Once the green of the sunflowers peeked through the earth, we became even more interested in our growing playhouse. Usually, we would each water the plot once a day. Soon the sun-

flowers were climbing skyward and the 'Heavenly Blue' morning glories were wrapping their tendrils around the stalk and heading upward too.

"I don't know how long it took before the sunflowers were at least twice as tall as us kids, but soon they were and Mother would come out with a big roll of used string we had saved up through the winter. 'John, you fetch the ladder and we'll get your roof going today,' Mother would say. My brother would drag out the big ladder and Mother would tie string to the top of one sunflower's neck. She would lace the string across that rectangle, back and forth, back and forth, 'til all we could see was a spider web of string against the blue Nebraska sky.

"In a matter of days, the Heavenly Blues would start journeying across the web, and soon the string was invisible. Looking up, all you could see was the gold of the sunflower faces, the green of all the leaves and like patches of the sky itself, the blue of those morning glories. I'll tell you there was nothing like crawling through the door of that playhouse and lying on the ground looking up through that incredi-

6'x 9'

THE
MORNING-
GLORY

❖

Wondrous interlacement!
Holding fast to threads by
green and silky rings,
With the dawn it spreads
its white and purple wings;
Generous in its bloom, and
sheltering while it climbs,
Sturdy morning-glory.

from
De Gardenne Boke

ble lacework of vines and flowers. I guess you could say that I spent the best days of my childhood playing, dreaming, and sleeping in that little shelter."

❖　　❖　　❖

How do you go about furnishing a house so special? Surely you cannot go to a store and buy anything that will fit properly into such a home.

The children searched fields and woods and found everything they needed. Their mother did not have to teach them to do this; they just knew, instinctively, what was right for their playhouse. What they chose was what their mother and father, grandmother and grandfather had used before them.

Acorn cup & Saucer

Rosehip teapot Thorn spout Twig Handle

For a table, they rolled in a large, flat rock. Perfect chairs came from the woodpile—short, fat stumps. Doll beds were made of corn husks and down-stuffed milkweed pods. For carpets, moss and lichens; for coverlets, great big leaves (sycamores were soft, but woolly lamb's ears and old-fashioned mullein were the best). Dinnerware was not a problem—round honesty plant pods were dishes, acorns

and caps made cups and saucers, a plump, red rosehip poked with a thorn became a teapot with a spout.

Filarees were scissors, wild walnut halves were the porridge bowls (look at the heart inside them), beech leaves were napkins, and a burr-basket (from burdock) filled with miniature wildflowers sat in the middle of the rock-table. The garden was an endless toy store.

At night, the children ran barefoot through the grass catching fireflies. Gently, so as not to injure the fragile, flickering lights, they tucked them into the blossoms of hollyhocks and knit the edges together with a long twig. Some of the hollyhock-firefly lanterns were hung inside the sunflower house. Others were used in fairy-like procession-als through the moist dark-ness of the garden.

"BOYS AND GIRLS,

COME OUT TO

PLAY,

THE MOON

IT SHINES

AS BRIGHT AS

DAY."

————

Lovejoy

Beans, Gourds, Pumpkins and Poles

Sweet summer dreams

In my runner bean tent

My friends who

played with me

Paid laughter for rent.

L O V E J O Y

Children love a place of their own to use as a hide-out. I once saw this wonderful teepee—a perfect place for summer play. Here's how to make it:

Set four to six poles in the ground at an angle and bring them together at the top, securely lashing them with some heavy twine to form a teepee shape. Run twine roughly around the teepee to form a ladder for scarlet runner beans or showy painted lady beans (both flowers and pods are edible) and varieties of gourds. Plant seeds all around the base of the teepee. As the vines begin to reach upward, the children will be fascinated with the climbing process and the searching tendrils. (Show them how some vines always wind clockwise and others always wind counterclockwise).

As the teepee fills in, it becomes a secluded, dream and play-inspiring hide-out. An added treat is that the children can use the gourds they have grown to make bird houses, bowls, nests, toys—the possibilities are endless, and they grew them themselves!

Sand Castles

"I SEE THE GARDEN THICKET'S SHADE

———

WHERE ALL THE SUMMER LONG WE PLAYED,

———

AND GARDENS SET AND HOUSES MADE

———

OUR EARLY WORK AND LATE."

———

MARY HOWITT

When I was a child growing up in the fragrant, golden hills of southern California, one of my favorite play areas was the wooden sandbox under our gnarled apricot tree. Flanking the sandbox were hollyhocks, carnations, iris, and rainbows of sweet peas—a palette of color for building castles.

Early dew-laced mornings would find me outside picking bouquets of blossoms to use in my construction project for the day. The night-moist sand was easy to mold and as I built, I studded the sides and roof with a mosaic of blossoms. Tips of bushes and ends of tree branches became a forest surrounding my creation. Tiny clumps of moss lined the path leading to the doorway—perfect bushes.

As the day progressed, friends joined in and helped add rooms and designs of flowers to the castle walls and pathways. At dusk, the last warning call came from our mothers—time to go inside now, or else! Deliberately and gleefully, we leapt into the center of our castle—every last vestige of our creation vanished. We felt no remorse, we knew our summer days stretched endlessly ahead. There would be other castles.

"That delightful thing, a sand-pit: it is a place of everlasting joy when one is small, and even when one is growing fairly biggish. We dig out arched recesses to sit in, and we build castles and all sorts of houses with the heap of loose sand at the bottom...And then we get some flowers and make quite a pretty garden round the house."

GERTRUDE JEKYLL, *from "Children and Gardens", CountryLife, 1908.*

WRITE A SECRET MESSAGE WITH LEMON JUICE OR MILK. WHEN IT IS DRY THE WORDS ARE INVISIBLE. TO READ THE MESSAGE, PRESS THE PAPER WITH A WARM IRON. THE WORDS COME BACK LIKE

MAGIC!

Ricky Beauclaire and I were the neighborhood whirlwinds. We were up in every tree, under every bush, and behind every rock. If there was trouble to be found, we found it (or maybe we caused it!).

We were inseparable, but when we were forced to be apart we found ways to communicate. Secret letters were tucked into a hole in our favorite old apricot tree and when Jackie Wingo found our hiding place we mystified him by writing with lemon juice "invisible ink". We put tiny, tiny messages inside the closed mouths of snapdragons, scratched letters onto mulberry leaves, and left cryptic trails of leaf messages on the sidewalk (which usually blew away before they were found).

Faerie Tea Parties

A recurring theme of faeries and woodlore cropped up in dozens of letters and reminiscences I received from throughout the country. And what would my own childhood have been without the secret hideaway of boughs in Grandmother's garden?

Dorothy Fitzcharles Weber, author of *Artistry in Avian Abodes*, wrote me, "Many of the nature crafts and lore I learned from scouting I practiced with my own children and then grandchildren at Crystal Lake in Maine.

"There were white birch trees, many unusual mosses, pink lady's slippers, curious rocks, hemlock cones, ferns and a multitude of natural materials.

"When Kim and Kelly were little girls we would have wonderful tea parties. The placemats were fern fronds, acorn cups were doll-sized tea cups, and then a choice of birchbark sandwiches filled with buttercup spread and tea brewed from soldier moss. Dessert was often pebbles á la mud."

From many miles away came this note from Susan

Deep in the wood
I made a house
Where no one knew the way;
I carpeted the floor with moss,
And there I loved to play.

———

I heard the bubbling of a brook;
At times an acorn fell,
And far away a robin sang
Deep in a lonely dell.

———

I set a rock with acorn cups;
So quietly I played
A rabbit hopped across the moss,
And did not seem afraid.

———

That night before I went to bed
I at my window stood,
And thought how dark my home
must be
Down in the lonesome wood.

———

K. Pyle

Jones Sprengnether, who grew up in St. Louis, Missouri.

"I clearly remember making homey places for the faeries who lived in the woods. These places were snuggled in amongst the roots of trees and mostly in mossy areas. We made dishes of acorn tops, cradles of walnut shells, leaves were cots or hammocks, and tables were made of twigs lashed together."

And from many, many years away:

"It was to please the faeries that, long before I had heard of naturalizing bulbs or knew the name and the fame of W. Robinson, I planted a ring of white crocuses in the grass round the bole of the wych elm one November. When the white circle appeared in spring, Mother said, 'Who put those crocuses in the grass? It must have been you, Nan.' I hung my head, expecting a wigging, but Mother smiled and said, 'Your grandmother used to do that in Bethnal Greens in 1820. What made you do it?' But I did not tell her, nor anyone else, that it was to please the faeries."

Poppy Maidens

Gretel Hanna Barnitz sat in my Heart's Ease gardens and shared childhood memories from the 1920s. As a child, she loved to sit beside her mother's shirley poppy bed and carefully turn down the silky petals of each poppy, exposing the little green seed pods for heads. Then, she would tie a blade of grass around their "waists", creating graceful, dancing, poppy maidens.

"Some afternoons we would spend hours carefully turning and tying all of the poppies in Mother's side garden," she said.

"One day Mother called me inside and as I turned to take a last look at my poppy ladies a breeze started stirring through them. All of the poppies began bowing and waving as though they were saying, "Goodbye, thanks for a great day of play!"

Poppy maidens

Bowing, swaying

Watched the girls

As they were playing.

Lovejoy

LOVELY DANCING GIRL
Please play with me
I'll make you leaf boats
To take you to sea

MY FILAREE SCISSORS
will cut you a shawl
Of dew studded spider webs
Dressed for the ball!

A HAT FROM A TINY PETAL
of blue
A peek of your anther
We'll call it your shoe!

A HOLLYHOCK DANCING SKIRT
Hearts ease for a face
Twigs for your arms—
Now, your hair's a disgrace!

LOVEJOY

Daisy Grandmothers

Years ago, I quizzed an elderly lady who still spends most of her time in her garden. My usual question, "What did you do with plants when you were a child?" was met with a bright, quick answer.

"We made daisy grandmothers," she said, smiling as she nodded her head in thought.

"Daisy grandmothers?" I asked, "I don't recall hearing of those before."

"Oh," she said, "that wakens fond memories of spring, when we four sisters would take scissors and a pencil and head out to the meadows searching for the best, fullest field of daisies."

She explained how the girls would spread out in a meadow and pick a handful of daisies and then "trim their bonnets". "We would work around the face of the daisy, cutting the petals in the shape of a bonnet," she said. "Generally, we left two long petals at the bottom of the daisy face. Those would be the bonnet ties. Oh, what great fun we had with our daisy grandmothers!"

Years later, my friend Christine Nybak Hill recounted tales of making daisy grandmothers out in the fields, too. Somehow, through time and conti-

SOMEHOW, THROUGH TIME AND CONTINENTS AND GENERALLY WITHOUT BENEFIT OF BOOKS, OUR FLOWER TRADITIONS ARE PASSED ON FROM GENERATION TO GENERATION.

nents and generally without benefit of books, our flower traditions are passed on from generation to generation.

I found this poem in a children's garden book from the late 1800s:

W e were sitting down in the grass,
deep in it, it was taller than we;
The daisies were there, close beside us,
In a circle they stood on a mound,
And Auntie took out her sharp scissors
And she snipped them around and around,
Until each had a white cap border,
And she left them two petals for strings;
And then next she found a lead pencil
In her bag with the rest of her things;
And with that, on each yellow center,
Auntie drew such a queer little face—
But look! You can see the grandmammas,
Here they are in the same grassy place!

Hollyhock Dolls

Hollyhock dolls were the plaything most commonly mentioned when I quizzed people about childhood play. "Oh, yes, my sisters and I always made hollyhock dolls," one lady told me. "There was an unlimited supply of hollyhocks next to our barn. Every morning we would go outside and pick buds and blossoms. We used them stacked on top of each other and held together with twigs. We loved to make them cloaks of violet leaves sewn together with thin strands of grass.

"Our big brother

HOLLYHOCKS

The hollyhocks greet you

Wherever they meet you,

With stiffest of bows

KATHERINE

H.

PERRY

made dolls for us using small cherry tomatoes as heads, but we liked our dolls to be all flowers. Canterbury bell blouses, petunia skirts, these were some of the other flowers we used."

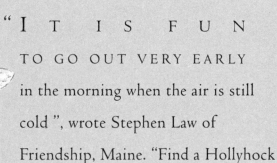

"IT IS FUN TO GO OUT VERY EARLY in the morning when the air is still cold ", wrote Stephen Law of Friendship, Maine. "Find a Hollyhock with a big, fat, black and yellow bumblebee sleeping in it and pet it!" (I've always caught them in the cup of my hands and have never been stung—the secret seems to be to handle them gently and let them just crawl about.)

Trumpet Flower Dolls

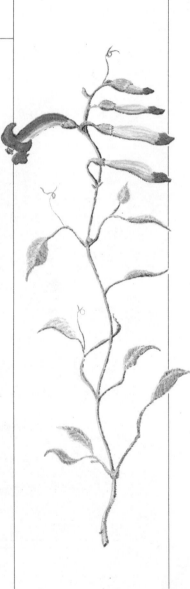

Grab yourself some trumpet flowers and leaves and we'll work on a doll for you," Gram said. I reached out and picked two blossoms and a handful of leaves.

Gram turned the bloom with the narrow end up, and stuck a sunny dandelion face into the mouth of the trumpet. Next, she bent a fresh, green leaf over the head and pinned it with a twig. "There, now she has a happy face and a beautiful bonnet," she said. Finally, we fashioned her a cloak out of one of the leaves, and a peach tree furnished her with twig arms. Gram made a dainty necklace of tiny pink clovers.

"Let's make her a sister," I said. "Let's dress her like a Hawaiian hula dancer," Gram chuckled, as we tied a long strand of grass around the dancer's waist. Then, we draped many strands of grass over the waistband and we had a hula skirt.

"Let's give this gal some dandelion curls on a rosehip head," she said as we split some dandelion stems, sucked on them, and made curls.

Our trumpet vine dolls danced and played all through a rainy, summer day. In the evening we took them down to the swollen creek and let them float away for an adventure of their own.

Pansy and Heart's Ease Dolls

In the 1800s, young ladies would often sit for hours and cut out strings of headless paper dolls. The paper was of two thicknesses; in other words, one piece was folded in half lengthwise, and the dolls cut out with the fold at the top. Then our Victorian friends would slip pansies or Heart's ease blossoms into place for heads, and the little ladies would be able to stand on their own. When paper was not available, leaves would suffice. They would simply pick a pansy or heart's ease, fold a leaf around the stem like a cloak, and poke twig arms through for a little pansy leaf doll. A leaf also could be folded in half, like a single paper doll, a hole slit for the head, and a pansy on a stem stuck into the hole.

PANSY FACES

*Each pansy has a smiling face
To greet me when I go
To work among them with my spade,
And help to make them grow.*

LOUISE MARSHALL HAYNES
Over the Rainbow Bridge

Trees for Wishing, Trees for Dreaming

My Tree

*Spreading wide
her skirt of leaves,*

*Stroking the wind,
Tickling clouds,*

*Chatting with
birds,*

*Sheltering children
on friendly boughs.*

Lovejoy

More than forty years ago a little boy with rosy cheeks and curly, cowlicked hair found his own tree. He didn't know that it was a sycamore tree, over a hundred years old, the last of dozens which had once arched over Wildcat Creek.

The tree became the boy's friend. When childhood problems overwhelmed him he ran to the tree, scrambled up its welcoming branches, and found comfort in its huge, sheltering presence. After a few years the one-sided conversations he had with his friend became part of a daily routine. The dependable old sycamore was always there to hear his wishes, dreams, and sorrows.

On the day his family left Indiana to move to California the little boy made one last trip to his friend. He hugged his tree and as he walked away, a strong wind stirred a piece of paper he had left in a hiding place. In childish writing the paper said, "I, John Arnold, love this tree."

John's Buttonwood tree.

A Tree For My Son

On the day I found out that I was pregnant, I bought a tree for my unborn son. During the months that Noah was growing inside me, the tree grew and flourished.

Afraid to plant the tree in the ground and leave it behind in a move, I planted it in a large terra cotta pot. To this day the Deodar cedar grows in a pot, gets fed regularly, and is talked to and nurtured like a child.

Give your child a birth tree. As the child grows, the tending of the tree can be a favored chore. The growth of the tree can be charted easily by tying a bit of colored string to the outermost tip of a branch each fall. During the spring and summer growth can be measured weekly.

DEAR LITTLE TREE that we plant today
What will you be when we're old and gray?

THE TREE ANSWERS

"The savings bank of the squirrel and mouse.
For robin and wren an apartment house,
The dressing-room of the butterfly's ball,
The locust's and katydid's concert hall,
The schoolboy's ladder in pleasant June,
The schoolgirl's tent in the July noon,
And my leaves shall whisper them merrily
A tale of the children who planted me."

UNKNOWN

What Dreams Are Made Of

*"LIFT YOUR LEAFY
ROOF FOR ME,
PART YOUR
YIELDING WALLS:
LET ME WANDER
LINGERINGLY
THROUGH YOUR
SCENTED HALLS."*

ETHELWYN
WETHERALD

Sunday mornings are my favorite time. I can curl up in bed and read and listen to the bird voices outside my window. I love to hear the quail coveys pattering across the roof—they sound like gentle rain.

Sunday mornings are when I do a lot of research from old garden and nature books. These are times of quiet discovery. Whenever I find a great garden poem, a story about children in the gardens and fields, or a story of a special garden, I feel as though I have uncovered a treasure.

Today I stumbled across an old etching of a Victorian garden. The etching depicted a huge catalpa tree. The tree had been pruned into the shape of a house—a true tree house! Windows and doors were simply cut through the outer leafy branches of the tree and the furniture was boughs. I could imagine half a dozen children eagerly climbing a rope ladder and entering the leafy bough house for an afternoon of sundappled dreaming and play.

The Need For A Swing

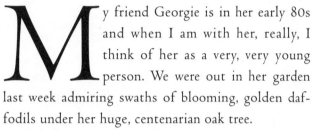

My friend Georgie is in her early 80s and when I am with her, really, I think of her as a very, very young person. We were out in her garden last week admiring swaths of blooming, golden daffodils under her huge, centenarian oak tree.

As we stood eyeing the daffodils she looked up into her tree and said, "I really think every child should have a tree swing, don't you?" I had to agree; I think a tree swing is one of the simplest and most wonderful garden pleasures.

"I used to love the freedom of swinging, and now that I think of it I really think that I NEED a swing in that tree. Yes, I NEED a swing," Georgie said emphatically.

I have always heard that there is a bread-and-water type of necessity and then there is soul-food necessity. I think that Georgie hit upon a definite soul-food garden necessity—a swing. It could be a tire hanging from a tree, even a plain rope hanging Tarzan style, or a swing with a wood plank seat.

However you do it, remember what it felt like to have the wind rushing past your ears as you tried, pumping harder and harder, to reach the very spot where the green earth ended and the blue sky began.

How do you like to go

up in a swing,

Up in the air so blue?

Oh, I do think it is the

pleasantest thing

Ever a child can do!

ROBERT LOUIS STEVENSON

A Living Gazebo Playhouse

I was wandering through the fragrant, meandering pathways at Lewis Mountain Herbs and Everlastings in Manchester, Ohio. As usual, my head was down, my eyes darting about at the variety of herbs and scented geraniums.

As I came to a Y in the path I looked up, trying to decide which fork to take, and gave a start of surprise. Ten feet in front of me was a lush, living gazebo of Ohio Melrose apple trees. The bough-canopied gazebo was punctuated by the straight trunks of the trees and festooned with slender arching branches. I headed for its sheltering circle.

I spent most of my afternoon sitting inside the gazebo surrounded by a curtain of shimmering leaves. A companionable brown towhee (we call them brown bettys in my family; the name seems to suit them) scratched through the soil, apple tree shadows playing across the ground and over her back.

To this day I think back to my afternoon in Ohio and realize what a haven that apple gazebo was for me. Imagine what it might mean to a child to find such a whimsical and playful space in the middle of an otherwise hands-off, grown-up garden.

A

Curtain of

SHIMMERING

leaves

The construction of the apple-tree gazebo was simple. John Lewis cultivated a circle and planted eight trees around its perimeter. Each one of the trees was sturdily staked to keep it straight. As the trees branched out, John pruned them to the shape he desired. Long branches were tied or wired to each other to form the arching canopy. Moderate trimming throughout the summer keeps the gazebo neat and inviting. I can't wait to plant this playhouse!

Crowns

A peculiar connecting thread runs through all the garden stories I've collected. Somehow, though fifty or sixty years might have passed, the child inside each person lightens and glows through ageless eyes as they tell their stories.

One sunny afternoon in May, I was sitting on the stone patio writing. A familiar voice greeted me and as I squinted into the sun I saw a snowy-white halo of hair. My friend, Millicent Truax Heath, sat down on a stool next to me. Millie's eyes brightened and her voice quality changed as she began telling me about her childhood summers in Rockport, Minnesota.

"My Aunt was Sarah E. Truax. She was a charter member of the San Diego Art Guild and she was an artist in everything she did. She was a wonderful lady! I remember what fun we had with her in the fields. She would take her easel out to paint and we children would go with her. She really made us look at nature and we would lie on the ground, peering through tangles of wildflowers trying to find the little people we knew were there. Sometimes she just put a crumb down on the ground and we watched, fascinated, as the ants picked up that boulder of a

Ivy and Roses
Woven around
Mary's a princess and
This is her crown

— ❦ —

Clover nasturtiums a
Bright passion flower
Sarah's a gypsy queen
This is her hour

A Tiara of Fireflies and Flowers

"Our Grandma always wore hair nets to keep her silver hair in place," a friend told me. "As the nets wore out or snagged, Gram would give them to us girls.

"On special evenings my sis and I would weave garlands of Daisies and wildflowers and pin them in our hair. Our brother would bring in a canning jar full of fireflies and we would tip it into Gram's hair nets, loosely fit them over our fancy hairdos, and have twinkling tiaras for an evening of garden play."

crumb and carried it away. We all got so much enjoyment out of everything!

"Aunt Sarah would pick a beautiful bouquet of the long stemmed pink clover that grew in the fields. Then she would make us crowns, necklaces, bracelets, and rings from clover braids."

Millie leaned over and picked some clover out of a patch of weeds. She laid three across my lap and began to braid them. As she braided, she added more blossoms until the braid was long enough to encircle a head. Then she poked the loose stems into the beginning, took a long stem of grass, and neatly tied the ends together to make our crown.

Millie said that once she and the other children learned how to make the braids, everything was fair game. They would stop alongside the road and braid bracelets and necklaces and stud them with violets, hepaticas and different colors of clover. They wore them everywhere—even to church.

Millie's sweet, clover-filled memories of seventy years past came alive for me as I learned to braid my own crown. Just as I was tying the ends together a young towheaded girl asked what I was doing. Before I knew what was happening, she was sitting on the stones, surrounded by a crazy quilt of flowers, slowly,

laboriously, braiding her own crown. "Look, it's per-fect," she said holding it up for all to see. "That's not a real crown," her older sister scoffed. "Yes, it is," she said, "it's the important kind!"

More Crowns

A few years ago Robert Ball, a former botany pro-fessor, told me the story of yerba buena crowns.

"When I was a child, our family would go on overnight camping trips," he told me. "My father always had us gather long strands of yerba buena and twine and weave them into crowns. We wore those to bed not only for fun and the good smell, but to ward off pesky mosquitoes."

Growing up in Grandmother's garden, the changing seasons brought me an endless variety of playthings. In the spring, I would string tiny Cecile Bruner rose buds to make necklaces and garlands. In the fall, I would string wild rose hips. I never realized that anyone else had ever thought to do this until I read what Gerard wrote in the late 1500s. "Children with delight make chains and pretty gewgaws of the fruit of roses."

YERBA BUENA
PICKED TODAY
HELPS TO CHASE
THE BUGS AWAY.

LOVEJOY

Clover Chains

Several years ago, I planned a day in the garden with two young friends, Sarah and MaryBeth Monger. As I walked up the pathway to their Grandma's house, I noticed Sarah sitting in the grass, head bent over her lap as she worked nonstop on something.

She was so engrossed in what she was doing that she didn't even see me watching her. Picking a clover, she would slit the stem just below the flowerhead with her thumbnail. Then she would push another clover stem through the slit until the head stopped it from going further. Doing this procedure over and over, she fashioned a five-foot-long rope of clover blooms.

Sarah looked up with a glowing face and said, "Look, Sharon, a day-long jump rope." And that is exactly what it was, lasting Sarah and Marybeth all afternoon. It was a simple pleasure, made fresh for each day of play.

Daisy chains, clover chains, flower braids, and wreaths—the simple, repetitive steps in making these timeless delights are known by children everywhere!

Sarah's Jumprope

Sarah waited patiently

Stringing clovers 1-2-3

Clover jump rope

For her play

It will last for

Just one day!

Lovejoy

Leaf Hats

In poking through old books of nature crafts and pastimes for children, I found a story of hats of leaves pinned with twigs. I planned to tell MaryBeth and Sarah about leaf hats, but they surprised me as I walked through the gate to their grandma's garden another time—they were both wearing hats of leaves that were pinned together with small twigs!

Sarah's hat was a large, elaborate leaf decorated with sprays of spiraea and tied under her chin by the stems. Mary's hat was smaller. She had used the stems to tie the leaves together in an overlapping, flower petal effect. Her hat was gaily decorated with sprigs of flowers inserted through slits in the leaves. (Imagine how beautiful and festive an autumn leaf hat would be!) The girls wore their hats most of the day, and when they were through with them they turned them into boats for their fuchsia dancing dolls!

During the long, summer afternoon, Sarah and MaryBeth foraged through Grandma's garden for more dress-up supplies. MaryBeth picked snapdragons from a tall stalk and used the individual "snaps" as clip-on earrings. Sarah chained clovers together to form a crown and as she worked, she tucked in nasturtiums

"THE TREES

DROP JEWELS

AT OUR FEET."

LUCY LARCOM

and passion flowers for "jewels." She looked like a flamboyant gypsy queen when she finished.

MaryBeth twined ivy and honeysuckle into a circlet and as she twined she wove rosebuds, forget-me-nots, and clover into its rim, she became a fairy princess crowned with rubies, sapphires, and diamonds.

Sarah in her hat of leaves

Sassafras Chains

"Although the years of the Second World War were tumultuous, somehow I remember them as the peaceful foundation of my life," Patricia Reppert told me. "My father was a surgeon who joined the service and was gone for five long years. To provide me and my brother with a home, my mother packed us up and we moved to my grandparents' farm, Whittenoak, in Charlottesville, Virginia.

Maple seed Spectacles are all the rage with the fashionable set.

"I remember that my father's letters were anticipated and treasured by all of us—he wrote to mother almost every day. It seemed as though our lives revolved around the daily mail delivery. "Every day, during nice weather, my mother, brother, and I would hike through the fields and wait alongside the road for our mailman. You see, the mail was our life-line.

"The roadsides were beautiful, a miniature, flower-filled garden, perfect for kids. The woods skirting the road were filled with bushes, and our favorite, the wonderful sassafras tree! Sometimes we would spend several hours waiting, and during that time we made flower and leaf toys to keep ourselves happy.

"My favorite things to play with were the sassafras leaves. They were large, almost hand shaped, and fun to make into chains and clothes. We would start by pinching the long stem off the first leaf. From then on we would pick another leaf (leaving this stem on) and we would overlap the leaves, using the long stem like a needle, piercing the leaf in small stem-stitches. They really did seem sewn together, and we would make vests, over-the-shoulder Carmen Miranda-type blouses, crowns, belts and long, long chains. I remember one chain that was about 15 feet long. My brother and I tried to walk all the way home without breaking the chain. We never tired of playing our leaf games!

L • E • A • V • E • S

The orange-tinted sassafras

With quaintest foliage

strews the grass;

Witch-hazel shakes her gold curls out,

'Mid the red maple's flying rout.

Mayday

May is such a joyous month for me. My gardens are brimming with new life. The perennial borders are a riot of color, towering hollyhocks, gray carpets of carnations, cerulean delphiniums, candelabras of foxglove, and everywhere columbine, the pastels of the little dove flower amidst the lacy foliage of love-in-a-mist. And my roses! Many of my antique roses are at their best. The scents from every corner of the garden are overwhelming.

I feel like a child again—that same quickening inside that I felt every May Day when I filled tiny baskets and cornucopias with flowers, hung them on my neighbors' door knobs, rang the bell, and ran for my life. Crouched down amongst huge bushes of sweet smelling, old-fashioned geraniums I would peek out, heart pounding wildly, and watch as Mamam Braden, Goldie Pickering, and old Mrs. Downs found their baskets. (Perhaps some of the flowers in the baskets were from their own gardens!)

May Day

If I were asked the season,
I could not tell today;
I should say it still was Winter—
The Calendar says May.

If this indeed be May-day,
I must be growing old;
For nothing I was used to
Do I today behold.

On May day in New England,
In that old town of ours,
We rose before the daybreak,
And went and gathered flowers.

And then in pretty baskets,
With little sprigs of green
We placed them, and stole homeward,
And hoped we were not seen.

RICHARD HENRY STODDARD

A simple gift of flowers filled me with joy—and I know now that my gift gave joy to some lonely neighbors. And today, spending time with people who tell me stories of their childhood, May Day always looms brightly in their memories. Their eyes light up while remembering May garlands, May poles, and secret May baskets left for friends and loved ones. And the question most often asked: "Whatever happened to May Day?"

I plan to find May Day again. This year, and every year hereafter, I will leave a May basket for someone who may be lonely and isolated. I want to feel that excited joy that made my heart pound as I crept up to doors and left my small gift of flowers.

MAY DAY MORNING

Oh, let's leave a basket of flowers today
For the little old lady who lives down our way!
We'll heap it with violets white and blue,
With Jack-in-the-pulpit and
Wildflowers too.

We'll make it of paper and line it with ferns
Then hide — and we'll watch her surprise when she turns
And opens her door and looks out to see
Who in the world it could possibly be.

VIRGINIA SCOTT MIKE

Wishes and Charms and Four-Leaf Clovers

An even-leaved

ash,

Even ash, I thee do pluck,
Hoping thus to meet good luck.
If no luck I get from thee,
I'll wish I'd left you on the tree.

DAISY DIVINATION

ONE FOR SORROW,

TWO FOR JOY,

THREE FOR A GIRL,

FOUR FOR A BOY,

FIVE FOR DIAMONDS,

SIX FOR GOLD,

SEVEN FOR A SECRET

NEVER TO BE TOLD.

And a four-

leaved clover,

White rose, white rose,
Bring me good luck.
Good luck to you, good luck to me,
Good luck to everyone I see.

You'll see

your love,

FIND A FOUR-LEAFED CLOVER AND PICK IT UP,
ALL THE DAY YOU'LL HAVE GOOD LUCK.

Down among the meadow grass,

Searching it all over,

GOOD LUCK!

'Fore the day

is over.

What a merry band are we,

Hunting four-leaf clover.

I wish, I wish is what you say as the dandelion blows away!

O N E I love, T W O I love,
T H R E E   I love, I say,
F O U R   I love with all my heart,
F I V E I cast away.
S I X he loves, S E V E N   she loves,
E I G H T   both love,
N I N E he comes, T E N   he tarries,
E L E V E N   he courts, T W E L V E he marries.

I know a place where the sun is like gold, And the cherry blooms burst with snow,

And down underneath is the loveliest nook Where the four leaf clovers grow.

*A clover, a clover of two,
Put in your right shoe,
The first young man you meet,
In field or lane or street,
You'll have him or one of his name.*

THREE WHITE
ROCKS,
AND THREE
RED BERRIES,
THREE YELLOW
DAISIES,
FROM THE
FIELD.
OVER YOUR
SHOULDER
INTO THE
STREAM
YOUR LOVE
WILL VISIT
WHEN NEXT
YOU DREAM.

Periwinkles

The soft, azure, star-like blooms of the periwinkle give the only color to be found in the shady recesses of the hillside below my garden. Even on the darkest California winter day I can usually depend on this faithful bloomer to enliven my herbal bouquets with a dash of quiet blue.

Over the years, I've asked flower lovers all over the United States and Britain for legends and lore about the humble periwinkle, but always to no avail. Sometimes we tend to overlook what's right under our noses. Such was the case with periwinkles and my friend Margaret Harper.

Margaret arrived one day smiling impishly, carrying a small bouquet of periwinkles. "Do you know the story of Perry Winkle's Paintbrush?" she asked. "It was told to me by Rossie Fairbairn. Her mother, Isabelle Evans, of Blue Lake, California, kept Rossie entertained when she was a child with stories of the wonders of plant life. Now, I share the story with my grandchildren, who never tire of it or of the search for the paintbrush."

Margaret set her bouquet down on a table and pulled out a single stem in bloom. As she began

Sometimes we

•

tend to overlook

•

what's right

•

under our noses

•

Such was the case

•

with periwinkles

telling the story, she carefully and slowly removed petal after petal.

Perry Winkle's Paint Brush

The first Spring descended upon the earth, and all of the new, young animals and shimmering green plants and trees were healthy and happy. The view from a hilltop across mile after mile of wildflowers with all different blossom and leaf shapes revealed one startling, glaringly obvious thing. Somehow, the finishing touch had been overlooked! All the flowers were one color—WHITE!

The very last flower to have been created was the humble periwinkle. Thus, he was the one called upon to solve the problem of coloring all of the flowers.

"Goodness, gracious," said Perry in a small, blue voice. "I am depressed. There is just no way a little flower like me could color all the flowers in the world."

"Perry," a deep, soft voice resounded, "what you need is a little faith! In this world everyone has a job and is expected to work. The job for you and your family will be to paint all the flowers every color to be found on our earth and in our sky."

In the language of flowers, the periwinkle is the symbol of pleasures, of memory and early friendship.

Dear fairies,
Grandma told me that you only read letters written with Perry's paintbrush. So, I am using one now! I saw you dancing with the fireflies last night!
Love,
🖌

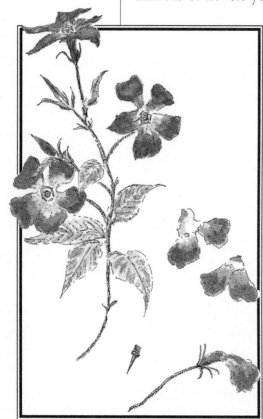

"But how can I do such a thing? There are not enough brushes or paint in the world to color the millions of flowers you have strewn on this planet," Perry said in a defeated tone.

"The rainbow will be your never-ending supply of colors. And listen closely: Slip your petals off, and you will see that I have given every periwinkle in my kingdom its very own paintbrush."

As Margaret ended her story, she slipped off the last pale blue petal and pulled out the tiniest, most fairy-like paintbrush I have ever seen. Since that day with Margaret, I have introduced dozens of children to the magical, hidden secret of the often-overlooked periwinkle.

Pansies

Nikolai Reimer was a nurseryman and plant lover who grew up in Czarist Russia and emigrated to Canada. His daughters Mary and Frieda say, "In the beginning, our father neither understood nor spoke the English language, but he was an expert in the universal language of flowers." Nikolai founded the now well-known Reimer's Nursery in Yarrow, British Columbia. When people in the area suggested that he spend more time growing fruit trees and other useful plants—plants that would provide food to eat—he would say, "When God created humankind, he gave each person two eyes, but only one mouth. Two eyes to appreciate doubly the beauty around us." He propagated great numbers of trees and shrubs, but flowers remained his first love.

> •• PANSIES ••
>
> *"I am thinking of you," is what the pansies say*
> *When they come to you from a friend;*
> *And, "I am thinking of you" is what they say*
> *When you the blossoms send.*
> *No need of words when pansies are near*
> *To carry the message for you—*
> *Just send a bunch of the blossoms fair,*
> *They'll speak plainly as you could do.*
> *All over the world in their simple way,*
> *No matter where they go,*
> *"I am thinking of you" is what they say,*
> *And all people their language know.*
>
> Margaret Coulson
> Walker

"Our father taught us many things about plants and flowers," say Frieda and Mary. "Among them was the story of the *Stiefmutterchen* (German for Little Stepmother, better known as the pansy). He would pick a pansy, and handling it with care so as not to injure its delicate beauty, proceed to introduce us to the little stepmother and her family":

"Today our father is 95 years old. He can no longer see the beauty of a flower. Recently we asked him if he would like to relive his life. 'Oh yes,' was the answer, 'if I could again be a gardener.'"

The Stiefmutterchen

The stepmother is number 1. You will note that she is wearing the most beautiful dress. Numbers 2 and 3 are her own daughters. They, too have lovely dresses, although not as beautiful as her own. Numbers 4 and 5 are her stepdaughters. They wear plain, unadorned dresses. If you turn the flower over, you will see the sepals which represent chairs. The stepmother has two chairs while her daughters, numbers 2 and 3, each have a chair to sit on. But sadly, her stepdaughters, numbers 4 and 5, must share one chair.

Poppies

A bby had been sick in bed for over a week. Cranky, aching, and tired of being indoors, she begged me to take her outside for a walk. "Sorry, Abby," I said, "Mom says you can't go outside until you are 100% well." "Oh, please, Sharon, please let's do something different. I am so tired of looking at the same thing every day, all day long!" "You are going to do something very different today," I replied. "You're going to watch a flower being born." I reached behind the door, pulled out a terra cotta pot filled with Iceland poppies, and set it on a sunny windowsill.

We read the morning away, and as we leafed through page after page of *The Secret Garden*, we watched a plump, hairy poppy bud slowly split, showing traces of orange along the seams. Then, quietly, almost sneaking by us, the pod fell away. During the next two hours we watched as the papery, orange petals unfurled and the wrinkles disappeared. I think that I was as excited and as touched by the poppy's birth as Abby was. I left the pot of poppies with her and every day she called me to give me a "poppy progress report".

In the silent language of flowers the poppy is the flower of CONSOLATION.

Dandelions

Millie Heath told me, "Every child knows how to tell the time by a dandelion clock. You blow as hard as you can, and you count each of the puffs left. An hour to a puff." (Dandelion clocks tell fairy time.)

Blow upon a dandelion,
Close thy eyes,
Chant
This year,
Next year,
Sometime,
Never,
If one clock remains,
We will be together.

OLD SONG

THE YOUNG DANDELION

I am a bold fellow
As ever was seen,
With my shield of yellow,
In the grass green.

You may unroot me
From field and from lane,
Trample me, cull me—
I spring up again.

I never flinch, sir,
Wherever I dwell;
Give me an inch, sir,
I'll soon take an ell.

Drive me from garden
In anger and pride,
I'll thrive and harden
By the road-side.

Dinah Mulock Craike

Dandelion Fortune Telling

It has been said that each of the tiny, feathery "clocks" on a dandelion has the power to tell time, divine emotions, and sail secret, winged messages to a loved one's soul.

Boys and girls of a hundred years ago picked "old man" dandelions, turned toward the direction of their faraway love, and blew once. If a single feathery seed remained, they knew they were not forgotten.

When children wanted to find out how many children they would someday have, they would pick a dandelion puff, close their eyes, and blow. If ten seeds remained, it foretold a large family!

From *Dandelion Clocks and Other Tales* by Julia Horatia Ewing London, 1894.

OVER THE CLIMBING MEADOWS WHERE SWALLOW SHADOWS FLOAT, THESE ARE THE SMALL GOLD BUTTONS ON EARTH'S GREEN WINDY COAT.

FRANCES FROST

Sweet Lavender

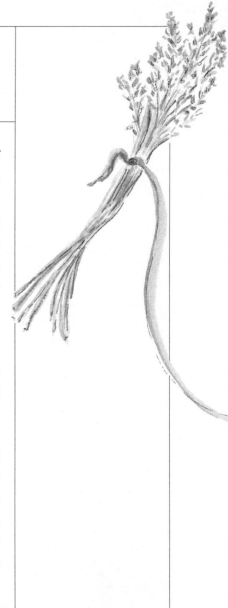

Lavender

hedges often were

planted around

cottages in

England.

It was believed

that they offered

protection

from evil....

There's nothing else like the scent of sweet lavender—fresh and clean straight from the garden in summer, or hauntingly nostalgic among the linens in winter. Lavender wands are so simple for children to make, and such a welcome gift for grandma or an older friend. Here's a story about lavender wands told to me years ago by a customer at Heart's Ease.

"Do you know I still have a lavender wand—sometimes we called them lavender cages—that I made over fifty years ago?" she said. "I keep it in a drawer and when I run across it I feel a whole flood of garden memories washing over me.

"Grandma would take us out into her cottage garden in the early morning as she cut her flowers and herbs for the day. I can still feel the warmth of the sun and I swear I can smell the lavender and the pinks. We would pick a handful of lavender and tie the heads together. Then, we would bend the stems back over the tied heads and tie them together—it looked like a little bottle. In fact, I think my neighbor called them bottles.

"Grandma would give us bits of ribbon from her sewing basket and we loved to weave the ribbon over

*I love thy flower
Of meek and
modest blue,
Which meets the morn and
evening hour,
The storm, the sunshine,
and the shower,
And changeth not
its hue.*

Agnes Strickland

and under the lavender stems. After the lavender wands were thoroughly dry we wrapped them in tissue paper and were so proud to give them to our schoolmistress the first day of school. We always had plenty to give as Christmas gifts too."

To make a lavender wand, pick an odd number of stalks in full bud, just before the flowers start to open all the way. Thirteen or fifteen stalks makes a nice fat wand. Bundle the stalks together and tie them firmly just below where the buds start. Holding the bundle with the stems pointing upward, carefully bend each stem down so that the buds are enclosed in a little "cage" of stems. Tie the stems together with ribbon just below the enclosed cluster of buds, or use a long piece of ribbon to weave over and under the stems, making a little basket to contain the buds.

Touch - Me - Not

During the past years the "grown-up kids" I have interviewed have often mentioned jewelweed. This plant seems to be one that tickles the dickens in all of us. I had my first experience with jewelweed at Audubon Camp in Maine. We were hiking the Roger Tory Peterson Bird Trail skirting a large pond. One of the men on the hike asked me if I liked jewelweed. I told him that I had never run into it and would love to look at it with my magnifier.

He pulled me over to a bush covered with beautiful yellow-spurred flowers spotted with red. Hanging from a fragile stem, swaying gently in the breeze, it was easy to see why these would be called jewelweed. Crouching over a blossom, not touching it, I looked up and asked why it was called "touch-me-not", too. My friend grinned from ear to ear, stretched his hand out to touch the flower, and ZING...like a firecracker exploding, seeds flew in all directions.

My question was answered and although I don't like to admit it, I did enjoy touching the "snapweed" all the rest of our hike. Sure feels good acting like an irrepressible kid again! I might mention that at least a dozen other "adults" on our hike were doing the same thing.

Eardrops

EARDROPS OF GOLD WITH

RED RUBIES BESET,

HANG FROM THE EARS OF A

DEAR LITTLE MAID.

"WHERE DID YOU GET THEM,

MY DARLING, MY PET?"

"DOWN BY THE BROOK YOU

CAN PICK THEM," SHE SAID.

Margaret Morley

Violets

*Who bends a knee
Where violets grow
A hundred secret
Things shall know*

You would think that the lovely, fragile violet would be the last thing a young boy would use to have a battle, wouldn't you? It was with a reluctant head shake and grin that Thomas Stanley related to me the violet tug-of-wars he fought in Shelbyville, Kentucky in the early 1900s.

"We would go out to the woods and pick a bunch of violets," he said. "You know that little hook they have on them where the petals are? Well, we would try to hook each other and see who could snag a violet head and rip it off. Whoever amassed the most violet heads was the winner of the violet tournament."

ORIGIN OF VIOLETS

I know, blue modest violets,
Gleaming with dew at morn—
I know the place you come from
And the way that you are born!

When God cut holes in Heaven,
The holes the stars look through,
He let the scraps fall down to earth,—
The little scraps are you.

———

ANONYMOUS

Bleeding Hearts

The true measure is the excited cry of joy and recognition when they notice the hearts.

Every spring, at the mossy base of my old sundial, a small miracle quietly unfolds. First, slender spears of green, then the heart-shaped leaves of old-fashioned violets appear. Amongst the violets another leaf shape emerges almost unnoticed. And one day, without fanfare, a fragile wand of parading bleeding hearts (*Dicentra spectabilis*) sways gently above my violets.

In my garden I can always calculate the degree of child left in a person by how they respond to my bleeding hearts. The true measure is the excited cry of joy and recognition when they notice the hearts. Then, the almost-instantaneous kneeling and close examination of the dangling flowers. I find that the only difference between the child of eight and the child of eighty is how long it takes to rise from that kneeling position!

Bleeding hearts are one of the most loved of the old-fashioned garden flowers. So many stories have been told to me about how the flowers were hung over ears as earrings, woven into hair as a dancing heart tiara, or dissected to reveal a lady-in-a-bathtub or a man-in-a-gondola.

My favorite is the story of the beautiful Princess

A browned, shadowy silhouette of a pressed stem of bleeding hearts marks this poem in the pages of my 1884 St. Nicholas magazine.

◆◆◆

"I know where there's a beautiful shoe—
Tiny and fair and ready for you;
It hides away in the balsam flower,
But I'll find you a pair in less than an hour."

"Thank you my laddie; now this I'll do,
I'll pluck a heart-flower just for you."

The hearts hang close on a

bending spray,

And every heart hides

a lyre away.

"How shall you find it? I'll

tell you true:

You gently sunder the heart

in two,

And, under the color,

as white as milk,

You'll find the lyre with its

strings of silk."

So now, child-at-heart, you see
that one man's princess is
another man's fairy-sized lyre.

Dicentra who wandered away from her walled garden and became lost in the darkness of an ancient forest. The princess fell prey to an evil crone angered to have her privacy disturbed. In an instant, Di was reduced to a fraction of her normal size and entrapped in the satiny pink folds of an oddly-shaped flower.

The old crone cackled happily and told Di that she was to remain forever imprisoned unless discovered and released by an innocent youngling.

Little did the crone know how tempting the Princess would be to any passing child! Only three days passed before a party of riders stopped for water in the forest. Drinking from a stream on bended knee, a boy glanced up, spied the dancing wand tipped by a pink and white heart, and plucked it (as innocent children will do). Short, plump fingers folded back Di's voluminous pink skirt, and the lovely princess was saved!

Dicentra is the perfect pressed flower. Picked early in the morning (after the dew has dried) and tucked between the pages of a thick dictionary, bible, or phone book, the flower is soon transformed into a perfect flat, papery little heart. After a few weeks of drying the bleeding hearts can be glued on greeting cards, valentines, or placecards for a special garden party.

IF YOU GENTLY FOLD BACK THE HOOP SKIRT OF THE BLEEDING HEART, INSIDE YOU WILL FIND PRINCESS "DI" CENTRA

Screechers

Millie Heckman Huffaker was raised on a ranch in Exeter, Tulare County, California, in the early 1900s. "We always had to make our own amusements and toys," she said, "and we always seemed to have plenty to do. The toys that were my favorites were my grass screechers.

"You pick a piece of Johnson grass and hold it between your thumb and first finger on each hand...like so. Pull it tight, hold it on its edge, and blow." Millie blew, and grinned from ear to ear; it was the first time she had tried it in sixty years. "You can make different sounds and screeches and whistles, depending how you breathe and blow. You can really get good at it and play tunes and fool people."

AFTERNOON ON A HILL

I will be the gladdest thing
Under the sun!
I will touch a hundred flowers
And not pick one.

I will look at cliffs and clouds
With quiet eyes,
Watch the wind bow down the grass,
And the grass rise.

EDNA ST. VINCENT MILLAY

---

*Hey, I've found some
moneywort.
Some day I'll be rich!
Or I wonder if it's
checkerberry?
I don't know
which is which.*

---

*Look, don't touch that
blade of grass,
Just keep away from it!
For see that frothy,
bubbly ball?
That's snake spit!*

---

*Cover your lips,
The darning needle
Loves to sew 'em up!
Who likes butter?
Lift your chin—
Here's a buttercup.*

---

*"D'ye ever whistle a
blade of grass?
Look, I got a fat one...
You slit it, see?
Here's one for you—
There's no snake spit
on that one."*

---

*Witter Bynner,
Child Life Magazine, 1937*

How To Make A Whistle

FIRST TAKE a willow bough,
Smooth and round and dark,
And cut a little ring
Just through the outside bark.

THEN TAP and rap it gently
With many a tap and pound,
To loosen up the bark,
So it may turn round.

SLIP THE bark off carefully,
So that it will not break,
And cut away the inside part.
And then a mouthpiece make.

NOW PUT the bark all nicely back,
And in a single minute
Just put it to your lips,
And blow the whistle in it!

ANONYMOUS

About Walnuts

John Arnold of Kokomo, Indiana, was famous for his walnut sailing vessels back in the 1940s. He'd fill a halved walnut with sap, glue, mud, or a gumdrop and stick in a toothpick, twig, or matchstick for a mast. Either a leaf or piece of paper would suffice for a sail, and he would spend hours sailing his fleet in Wildcat Creek, any rain-swollen gutter, or even Gram's wash-tub. When John had a son, he found himself construct-ing walnut boats again and delighting not only his son and his young friends, but himself as well!

Sailing off to

unknown seas

Walnut boats

with sails of

leaves

I once heard a story about a little girl who was very poor. Her birthday arrived and her family had no money to buy the sugar, flour, and eggs to bake her a cake. Missing out on a cake didn't bother her, but she was heartbroken about not having candles to wish upon.

When suppertime arrived, the girl swallowed the lump in her throat and resolved not to cry. Dinner was very meager, white bread with lard, poke greens, and a pot of navy beans...without ham. The little girl bravely ate her dinner and bantered cheerfully with her brothers and sisters.

After the table was cleared, just about the time the cake should have been served, the lights went out without warning. Mother, father, and all of the children paraded into the room holding the huge old crockery mixing bowl filled with water and a flotilla of walnut boats. Inside each walnut boat (one for each year of her life) was a small birthday candle glowing brightly. The little girl closed her eyes tightly, made a wish, and blew so hard the little boats scudded around the edges of the bowl as each and every candle was extinguished.

Walnut Baskets

Sometimes the simplest of gifts can give the most joy. My friends David, Julee, and Summer Krause stopped by on Christmas Eve and delivered a tray of cookies and a beautifully decorated golden box. I couldn't imagine what was inside. Jewelry? Really, there was nothing I needed.

On Christmas morning I eagerly unwrapped the gift from the Krause family and let out a shriek of excitement. Inside the box was a set of six tiny walnut baskets. Each basket was carved by David, and then Julee and Summer trimmed them with

miniature tablecloths and tied the handles with small red bows. It looked like a perfect picnic ensemble for a family of mice.

Now, every year I fill the baskets with pearly pink berries and hang them from our Christmas tree.

Today my dear friend Julie Whitmore brought my birthday gift—a tiny, tiny peach pit basket on an old and faded pink satin ribbon. Obviously, this was once somebody's prize necklace. I have set it next to my walnut baskets and it is positively dwarfed by them. Someone lovingly sanded, carved, and polished this little gem. I only wish I knew its story: from what garden, in what state, and carved by whom? I shall treasure it always!

Acorns

Who could help being intrigued by acorns in their little caps? I still enjoy walking through the woods and stuffing my coat pockets full of them!

THE BATTLE OF THE ACORN TOPS

Pick freshly fallen acorns and run a toothpick or nail through the acorn cap and halfway into the acorn (you must pre-drill a hole). The acorn top game may be played alone or with a friend.

First you empty a tabletop and set some of your acorn tops spinning. They may bump into each other and spin off of each other, but this is part of the battle. If one spins off of the table he is the loser. Whoever spins longest on the table is the winner. Whole armies of acorn tops may be made and set to spinning at the same time. Flowers of a certain color can be impaled on each tip. Perhaps red geraniums could top one army and blue cornflowers top another. Whichever army has the most spinners at the end of the battle wins. It is a sight to see all of the tops wildly spinning with vivid colors!

Gourds, Gourds And More Gourds

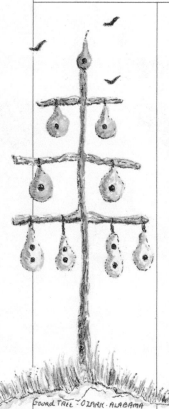

Gourd Tree - Ozark - Alabama

This story was told to me by Dorothy Greeman Peterson, who grew up in Turner County, Georgia, on a 200-acre peanut farm.

"In the springtime we would make houses out of gourds for the martins, sparrows, and other birds to lay their eggs in and raise their young. It was a beautiful sight to watch those birds flutter around the gourd houses and build nests. And they made such beautiful music!

"To make gourd houses you take green gourds, cut holes in them the shape of windows and doors, big enough for a bird to get through, scrape out the seeds and pulp, and hang them up to dry. We would poke holes through the tops and run wires through so we could hang them from a gourd tree after they dried.

"It was so much fun to make the gourd houses and watch the goings on. In the South gourds grow wild, usually among the watermelons or on the side of the road. We used leftover gourds as dippers on the back porch: just cut the gourd in half and dig out the pulp and seed and let it dry out. Oh, but the birdhouses were my favorite."

IT WAS A BEAUTIFUL SIGHT TO WATCH THOSE BIRDS FLUTTER AROUND THE GOURD HOUSES AND BUILD NESTS.

Here is a tip from an 1850s seed catalogue: "If, after a few gourds have set, the ends are pinched off the vines, the gourds will grow larger and better. Harvest the fruits before frost and when fully ripe, handling carefully to avoid bruising. Then, with a sharp knife slice away the unwanted parts to form the container, dipper, or whatever. Remove seeds, wash the gourd with a strong household disinfectant, and put it in a dry and ventilated place. Turn it every few days while drying, which will take weeks and in some cases months. You can polish it with paste wax."

•

YOU CAN

b a s k e t s

MAKE LOTS

b i r d h o u s e s

OF GREAT

s p o o n s

THINGS

r a t t l e s

USING

t o y s

GOURDS

•

If you haven't tried raising gourds you are missing a wonderful experience. Gourds provide a fragrant, fast growing shade screen, and the flowers are lovely. At Lewis Mountain Herbs in Ohio, a corner of the garden has a simple wooden framework totally covered with gourd vines and hung gaily with huge, ripening gourds. The gourds are harvested and dried for use as planters, birdhouses and other things, but during the summer the vines provide a delightful shady spot.

An old Burpee catalog for 1887 states, "Sugar trough gourds are useful for many household purposes such as buckets, baskets, nest-boxes, soap and salt dishes. They grow to hold from four to ten gallons each, have thick, hard shells, very light but durable, having been kept in use as long as ten years." Dippers and birdhouses were made from the dipper gourd, spoons were made from the spoon gourd (or it was left whole to form a darning egg for stockings or to become a rattle for the baby because of the dried seeds inside). Dippers and spoons made from gourds had the advantage of handles that don't get hot.

"A wonderful gourd toy that was often made in the late 1800s was a gourd man. He was simply stuck with twigs for arms and legs and a little face was painted or scratched on the top. But my favorite gourd toys were the coach gourds. An elongated gourd would have one quarter of the narrow part cut off so that it then resembled a coach shape. The pulp would be cleaned out and a long twig pushed through for an axle for the coach's wheels. The wheels could be made of thin log rounds, sliced buckeyes, or slices of cucumber.

The horses were easy to make out of peanuts with twig legs and drawn-on faces. Long strands of grass were tied around the peanuts to hold the harness in place. Driving the coach could be a lovely flower lady or a peanut lady or even a corncob lady. Whoever drove it, the ride would be fun!

In the 1880s, a favorite flower lady doll was made of gourd flowers! Harvest the tiny gourd just as it begins to form. This will be the doll's head. A gourd leaf is used as her clothing, and a hat can be made from another leaf. Twigs or toothpicks can be used to hold all of the parts of this lady together.

Betting On Hops

On a hot, clear, spring afternoon I was sitting on Georgie Van de Kamp's veranda with a group of gardening friends. We were discussing gardens and things we remembered about gardens and Carol Bateman piped up, "We used to place bets on hops!"

"Bets on hops?" I asked, "What in the world do you mean?" Carol laughed and said that hops vines grow so fast you can almost see them climbing.

"During our family's summers in Yosemite we would place bets on how much the hop vine would grow during the night," she said. "In the morning, we would go out and measure and do you know that some nights it would actually grow 6 or 7 inches!"

> HOP VINES GROW SO
>
>
>
> FAST YOU CAN ALMOST
>
>
>
> SEE THEM CLIMBING

Thomas Stanley was in his late 70s when he told me the story of how he and his friends turned grass into hearts and fooled the girls.

"We would pick a bunch of shepherd's purse—you know how it has the flat seedpods that look like little hearts? Well, we would hide the hearts under our tongues. Then we would stand in front of the girls and pick a handful of grass and say, 'We can chew grass and spit out hearts.'

"The girls would always laugh at us and tell us we couldn't, whereupon we would gobble up the blades of grass and spit out the shepherd's purse hearts. Got 'em every time!"

Trumpet Flower Bubbles

"we spent all of our time on the huge front ❖ porch which was draped and ❖ shaded by an old trumpet vine."

Margaret Crittenden Sparks told me this story about growing up in Topeka, Kansas, in the 1920s.

"Grandma always said that summers in Topeka were so hot and the air so thick and heavy that the wheat could stand up on its own after it was cut.

"Playing out in the sunshine or in the house was unbearable. It seemed as though we spent all of our time on the huge front porch which was draped and shaded by an old trumpet vine.

"My sisters and brothers and I had mixed up a bucket of soap flakes and water. We were planning to spend the day blowing bubbles, but much to our dismay we could find only one bubble pipe.

"For some reason, our eyes all seemed to settle on the red trumpet flowers at the same time. We each picked one, pulled out the stamens to create a little hole, pinched the hole closed, poured in the soapy water, tilted the blossom up, and blew from the wide part of the petals. It worked perfectly! We never argued over the bubble pipe again— we had an unlimited supply!"

The Magical Pumpkin Patch

This story was related to me in the early 1970s. Mammy is no longer living, but her story is as delightful today as when I first heard it.

"When we were little kids in Alabama we just didn't have any money or any toys like kids have now. We had to make all our own fun and mischief—and we did! Let me tell you the pumpkin patch story.

"The kids in my family were pranksters. We could stir up a storm without a cloud in the sky. We would sneak out on moonlit nights and head straight for old John Henry's watermelon and pumpkin patch. Sometimes we would just cut the heart out of the biggest melons in the patch and gorge ourselves on that juicy, sweet heart and then we would giggle and roll around so stuffed and proud of ourselves. Isn't this a shameful tale? Anyhow, we loved to pull his biggest pumpkins out of the patch and roll them down the hills. Sometimes we would build pumpkin walls from one side of the road to the other. We never, ever thought that John Henry would dream we were the culprits.

"One dark October night we stole over the fences and through the kudzu thickets into John's pumpkin patch. We went out into the middle and headed for the biggest pumpkin there. My brother Asa rolled that huge pumpkin over and there, in huge letters carved right in the pumpkin were the words...'THOU SHALT NOT STEAL'! We were right frightened! We turned over another one...'HE SEES ALL'! At this we looked up and around, let out screams, and high-tailed it back through the kudzu and home faster than we'd ever travelled before.

"Well, now I'm older and wiser. I know that old John had us figured out pretty early on. Finally, fed up with all our pranks, he had picked out the fairest dozen pumpkins in his patch and had scratched warnings into their soft skins as they were growing. As they grew so did the warnings and by the time we saw them they were darn near as big as billboards.

"Raising my own family, I always let the kids plant a pumpkin patch of their own. They are so comely and lovable, those huge old pumpkins. I love to scratch my grandchildren's names and their birthdates and sometimes phrases into the pumpkins as they are just starting to put on their growth. The kids love them, and they are always so tickled to have their own namesake pumpkin!"

Why don't you do this for your children? Give them their own magical pumpkin, named especially for them, and watch their wonder and joy. Recently, I saw a pumpkin patch where a farmer had customized his crop. He took orders in the spring and actually scratched names and addresses or phrases on the pumpkin. For example: WELCOME FRIENDS! These pumpkins last a long time; you could have one sitting on your front porch or doorstep all through the autumn and sometimes even into late spring.

Grass Slides

"MY HEART

WOULD RACE AS I

MADE THE

SEASON-OPENING,

BUMPY RIDE

DOWN THE HILL."

I grew up in a tiny valley surrounded by high, grass-covered hills. Every spring, when the grass got about up to our waists, an excited wave of anticipation swept through the valley. Time for the grass slides—time to start collecting cardboard boxes. Everyone's trash became fair game. Early on Saturday morning we would rally together with boxes of all sizes. We tore the boxes down, stamped them flat, and then the fun began.

The ascent up the green hillside was slippery and riotous. When we reached the top and looked down, our houses were toy-sized and the people working in their yards looked like bugs. The first ride down was the roughest. We drew straws to determine who would make the "rough run". I usually lost; in fact, I think I always lost. Could it be because I was the only girl in the gang? My heart would race as I made the season-opening, bumpy ride down the hill. Our whoops and hollers could be heard from one end of the valley to the other as our spring-time sledding party slipped through the sweet, green day.

Yesterday I was talking to some friends about grass slides. Kim Cory remembered racing down Laguna hillsides over a carpet of pungent, wickedly

slick eucalyptus leaves. Carolyn Germain described wild runs down Plymouth Avenue in St. Francis Woods in San Francisco in the early 1950s. "And those hills were *really* terrifyingly steep," she said. Jeff Prostovich remembered that when spring arrived and sliding began, he had to find numerous excuses for arriving home late with grass stained pants. I wonder if any of us would have the courage to do it now?

Dragonflies

This is a
DAMSELFLY.
They are smaller
than dragonflies
and when they rest,
they fold back their
wings - which is
something
dragonflies
don't do.

page 130

When I was a youngster maybe four or five years old, I was terrified to run along the hollyhock trail to Grandmother's house. I would peek out of our screen door, check to make sure the coast was clear, and then streak through the garden to Grandmother's back porch. One day I nearly bowled her over as I leapt up the stairs and into her kitchen.

"What on earth is scaring you, dear? she asked. "The dragon monsters," I replied, with my head bowed in shame. "Do you mean our friend the dragonfly?" she asked. I nodded, ashamed to have finally confessed my biggest fear. "Let me tell you about dragonflies, my dear," she said. "They are great hunters and while you are playing outside in the garden they are your guardian angels. They patrol the sky above you and snatch insects out of the air before they can bite you or bother you. Indians believed that the dragonflies, which are sometimes called darners, passed back and forth between the water and the air and stitched the rain clouds into the sky. When it rains it is because the dragonflies have decided to rest for a day and they don't attend to their duties of cloud-darning. On their day of rest the clouds loosen up and drop their rain on the dry earth, awakening sleeping seeds and giving birth to all of the beautiful flowers in our garden. Do you remember the dragonflies ever being out on a rainy day?" I puzzled over that question for a minute and then had to admit that I didn't.

"So, they're my guardian angels and they're protecting me from insects and they put clouds in the sky and they help us have flowers in our garden," I stated bravely. "Then I won't ever be afraid of them again." I turned, walked slowly down the steps, past the iris bed and straight over to the platoon of hollyhocks on the pathway. A pair of jewel-colored dragonflies clattered noisily into each other defending their territories. My heart jumped, but only once, as I turned and waved to Grandmother.

A living

rush

of light

he

flew

TENNYSON

Riddles

JONQUIL

FLAG

MAIDENHAIR FERN

POPPY

CARNATION

TIGER LILY

LAMB'S QUARTERS OR

PHLOX

JACK-IN-THE-PULPIT

FOUR-O'CLOCKS

LILAC

ANGEL'S TRUMPET

This flower riddle was given to me by Margie de Lyser of Cambria, California. The unsolved riddle was found folded up in a box of old letters hidden in a trunk. Can you match the clues with the flowers named here? Answers are on page 144.

GRANDMOTHER'S GARDEN

In Grandmother's garden strange plants you will see,
And if you guess rightly you'll find twenty-three.
They are all out of order for climate and time,
And arranged in this manner to give the words rhyme.
Just inside the gateway some clergymen stand (1)

With a bugler who plays in the heavenly band (2).

The name of a boy and an old-fashioned weapon (3),

You will find with the cares of all single men (4)

In Grandmother's garden we likewise behold,
Some plants that remind us of sheep in the fold (5).

And near them all standing, too stately to bend,
That which the soldier has died to defend (6).

A state in the South and a one-year-old child (7),

Form a beautiful background in this garden wild.
Here too, with its head held haughty and high,
The dread of the jungle lurking near by (8).

Yet farther, a fairy wand all made of gold (9),

And the pride of the mermaid so fabled of old (10).

A little white sin and a spinster's pet charm (11),

In yon shady thicket is sheltered from harm.
A time of the day (12) and a little frog's walk (13),

And a part of the face we use when we talk (14),

The child of a suffragette known in our land,
With one letter changed to good spelling command (15).

A pet name for father (16) and an embrace so sweet (17),

Are all to be found in this quiet retreat.
But ah! Here a beauty so perfect to see—
The serf of a Mexican followed by "e" (18).

The hope of our Pilgrims (19), an attempt made to
bite,

And a hideous monster once slain by a knight (20),

A mode of conveyance, a word meaning tribe,
Attracts our attention, and is Grandma's pride (21).

A shot from a cannon, and part of the foot (22),

While along the rough pathway Grandma has put
A pleasant expression, and one sharp-edged tool (23).

Now please try to guess them and stick to the rule.

MAYFLOWER

TULIPS

HOPS

CRESS

PEONY

SUN ROSE

GOLDENROD

BACHELOR BUTTON

VIRGINIA CREEPER

SNAPDRAGON

SMILAX

MISTLETOE

London pride
Lad's love
Black-eyed Susan
Jacob's ladder
Bishop's hat
Blush rose
Speedwell
Eyebright
Fair maids of France
Poppy
Love-in-a-mist
Sweet William
Wake robin
Thrift
Marguerite
Johnny jump-up
Maiden pink
Bleeding heart
Coxcomb
Wallflower
Rambler
Bachelor's buttons
Ladies tresses
English daisy
Four o'clock
Lady's slippers
Spring beauty
Goldenrod
Honesty
Tulips

LOVE AMONG THE ROSES

This was sent to me by Julie Whitmore. She found it in an old issue of *Modern Priscilla Magazine* dated 1928. Answers are on page 144.

Yellow was especially becoming to little (1), and so when (2) that dashing (3), invited her to a party at (4), she gratefully accepted this proof of the (5), and put on her yellow dress and yellow (6) in honor of the occasion. First, she carefully arranged her (7), and then tiptoed softly out of the house so as not to (8), her little brother. The mirror in the hall showed her that she was a (9), and that if her name had only been (10), she would have been a real (11). Her escort's (12) leaped high as he saw her, though, not to be outdone, he had with careful (13) polished his own (14) until they shone like a (15). "Not one of the (16) can equal your appearance!" he exclaimed proudly. "England forever!" A tinge of (17) showed on her face as he spoke with such (18), for behind it she read aright his (19). But she only answered him demurely, "I hope I shall not be a (20)." "Far from it," he answered warmly. " I would scale (21) itself for a dance from you." By that time they were at the party. "(22) exclaimed her escort to a boy at the door, "and give her your seat!" "Never," answered the young (23) disagreeably, and when pressed, he gave her lover such a blow that he saw his (24). But when he saw the (25) approaching he ran away. "Oh, Billy, are you hurt?" she sobbed wildly. He opened his (26) with love and answered feebly "Will you be mine?" "Ask (27)," she answered shyly; while a (28) to her cheek. His (29) answered in the old, old way and all we can do is to wish them (30).

T E N C U R I O U S B E R R I E S

There's a berry which makes my pony's bed;

And another one which is green when red;

And there's one which rubs you all the wrong way;

And another which swims and quacks all day;

There's one you can play, to beguile your care;

And one at their necks the ladies wear;

There's a berry which seems to be much depressed;

And one is a bird with a speckled breast;

There's one we can see when the tide is low,

And the last you will be when you older grow.

Some fill me,
Some beat me,
Some kill me,
Some eat me;
I creep and I fly,
And my color is
green;
And though I'm a
season
There's quite a good
reason
Why my end or
beginning there's no
man hath seen.

As soft as silk,
As white as milk,
As bitter as gall,
I'm rather tall,
And a green coat
covers me all!

———

Answer –
The milkweed pod

ANSWERS: *Strawberry, Blackberry, Raspberry, Gooseberry, Checkerberry,*
Mulberry, Blueberry, Partridge-berry, Barberry, Elderberry.

Answer – Thyme

Epilogue

I am young again and sitting in the cool darkness of Grandmother's early California bungalow. The smells of oatmeal cookies and simmering marmalade are wrapped around me like warm hands.

Outside, hummingbirds are dipping into the brilliant, red bottlebrush as Grandmother grabs her old straw hat and looks over at me. I wait for the familiar words, "Let's get busy, Sharon, time to go outside and see just what's happening in our garden."

My heart still soars when I smell oatmeal cookies, freshly turned spring earth, carnations in full sunshine. I relive over and over the joys and surprises of each day in our garden. I can sit quietly and string those sweet garden thoughts together, memory upon memory, like my summer garlands of tiny, pink rosebuds.

I know now that the gift my Grandmother Lovejoy gave me is an ancient one that runs like a tenacious woodbine through the childhoods of the hundreds of gardeners who have contributed to my book. A gift which has been quietly passed on from loving aunts and uncles, neighborhood friends, mothers, fathers, grandmothers and grandfathers, teachers, naturalists—it is the magical gift of sharing, a sharing of the reverence for the

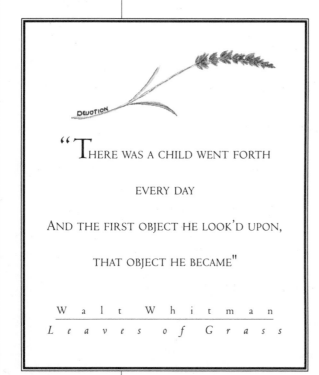

"THERE WAS A CHILD WENT FORTH

EVERY DAY

AND THE FIRST OBJECT HE LOOK'D UPON,

THAT OBJECT HE BECAME"

Walt Whitman
Leaves of Grass

earth and of the simple miracles of each unfolding day. Sharing the faces in a pansy, the opening of a poppy blossom, the taste of fresh hollyhock cheeses, or a pumpkin big as Cinderella's coach—small, seemingly insignificant sharings that will pop into our children's minds when they smell a familiar flower, or watch the sunflower's slow dance through the day. And they will say to their children, "Come over here, did you ever play tops with an acorn? Want to make a day-long jump rope?" And the traditions and love will keep lengthening, like my never-ending chains of summer rosebuds.

F A R E T H E E W E L L !

Let our children look upon the flowers of the garden.....

Bibliography

Blanchard and Lea. *The Handbook of the Sentiment of Flowers.* Philadelphia: 1847.

Bailey, Liberty Hyde, and Ethel Zoe. *Hortus Third.* New York: Macmillan Publishing, 1978.

Barrett, E.L. *The Doll's Own House.* Springfield, Ohio: G.C. Hall and Company, 1882.

Barrows, Marjorie. *One Hundred Best Poems for Boys and Girls.* Racine, Wisconsin: Whitman Publishing Co., 1930.

Beard, Adelia, and Lina Beard. *The American Girl's Handy Book.* New York: Charles Scribner's Sons, 1887.

Bralliar, Floyd. *Knowing Insects Through Stories.* New York: Funk and Wagnalls Company, 1918.

Brickell, Christopher, and John Elsley. *The American Horticultural Society Encyclopedia of Garden Plants.* New York, Macmillan Publishing, 1989.

Burgess, Thornton. *The Burgess Flower Book for Children.* Boston: Little, Brown and Co., 1923.

Bynner, Witter. "Read Aloud Time". *Child Life Magazine,* May, 1937.

Crane, Walter T. *Flowers from Shakespeare's Garden.* London: Cassell and Co., 1906.

_____. *Flora's Feast.* London: Cassell and Co., 1899.

Curtis, Mary I. *Stories in Trees.* New York: Lyons and Carnahan, 1925.

Earle, Alice Morse. *Child Life in Colonial Days.* New York: Macmillan Publishing, 1899.

_____. *Home Life in Colonial Days.* New York: Macmillan Publishing, 1900.

_____. *Old Time Gardens.* New York: Macmillan Publishing, 1901.

_____. *Sun Dials and Roses of Yesterday.* New York: Macmillan Publishing, 1902.

Ellacombe, Canon. *In a Gloucestershire Garden.* London: Edward Arnold, 1895.

Ewing, Juliana Horatia. *Dandelion Clocks and Other Tales.* New York: E. & J.B. Young and Co., 1894.

"Fairies in a Surbiton Garden". *The Garden,* August 24, 1918.

Gerard, John. *The Herbal.* New York: Dover Publishing, 1980. First published in 1633.

Gibson, William Hamilton. *Sharp Eyes: A Rambler's Journal.* New York: Harper and Brothers, 1892.

Gordon, Elizabeth. *Flower Children.* New York: Wise and Parslow Co., 1939.

Greenwood, Laura. *The Rural Wreath: Life Among the Flowers.* Boston: Wentworth and Co., 1856.

Hadfield, Miles. *The Gardener's Companion.* London: J.M. Dent and Sons, Ltd., 1936.

Haines, Jennie Day. *De Gardenne Boke*. San Francisco: Paul Elder and Co., 1906.

Haynes, Louise Marshall. *Over the Rainbow Bridge*. Illinois: P.F. Volland Col, 1920.

Howe, Elias. *The Language of Flowers*. New York: Leavitt and Allen, 1847.

Jekyll, Gertrude. *Children and Gardens*. Suffolk, England: Antique Collector Club, 1984. First published in 1908.

Johnson, A.T. "The Country of the Little People". *The Garden*, May 18, 1918.

Kelman, Janet, and Olive Allen. *Gardens Shown to the Children*. New York: Platt and Peck Co., 1899.

Lawrence, Elizabeth. *Gardening for Love*. Durham, North Carolina: Duke University Press, 1987.

Leist, Velista Preston. "Unbuttoning the Peas". *Child Life Magazine*, May, 1937.

Lounsberry, Alice. *The Wildflower Book for Young People*. New York: Frederick A. Stokes Co., 1906.

Miller, Olive Beaupre. *Through the Gate*. Vol. IV, My Book House. Chicago: The Book House for Children, 1920.

Morley, Margaret W. *Flowers and Their Friends*. Boston and New York: Ginn and Co., 1897.

Mulets, Lenore E. *Tree Stories*. Boston: L.C. Page and Co., 1904.

Paine, Albert B. *A Little Garden Calendar*. Philadelphia: Henry Altemus Co., 1905.

Rohde, Eleanour Sinclair. *A Chaplet of Flowers*. London: Medici Society, n.d.

Shafer, Sara Andrew. *A White Paper Garden*. Chicago: A.C. McClurg and Co., 1910.

Stack, Frederick William. *Wildflowers Every Child Should Know*. New York: Doubleday, Page and Co., 1909.

Stevenson, Robert Louis. *A Child's Garden of Verses*. Boston: L.C. Page and Co., 1900.

"Sunflower Competition, The". *The Garden*, October 12, 1918.

Tice, Patricia M. *Gardening in America 1830-1910*. Rochester, New York: The Strong Museum, 1984.

Walker, Margaret Coulson. *Lady Hollyhock and Her Friends*. New York: The Baker and Taylor Co., n.d.

Waterman, Catharine. *Flora's Lexicon, or The Language and Sentiment of Flowers*. Philadelphia: Hooker and Claxton, 1839.

Waugh, Ida. *Holly Berries*. New York: E.P. Dutton Co., 1881.

Glossary of Plant Names

African marigold   *Tagetes erecta*
Alpine strawberry   *Fragaria vesca*
Angel's trumpet   *Datura inoxia*
Anise hyssop   *Agastache foeniculum*
Bachelor's button   *Centaurea cyanus*
Balloon flower   *Platycodon grandiflorus*
Beauty-of-the-night (see Four o'clock)
Bee balm   *Monarda didyma*
Bishop's hat   *Astrophytum myriostigma*
Black eyed susan   *Rudbeckia hirta*
Bleeding heart   *Dicentra spectabilis*
Box   *Buxus sempervirens*
Brampton, queen's stock   *Matthiola incana*
Buttercup   *Ranunculus*
Cabbage   *Brassica oleracea*
Calendula, mary's gold   *Calendula officinalis,
    C. arvensis*
California poppy   *Eschscholzia californica*
Campion   *Silene alba*
Canterbury bell   *Campanula medium*
Cape marigold   *Dimorphotheca* spp.
Carnation   *Dianthus cariophyllus*
Carrot   *Daucus carota*
Catalpa   *Catalpa bignoniodes*
Cat's ear   *Hypochoeris maculosa*
Cedar   *Cedrus* spp.
Chamomile   *Chamaemelum nobile*
Chickweed   *Stellaria media*
Chicory   *Cichorium intybus*
Chinese lantern   *Physalis alkekengi*
Clover   *Trifolium*
Cockscomb, coxcomb   *Celosia cristata*

Colts foot   *Galax urceolata*
Columbine   *Aquilegia* spp.
Convolvulus   *Convolvulus*
Coral bells   *Heuchera sanguinea*
Cornflower (see Bachelor's button)
Cosmos   *Cosmos bipinnatus*
Cowbell   *Uvularia*
Cowslip   *Primula veris*
Cress (see Garden cress)
Crocus   *Crocus vernus*
Cucumber   *Cucumis sativus*
Cup-and-saucer vine   *Cobaea scandens*
Daffodil   *Narcissus*
Dandelion   *Taraxicum officinalis*
Daisy   *Erigeron annuus*
Daughter-of-the-evening (see Sweet rocket)
Day lily   *Hemerocallis* spp.
    (night blooming)   *H. altissima*
Delphinium   *Delphinium*
Dogwood   *Cornus stolonifera*
Dollar plant (see Money plant)
Easter egg eggplant   *Solanum melongena*
Egyptian water lily   *Nymphaea lotus*
Emilia   *Emilia sonchifolia*
English daisy   *Bellis perennis*
English wallflower   *Cheiranthus cheiri*
Evening lychnis (see Campion)
Evening primrose   *Oenothera marginata, O. hookeri*
Evening-scented stock (see Night blooming stock)
Fairy berry (see Alpine strawberry)
False dragonhead   *Physostegia virginiana*
Fennel   *Foeniculum vulgare*

Field marigold   *Calendula arvensis*
Fig marigold   *Glottiphylum depressum*
Filaree   *Erodium cicutarium*
Flag (see Iris)
Flanders poppy (see Shirley poppy)
Flax   *Linum grandifolium*
Forget-me-not   *Myosotis sylvatica*
Four o'clock   *Mirabilis jalapa*
Foxglove   *Digitalis purpurea*
Fraises des bois (see Alpine strawberry)
Fringed pink   *Silene laciniata*
Fuchsia   *Fuchsia*
Garden cress   *Lepidium sativum*
Garden verbena (see Verbena)
Gazania   *Gazania rigens*
Geranium   *Pelargonium* spp.
Germander   *Teucrium* spp.
Gladiolus   *Gladiolus*
Goat's beard   *Tragopogon pratensis*
Goldenrod   *Solidago odora*
Golden star   *Bloomeria crocea*
Gooseberry   *Ribes uva-crispa*
Goose grass   *Eleusine indica*
Gourd   *Lagenaria* spp.
Granny's bonnet (see Columbine)
Grape hyacinth   *Muscari botryoides*
Hawkbit   *Leontodon*
Heart's ease   *Viola tricolor*
Heavenly blue morning glory   *Ipomoea rubrocaerule*
Hens-and-chicks   *Echeveria*
Hepatica   *Hepatica americana*
Hollyhock   *Alcea rosea*

Honesty (see Money plant)
Honeysuckle   *Lonicera japonica*
Hops   *Humulus lupulus*
Horehound   *Marrubium vulgare*
Horseradish   *Armoracia rusticana*
Hyssop (see Anise hyssop)
Ice plant   *Mesembryanthemum crystallinum*
Iceland poppy   *Papaver nudicale*
Indian corn   *Zea mays*
Iris   *Iris*
Ivy   *Hedera helix*
Jack-go-to-bed-at-noon (see Goat's beard)
Jack-in-the-pulpit   *Arisaema triphyllum*
Jacob's ladder   *Pedilanthus tithymaloides*
Jewelweed   *Impatiens capensis*
Jimson weed   *Datura inoxia*
Johnny-jump-up (see Heart's ease)
Jonquil (see Daffodil)
Jupiter's beard   *Centranthus ruber*
Kale   *Brassica oleracea*
Ladies' tresses   *Spiranthes cernua*
Lady's mantle   *Alchemilla* spp.
Lady's slipper   *Cypripedium acaule*
Lamb's ear   *Stachys byzantina*
Lamb's quarters   *Chenopodium album*
Lantana   *Lantana camara*
Lavender   *Lavandula* spp.
Lemon verbena   *Aloysia triphylla*
Lilac   *Syringa vulgaris*
Little doves (see Columbine)
London pride   *Lychnis chalcedonica*
Love-in-a-mist   *Nigella damascena*

Madwort   *Aurinia saxatilis*
Maidenhair fern   *Adiantum*
Maiden pink   *Dianthus deltoides*
Mallow   *Malva* spp.
Marguerite   *Chrysanthemum frutescens*
Marigold   *Tagetes* spp.
Marvel of Peru (see Four o'clock)
Mayflower   *Cardamine praetensis*
Mint   *Mentha* spp.
Miss-go-to-bed-at-noon (see Chicory)
Mistletoe   *Phoradendron serotinum*
Money plant   *Lunaria annua, L. rediviva*
Moon flower   *Ipomoea alba*
Morning glory   *Ipomoea purpurea*
Moss rose   *Portulaca grandiflora*
Muskmelon   *Cucumis melo*
Nasturtium   *Tropaeolum majus*
Nicotiana   *Nicotiana alata*
Night-blooming cereus   *Selenicereus grandiflorus*
Night primrose   *Oenothera biennis*
Night-flowering campion   *Silene noctiflora*
Night blooming stock   *Matthiola longipetala*
Nottingham catchfly   *Silene nutans*
Oak   *Quercus* spp.
Obedient plant (see False dragonhead)
Onion   *Allium fistulosum*
Oriental poppy (see Poppy)
Ox-eye daisy   *Chrysanthemum leucanthemum*
Painted lady bean   *Phaseolus coccineus*
Pansy   *Viola x wittrockiana*
Parsley   *Petroselinium crispum*
Passion flower   *Passiflora alata*

Peony   *Paeonia lactiflora*
Peppergrass (see Garden cress)
Peppermint   *Mentha x piperata*
Periwinkle   *Vinca minor*
Petunia   *Petunia*
Phlox   *Phlox*
Pigweed   *Chenopodium album*
Pineapple sage   *Salvia elegans*
Pink   *Dianthus* spp.
Pink clover   *Trifolium pratense*
Pink sandwort   *Arenaria purpurascens*
Poor-man's-weatherglass (see Scarlet pimpernel)
Popcorn   *Zea mays* var.
Poppy   *Papaver orientale*
Portulaca (see Moss rose)
Postage stamp plant   *Schizopetalon walkeri*
Pumpkin   *Cucurbita pepo*
Pussy willow   *Salix caprea*
Queen-Anne's-lace   *Daucus carota*
Queen-of-the-night (see Night-blooming cereus)
Radish   *Raphanus sativus*
Ragged sailors (see Chicory)
Rocket (see Sweet rocket)
Rose   *Rosa* spp., *Rosa rugosa*
Rose geranium   *Pelargonium graveolens*
Sage   *Salvia officinalis*
St. Bernard's lily   *Anthericum liliago*
Sand spurry   *Spergularia*
Salvia   *Salvia* spp.
Saxifrage   *Saxifraga*
Scarlet pimpernel   *Anagalis arvensis*
Scarlet runner bean   *Phaseolus coccineus*

Scented geranium   *Pelargonium* spp.
Shepherd's purse   *Capsella bursa pastoris*
Shirley poppy   *Papaver rhoeas*
Smilax   *Smilax*
Snapdragon   *Antirrhinum majus*
Snow drop   *Galanthus*
Sow thistle   *Sonchus oleraceus*
Spaghetti squash   *Cucurbita* var.
Spearmint   *Mentha spicata*
Speedwell   *Veronica officinalis*
Spiderwort   *Tradescantia virginiana*
Spiraea   *Astilbe japonica*
Spring beauty   *Claytonia virginica*
Star-of-Bethlehem   *Ornithogalum umbellatum*
Stock   *Matthiola incana*
Strawberry   *Fragaria x ananassa*
Strawberry popcorn   *Zea mays* var.
Sunflower   *Helianthus annuus*
Sun rose   *Helianthemum*
Sweet alyssum   *Lobularia maritima*
Sweet fennel (see Fennel)
Sweet pea   *Lathyrus odoratus*
Sweet rocket   *Hesperis matronalis*
Sweet violet (see Violet)
Sweet white tobacco   *Nicotiana alata*
Sweet william   *Dianthus barbatus*
Sycamore   *Platanus occidentalis*
Tansy   *Tanacetum vulgare*
Tasselflower (see Emilia)
Thrift   *Armeria*
Thyme   *Thymus* spp.
Tiger lily   *Lilium lancifolium*

Tomato   *Lycopersicum* spp.
Touch-me-not (see Jewelweed)
Trumpet vine   *Campsis radicans, C. grandiflora*
Tulip   *Tulipa* spp.
Ursinia   *Ursinia*
Verbena   *Verbena x hybrida*
Vesper iris   *Pardanthopis dichotoma*
Walnut   *Juglans nigra*
Water lily   *Nymphaea* spp.
Violet   *Viola odorata*
Virginia creeper   *Parthenocissus quinquefolia*
Wake robin   *Trillium*
Wallflower   *Cheiranthus cheiri*
White lychnis   *Viscaria elegans*
White water lily   *Nymphaea odorata*
Woolly lamb's ear   *Stachys byzantina*
Wormwood   *Artemisia absinthium*
Xeranthemum   *Xeranthemum*
Yarrow   *Achillea millefolia*
Yellow lark's heels (see Nasturtium)
Yerba buena   *Satureja douglasii*
Zinnia   *Zinnia elegans*
Zucchini   *Cucurbita pepo* var.

ANSWERS TO GRANDMOTHER'S GARDEN:
1. *Jack-in-the-pulpit* 2. *Angel's trumpet* 3. *Jonquil (John Quill)* 4. *Bachelor's button* 5. *Lamb's quarters or Phlox* 6. *Flag (Iris)* 7. *Virginia creeper* 8. *Tiger lily* 9. *Goldenrod* 10. *Maidenhair fern* 11. *Lilac (lie Lock)* 12. *Four-o'clock* 13. *Hops* 14. *Tulips (two lips)* 15. *Sun rose* 16. *Poppy* 17. *Cress (Caress)* 18. *Peony* 19. *Mayflower* 20. *Snapdragon* 21. *Carnation (Car and Nation)* 22. *Mistletoe* 23. *Smilax*

ANSWERS TO "LOVE AMONG THE ROSES":
1. *Black-eyed Susan* 2. *Sweet William* 3. *Rambler* 4. *Four o'clock* 5. *Lad's love* 6. *Lady's slippers* 7. *Ladies' tresses* 8. *Wake robin* 9. *Spring beauty* 10. *Marguerite* 11. *English daisy* 12. *London pride* 13. *Thrift* 14. *Bachelor's buttons* 15. *Goldenrod* 16. *Fair maids of France* 17. *Maiden pink* 18. *Honesty* 19. *Bleeding heart* 20. *Wallflower* 21. *Jacob's ladder* 22. *Johnny-jump-up* 23. *Coxcomb (cockscomb)* 24. *Love-in-a-mist* 25. *Bishop's hat* 26. *Eyebright* 27. *Poppy* 28. *Blush rose* 29. *Tulips* 30. *Speedwell*

SCUBA DIVING

Dennis K. Graver

Human Kinetics Publishers

Library of Congress Cataloging-in-Publication Data

Graver, Dennis.
    Scuba diving / Dennis K. Graver.
       p.   cm.
    Includes bibliographical references and index.
    ISBN 0-87322-431-0
    1. Scuba diving. I. Title.
    GV840.S78G675   1993
    797.2'3--dc20
                                        92-43353
                                             CIP

ISBN: 0-87322-431-0

Developmental Editor: Holly Gilly
Assistant Editor: Dawn Roselund
Copyeditor: Jane Bowers
Proofreader: Valerie Hall
Production Director: Ernie Noa
Typesetter and Text Layout: Kathleen Boudreau-Fuoss
Paste Up: Tara Welsch
Text Design: Keith Blomberg
Cover and Interior Photos: Dennis Graver
Interior Art: Thomas · Bradley Illustration and Design
Printer: Sung In Printing America, Inc.

Human Kinetics books are available at special discounts for bulk purchase. Special editions or book excerpts can also be created to specification. For details, contact the Special Sales Manager at Human Kinetics.

Printed in Korea   10 9 8 7 6 5 4

Human Kinetics
Web site: http://www.humankinetics.com/

United States: Human Kinetics, P.O. Box 5076, Champaign, IL 61825-5076
1-800-747-4457

Canada: Human Kinetics, Box 24040, Windsor, ON N8Y 4Y9
1-800-465-7301 (in Canada only)

Europe: Human Kinetics, P.O. Box IW14, Leeds LS16 6TR, United Kingdom
(44) 1132 781708

Australia: Human Kinetics, 57A Price Avenue, Lower Mitcham, South Australia 5062
(088) 277 1555

New Zealand: Human Kinetics, P.O. Box 105-231, Auckland 1
(09) 523 3462

SCUBA DIVING

Contents

About the Author

With a quarter century of experience as a scuba instructor and instructor trainer, Dennis Graver, pictured here with his wife Barbara, is uniquely qualified to write this book. From master diver to award-winning underwater photographer, he is skilled in all aspects of scuba diving.

Dennis has authored over 25 books and manuals on the subject of scuba diving. In his position as director of training for the Professional Association of Diving Instructors (PADI), he designed the PADI modular scuba course and wrote the PADI Dive Manual, which revolutionized scuba instruction. During his tenure as director of education for the National Association of Underwater Instructors (NAUI), Dennis wrote the NAUI Openwater I Scuba Diver Course Instructor Guide. He has also contributed hundreds of published articles on diving in such magazines as *Skin Diver*, *Sources*, and *Undercurrents* and several NAUI technical publications.

Dennis has been an underwater photographer since 1970 and has won numerous awards from the Underwater Photographic Society. His photos have graced the covers of many magazines and illustrated several diving texts and audiovisual education programs.

Graver also influenced scuba diving with his development of a dive table multilevel diving technique for recreational diving and a breathing mask technique for diving rescue. In addition, he designed the NAUI Dive Time Calculator and the first PADI dive tables.

Dennis is a member of NAUI, PADI, the Handicapped Scuba Association, the Undersea Hyperbaric and Medical Society, the American Academy of Underwater Sciences, Diver's Alert Network, the Underwater Photographic Society, and the Underwater Society of America.

Preface

My goals in writing this book were to create the most complete, up-to-date text available for entry-level scuba diving and to improve diving safety through education. Toward those ends, I've written *Scuba Diving* for beginners who want to learn to scuba dive and for certified divers who want to refresh their memories and update their knowledge. I've presented the information so that the book will be easy for diving instructors to use with their classes regardless of the training organization the instructor is affiliated with.

In recent years, the trend has been to simplify diving instruction. Simultaneously, advances in diving medicine, diving equipment, and dive-planning devices have complicated the task of educating the beginning diver. This book provides more information than many scuba texts now available and addresses current issues and topics. Specifically, *Scuba Diving* has several unique features, including

- full-color illustrations and photographs,
- explanations of diving science the average person can understand,
- emphasis on the practical skills of diving,
- modern environmental concerns,
- a detailed explanation of equipment for diving in both warm and cold water,
- new, easy-to-understand dive-planning tables, and
- a thorough, yet nonfrightening, explanation of the risks and hazards of diving.

Two other elements that require a bit of explanation are the *new terms* and the *study goals*. There are many terms used in scuba diving and by scuba divers. The new terms appear in the text in aqua ink and their definitions are in aqua boxes in the margins of the pages. Be sure you are familiar with the terms in a chapter before you proceed to the next chapter. You will find the study goals in the coral boxes in the margins of the pages. These goals ask specific questions that you should be able to answer after reading the nearby text. Review these elements carefully; they are learning targets that will help you to channel your study.

The eight chapters of this book introduce you to the scuba diving "community," the diving environment, and diving science, equipment, skills, planning, and opportunities. Everything today's entry-level diver needs to know to enjoy scuba diving in comfort and safety is in *Scuba Diving*. However, you cannot learn everything you need to know as a scuba diver in a single course. My focus in this book is on teaching you to dive in average water conditions. You will learn about specialty diving, such as ice diving, night diving, or wreck diving, when you complete intermediate and advanced scuba diving courses. Do not attempt to teach yourself to scuba dive. Do not have a friend who scuba dives teach you. If you want to become a scuba diver, you must complete a sanctioned course of instruction taught by a professional scuba instructor who has been certified by a reputable diver-training organization.

If you are unsure whether or not scuba is something you would enjoy, many diving businesses offer introductory scuba lessons. You can try scuba diving in shallow water to see if you would like to learn more. Contact a local diving professional and ask about an introductory scuba experience, which requires only a few hours and often is free of charge. By giving yourself the experience, you will introduce yourself to one of the most exciting and enjoyable leisure activities available. Diving evokes feelings of peace and joy that you can experience as soon as you qualify as a scuba diver. Sign up for a course today and start reading!

Dennis K. Graver

WARNING:

DO NOT ATTEMPT TO LEARN SCUBA DIVING WITHOUT INSTRUCTION FROM A PROFESSIONAL DIVING INSTRUCTOR.

Acknowledgments

I am grateful to many individuals and organizations for their assistance with this book. My first thanks go to Rainer Martens, publisher at Human Kinetics, for his persistence in persuading me to write *Scuba Diving*. It also was a pleasure to work with Holly Gilly, the best developmental editor an author could hope to have, and the rest of the Human Kinetics staff—they are extremely professional.

Many people contributed to the photos in *Scuba Diving*. I wish to thank Bill Oliver of SeaQuest, who provided diving equipment for the models, and Harry Truitt of Lighthouse Diving Center and Dick Long of DUI, who both loaned equipment for photos. I am especially grateful to Skip Commagere, owner of Force E, who provided diving support and photographic models. Cliff Newell of NOAA in Seattle allowed me to photograph the recompression chambers at the NOAA facility. My long-time friend and diving buddy, Fred Humphrey, provided surf entry and exit shots, and

Wayne Hasson of the Aggressor Fleet supplied the photos of live-aboard boats. While many divers appear throughout the book, I want to thank these in particular: Michelle Anderson, Bill Black, Skip Commagere, Beth Farley, Barbara Graver, Scott Harrison, and Tom McCrudden.

The reviewers have my sincere appreciation, but my deepest gratitude is for the members of the diving community who have taught me for the past 28 years and who continue to teach me now. It is a pleasure to be able to pass on to others some of what I have learned.

Finally, I would like to say a special thank you to my loving wife, Barbara, for all the support she gave me while I completed *Scuba Diving*.

Dennis K. Graver

Equipment courtesy of

1 Getting Your Feet Wet

When you descend beneath the surface of the water, you enter a new and beautiful world. You have opportunities to view incredible life-forms that only a few ever see. Imagine swimming in a giant aquarium, and you can glimpse what you will experience in the underwater world.

The Joys of Diving

As a diver you are weightless and can move in all directions. You approach the freedom of a bird as you move in three dimensions in a fluid environment. Swimming weightless in clear water in a forest of underwater plants with sunlight streaming through is only one of many unforgettable experiences awaiting you.

Just as there are mountains, plains, and differing environments above water, there are a variety of environments for you to explore underwater. Coral reefs, kelp forests, incredible rock formations, and other natural wonders await divers in various geographical regions. Add to this piers, jetties, quarries, mysterious shipwrecks, and other human-made structures, and you can see how the breadth of underwater sights is limitless. There is more to view underwater than any diver could see in a lifetime.

Along with the variety of diving environments comes a wide range of activities. With pursuits like photography, hunting, and collecting, diving is challenging and rewarding. There is an activity to interest everyone. And the camaraderie of divers is well known. If you take up scuba diving, you will meet fine people and develop lasting friendships. Diving is a sharing activity, and there is much to share.

If you enjoy traveling, you will love diving. Dive travel is the Number 1 business of recreational diving, and reasonably priced vacations to exotic islands abound. Many divers plan one or more diving vacations each year.

The feelings and sensations of diving are fantastic, but they can be difficult to explain. Words are inadequate to describe the peaceful solitude of inner space one feels underwater. Diving can help reduce work-related stress, can increase self-esteem, and

Figure 1.1 Kelp forests are just one of many beautiful sights you'll encounter as a scuba diver.

Figure 1.2 Wrecks teem with underwater life.

can make you feel great. Soon you will experience the emotions and sensations for yourself. You'll then begin to know the joys of diving.

Learning About the Diving Community

The recreational diving community includes equipment manufacturers, diving retailers, diving educators, diver-training organizations, dive resorts, diving supervisors, dive guides, dive boats, dive clubs and associations, publishing companies, and certified divers. Commercial, scientific, and highly technical professional diving are not considered recreational pursuits; people involved in these diving activities belong to separate "communities."

There are few laws pertaining to scuba diving, and those that do exist do not govern who may dive. The diving industry is self-regulating. Those in the diving community realize that it is dangerous for anyone who has not completed a sanctioned course of instruction to attempt scuba diving. Dive businesses require proof of completion of training before they allow people to have scuba tanks filled or to participate in diving activities. Many dive operations also require proof of recent experience, documented in a diving log book. If you have not been diving for a year or more, you may be required to do at least one dive under the supervision of a diving professional. This supervised dive requirement helps increase the safety of divers whose skills may need refreshing.

Figure 1.3 You will need to show proof of certification before dive businesses will fill your scuba cylinders.

When you complete your training requirements as a scuba diver, you receive a certification card, called a *C-card*. Most C-cards do not require renewal, but the recreational diving community universally recommends refresher training following a period of inactivity longer than 6 months.

Certified divers can dive without supervision, but they may employ the services of a diving guide. But don't assume that because there is a divemaster or diving supervisor aboard a dive boat, that person will dive with you as a guide. Guiding services are not necessarily included with dive trips. If you want a guide to lead you about underwater and show you the sights, arrange for that service in advance.

You will learn more about the diving community as your experience increases. There are many opportunities for adventure and enjoyment. Get actively involved in the community when you complete your training and officially qualify as a scuba diver.

Learning About Diver Training

Your training must be sanctioned by one of the diver-training organizations. These organizations establish standards of training that you must meet to obtain a C-card. See the appendix for a list of diver-training organizations.

To be qualified to teach and certify divers, an instructor must have a current membership in a training organization. Confirm the qualifications of your instructor.

Your entry-level training course will follow a logical progression common for all approved diver-training courses. You'll learn through academic sessions, pool or confined-water (pool-like conditions in open water) sessions, and open-water training in actual diving locations. You will learn theory in the classroom and skills in controlled conditions, and then you'll apply your skills in the diving environment. The minimum training requirements are four academic sessions, four pool sessions, and four scuba dives in open water. You should make no more than two scuba training dives per day.

What are the three phases of entry-level training for scuba divers?

Figure 1.4 You should make at least four dives in open water during your scuba training.

Your initial training should include 30 to 40 hours of instruction, preferably over a period of several weeks instead of a few days. The time between classes allows you to reflect on your training and helps you absorb and retain the knowledge and skills better than a concentrated training schedule would.

Diving Prerequisites

Anyone who is at least 12 years old, has normal health, and is reasonably physically fit can undertake diving (12 is the minimum age for scuba certification). You do not need to be a competitive swimmer, but you do need to be able to swim 200 yd (183 m) nonstop using any combination of strokes. There is no time requirement for the swim; being comfortable in the water is more important than being able to swim fast.

You have normal health if your heart, lungs, and circulation are normal and you do not have any serious diseases such as epilepsy,

What kinds of medical conditions would disqualify an individual from scuba diving?

Commit these phone numbers to memory, or carry them with you when diving:

DIVERS ALERT NETWORK

Diving Emergencies Only
24 HOURS   919-684-8111

Information M-F   9-5 E.T.
919-684-2948

asthma, or diabetes. Any medical condition—even if controllable under normal conditions—that might incapacitate you in the water could cause you to drown while scuba diving. The air spaces in your body—sinuses, ears, and lungs—must be normal because changes in pressure affect them. People with physical disabilities may dive if they have medical approval from a physician.

Women who are pregnant should not scuba dive because the increased pressure can adversely affect an unborn child. But pregnant women may participate in snorkeling. Women often ask if they may dive during menstruation. A woman's menstrual cycle does not exclude her from diving if her health permits participation in other sports during that time.

Diving requires emotional as well as physical fitness. If you are terrified of water or of feeling confined, you probably should not pursue diving. Normal concerns are to be expected, but panic is dangerous underwater.

You should have a physical examination before you begin your training, especially if it has been more than a year since your last exam. It is best if a diving physician recommended by your instructor does the exam. Sometimes regular physicians who do not understand the physiology of scuba diving grant approval to scuba dive for individuals who have medical conditions that place them at great risk in and under the water. If your physician grants you medical approval for diving, but your instructor says your medical condition is contrary to safe diving, listen to your instructor.

The Risks of Diving

Figure 1.5 Being comfortable in the water is important to your enjoyment and safety.

All activities have risk. There is risk in walking across the street, driving a car, or water skiing. To avoid injury, we take precautions for our safety. There are precautions for scuba diving just as there are for any other pursuit.

Diving is similar to flying. Both are low-risk activities when done with well-maintained equipment, according to established rules, and in good environmental conditions. But both are unforgiving if you ignore the rules and safety recommendations.

In this book I discuss injuries that can happen to scuba divers. By being aware of the hazards, you can learn how to avoid injury. If you do as you are taught, your risk will be minimal and your diving experiences are likely to be pleasant.

One hazard of diving concerns the changes in pressure that occur with changes in depth. Changes in pressure can injure body air spaces severely if you are not in good health or if you fail to keep the pressure in the air spaces equalized with the surrounding pressure. You will learn equalizing techniques in your training.

You normally have gases dissolved in your body. Increased pressure at depth increases the amount of gas dissolved in the body. If you ascend too rapidly from a dive, the gases in your system can form bubbles and produce a serious illness known as **decompres-**

decompression sickness (DCS)
Illness caused by gas bubbles forming in the tissues or blood before the gas can be diffused into the lungs and eliminated; also called venous gas emboli (VGE) and "bends."

sion sickness (DCS). By regulating your depths, the times of your dives, and your rates of ascent, you can minimize the likelihood of DCS. Failure to heed depth and time schedules and ascent rates can cause serious, permanent injuries.

Diving can be strenuous at times. You need sufficient physical fitness and stamina to handle long swims, currents, and other situations. If you become winded from climbing a flight of stairs, you may need to improve your fitness level before you learn to scuba dive. Exhaustion in and under the water is hazardous.

Diving takes place in water, an alien environment. Aquatic skills are essential in and around water. You'll use life support equipment to dive, but you cannot depend entirely on the equipment for your well-being. A person with weak aquatic ability can drown when minor equipment problems occur—problems that could easily be handled by a person with good water competence. You must be comfortable in water to be a scuba diver.

Any activity involves risk. Don't be overly concerned with them because the risk of diving injuries can be minimized. Your training will teach you how to dive safely. You will learn how to minimize the risk of injury and maximize your enjoyment of the underwater world.

How to Choose a Dive Course

There are many diver-training organizations and thousands of professional diving educators. Check your phone book for diving businesses offering sanctioned courses. Many community colleges, YMCAs, and recreational departments also offer scuba courses. Ask about the qualifications, experience, and reputation of several diving instructors in your area before selecting a course. To find the best possible training, you will want to ask the following questions:

- Which diver-training agency sanctions the training?
- How long has the instructor been teaching scuba diving?

Figure 1.6 You should purchase a mask, snorkel, fins, boots, and gloves for use during your scuba diving training.

- What levels of training is the instructor qualified to teach?
- May you speak with the graduates of a recent class?
- Why is this course better than others in the area?

The tuition for diving instruction is usually between $200 and $300. The lowest priced course may not necessarily be a bargain. Find out what the course fee includes and, more importantly, what the total cost will be for you to become certified as a scuba diver. You will not have to purchase all of the equipment needed to scuba dive, but you will need to have mask, snorkel, fins, and usually boots and gloves for your training. Use of the additional required equipment typically is part of the course tuition.

Find out if the course price includes costs for educational materials and certification. There may be additional costs for travel, lodging, parking, boat fees, and equipment rental for open-water training. Determine the complete cost before enrolling in a course.

When you enroll in a course, you should receive a reading assignment for your first session. If you are not given an assignment, ask about it. You will learn much better if you read in advance about the topics to be presented in class. Good diving instructors provide a handout with reading assignments.

Select a course and enroll right away. A fantastic world awaits you underwater. Scuba training is exhilarating, challenging, and enjoyable.

Being a Responsible Diver

What responsibilities do you assume when you become a scuba diver?

When you qualify as a scuba diver, you assume many responsibilities—for your safety, for the safety of those with whom you dive, for the image of scuba divers, and for the preservation of the diving environment. The diving community, which you'll be part of, encourages divers to accept responsibility for their actions. Each chapter of this book emphasizes various responsibilities; a summary of them is provided in the appendix. Learn what you should do, then *do* what you have learned.

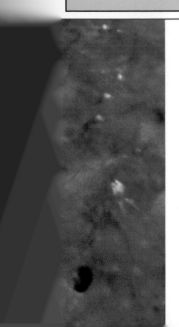

2 The Underwater World

Learning to dive gives you an opportunity to explore the aquatic environment, which covers more than 70% of the earth's surface. The underwater world is fascinating. This section introduces you to the biological and physical conditions of the diving environment. You will learn about people's effect on the environment and the environment's effect on people. You affect the underwater world more than you might imagine.

Introduction to Aquatic Biology

The plants and animals of the underwater world are wondrous and diverse. The millions of plants and animals in the aquatic realm range from microscopic size to creatures weighing tons. To appreciate, respect, and enjoy aquatic life, you need to learn certain aspects of biology. This section familiarizes you with the flora and fauna of the aquatic realm. Aquatic life fits into three categories: life-forms that drift with the currents, those that swim freely and are able to move against the currents, and those that dwell on the bottom.

Drifters

The drifters are called *plankton*. Animals that drift are called zooplankton; plants that drift are called phytoplankton. Plankton begins the food cycle in the waters (see Figure 2.1). Small animals eat plankton, and larger animals eat the smaller animals. When the large animals die, their remains sink to the bottom and they decompose. The decomposed material rises to the surface, where it becomes food for the plankton.

Warm water and nutrients cause some plankton to multiply. Overpopulations of plankton, called *blooms*, can color the water, destroy underwater visibility, and form toxins in animals that feed by filtering water. Toxin from blooms makes clams and mussels unsafe for consumption during summer months in some areas. One type of red phytoplankton often creates blooms, known as *red tide*, in the seas. Diving conditions are poor in areas affected by plankton blooms.

> **Describe the aquatic food cycle and how the process contributes to red tide.**

Another type of phytoplankton, called algae, is an important part of the aquatic world. Plants use light to produce their own food and become food for animals. They convert water and carbon dioxide (CO_2) to oxygen and carbohydrates through photosynthesis. Various types of algae are found in underwater areas where light is available. Most algae grow in shallow water where light is most abundant. Thick moss drapes objects in some freshwater areas. A grasslike, green, tropical saltwater algae that provides a habitat for many forms of life is called turtle grass. Some cold-water, shallow-water types of long, flowing algae, such as surf grass or eel grass, can cause you to trip if you try to walk against them. Slippery plants covering rocks can cause you to slip and fall unless you move cautiously.

Giant algae, called *kelp*, produce long strands, called *stipes*, in which you can become entangled, but you can learn how to avoid and how to deal with this problem. A rootlike structure, called a *holdfast*, anchors kelp to the

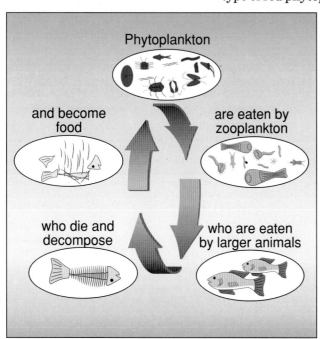

Figure 2.1 The underwater food cycle.

Phytoplankton

are eaten by zooplankton

who are eaten by larger animals

who die and decompose

and become food

bottom; numerous gas bladders, called floats, lift kelp toward the surface. What appear to be the leaves of kelp are *fronds*. Large areas of kelp, known as kelp beds, have thick canopies that blanket the surface of the water (see Figure 2.2). It is difficult to swim through a kelp canopy at the surface, but it is easy to swim between the clumps of stipes beneath the surface. Underwater navigational skills are important when diving in areas where kelp is dense. Kelp "forests" are popular diving areas because they contain lots of life.

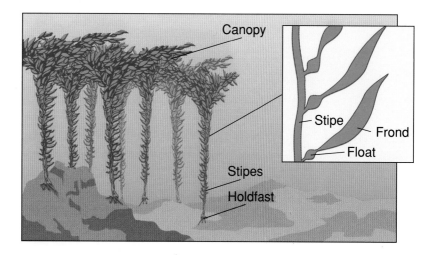

Figure 2.2 A typical kelp bed.

Swimmers

What is the best way to observe fish?

One of the rewards of diving is seeing fish. There are fish in nearly all the waters of the earth. You cannot outswim the slowest fish, so do not chase them. If you want to observe fish closely, blend into the environment. Fish will get closer to you than you could ever get to them.

Collecting for aquariums requires specialized knowledge and procedures. Most fish have an internal air bladder for buoyancy control. If the fish is taken to the surface too quickly, the air bladder expands and kills the animal. Avoid handling fish because the experience can be traumatic, as well as physically damaging, to the animal.

And eating some types of fish can harm you. Some fish are poisonous. Types of fish poisoning include ciguatera, scombroid, and tetrodotoxin. Ciguatera results from eating fish that consume a certain species of algae. Ciguatera poisoning causes gastro-intestinal problems within 6 to 12 hours. Scombroid poisoning, which produces nausea and vomiting within an hour, can result if you eat fish that have not been kept chilled. Tetrodotoxin, the most serious fish poisoning, results from eating exotic fish such as a pufferfish or blowfish (Figure 2.3 shows an example of a pufferfish). Tetrodotoxin poisoning can cause death within minutes. Avoid eating large and unusual-looking fish. Check with local fishermen to determine which fish are safe for consumption.

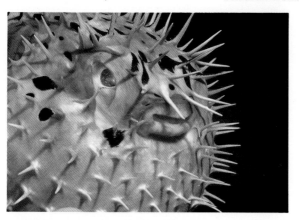

Figure 2.3 Eating pufferfish will cause poisoning that could result in death.

Many large, swimming mammals—sea lions, seals, dolphins, whales, and manatees—inhabit the water world. They are graceful, beautiful, and sometimes awesome in appearance. Some are curious and will approach you. Aquatic mammals usually will not harm you in the water if you leave them alone, but sea lions and seals are defensive on land and might bite if you get too close.

Bottom Dwellers

Bottom dwellers include animals that are stationary, such as sea fans and some hydroids, as well as animals that move about, such as crabs and lobsters. Generally speaking, living stationary bottom dwellers are not included in fish and game regulations, and you should not take them. Don't take coral, sea fans, or animals that appear stationary, such as starfish. Many people seek crabs and lobsters for food because the animals are delicious to eat. If you hunt these creatures, know how to determine their sex, how to catch them without harming them, and how to measure them for minimum size. Do not take females, particularly those bearing eggs. Some divers take only one claw from a crab, to conserve the species. A crab can feed and defend itself with one claw and can regenerate a new claw to replace the one taken.

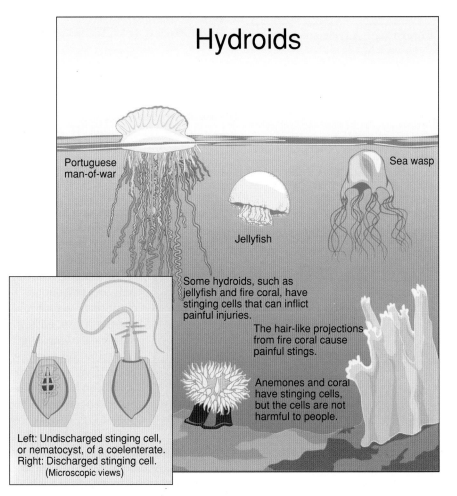

Figure 2.4 There are several types of hydroids, which have stinging cells.

Hydroids

If you dive in salt water, you should know about hydroids, a category of animals that includes bottom dwellers, such as coral, and swimmers, such as jellyfish (see Figure 2.4). Some hydroids, like the beautiful sea anemone, have a round, columnlike body with a mouth surrounded by tentacles. This is a polyp form of hydroid. Another type, the colonial form, can assume many different shapes. Colonies of hydroids can encrust a surface, and groups of colonies form jellyfish.

Potentially Dangerous Aquatic Animals

Aquatic animals use a variety of mechanisms to obtain food and to defend themselves from attack. You can minimize your chances of injury by being familiar with the ways in which animals inflict injury. Aquatic animals are rarely aggressive toward humans; they flee, hide, or stand still as you approach. If you do not touch, threaten, or provoke an animal, it is unlikely it will injure you intentionally. But remember, aquatic animals are wild animals. If you feed them and they bite you in the process, you should not blame the animals. Figure 2.5 lists types of injuries you could sustain from aquatic animals and recommended first aid.

Animals That Cause Abrasions or Cuts

Many animals, such as some types of coral and barnacles, are sharp, hard structures that easily cut flesh. Such cuts can be painful and slow to heal and can get infected. Avoid contact with reefs and rocks covered with sharp animals.

Also, some fish have knifelike protusions on their gill plates or at the base of their tails. They defend themselves by flailing rapidly back and forth and slashing anything near them.

> **What are the ways divers can be injured by aquatic life?**

Animals That Puncture

Sea urchins are the porcupines of the seas. Cold-water urchins have short, thick spines, whereas warm-water urchins have spines that are long and thin. The spines of all urchins can penetrate an exposure suit if you bump into them. The spines break off in your flesh and produce a painful, red, swollen wound. The spines can be difficult to remove, so if you are unable to avoid a sea urchin injury, see a physician to have the spines removed.

Some fish have a row of long, sharp spines along their backs. The scorpion fish has hollow dorsal spines, at the base of which are sacs filled with venom. If you are punctured by the spines and compress the venom sacs, you inject yourself with a toxin. The toxin of some species, such as the stonefish, can cause serious symptoms. The lionfish (also called a turkey fish or a zebra fish) has spines in other fins, and its toxin produces serious symptoms in humans.

A tropical marine worm called a bristle worm has tufted, silky bristles along the sides of its body. The bristles, which are fine and

Coral

Fire coral

Sea urchin

Moray eel

Injury	First Aid
Abrasions or cuts	
Barnacle	Scrub and disinfect the wound.
Coral	
Bites	
Barracuda	Stop the bleeding, clean and
Moray eel	disinfect the wound. For a sea snake
Sea snake	bite, apply pressure, immobilize the
Shark	area, and get prompt medical
Turtle/muskrat/alligator	attention.
Stings	
Bristle worm	Soak the injured area in
Cone shell	vinegar. For a cone shell sting,
Fire coral	apply pressure and immobilize the
Jellyfish	injured area.
Puncture	
Sea urchin	Soak the injured area in hot water.
Venomous fish	
Laceration	
Stingray	Soak the injured area in hot water.

*Get medical attention as needed for all injuries.

Figure 2.5 Potentially dangerous aquatic animals.

Stingray

brittle, penetrate the skin easily, are difficult to remove, and cause a burning sensation. Do not handle these worms.

Some seashells, called cone shells, have a venom apparatus they use to kill animals for food. The venom is highly toxic, and the animals can inject their venom into a human. Do not handle conical shells in tropical waters.

Animals That Bite

Use discretion to avoid being bitten in the water. A large freshwater fish that can bite is the gar. Turtles can inflict serious wounds, muskrats may attack in defense, and moray eels in the ocean can deliver a serious bite. Alligators also have the potential to inflict injury but have not been known to hurt divers. Sharks can bite, but attacks on scuba divers are nearly nonexistent. Hollywood has greatly exaggerated the danger of sharks; only a few species of sharks are aggressive, and it is rare to encounter these types in the waters visited by divers. Most divers would be delighted to see a shark because the animals usually retreat from areas frequented by scuba divers.

Retreat from snakes if you encounter them. Do not handle them. Sea snakes in tropical waters are extremely venomous; a sea snake bite can produce a life-threatening emergency. Some freshwater snakes, such as the cottonmouth, also are venomous.

Animals That Cause Lacerations

Rays are round, flat bottom dwellers. Some rays have a sharp, serrated barb at the base of the tail. The rays blend into the bottom. When someone disturbs a ray, it defends itself by arching its back and thrusting its barb into the attacker. A sheath, which often remains in the laceration wound, covers the barb and contains a toxin. Stingray wounds in the ankles of divers, waders, and swimmers are common in some areas. Avoid stingray wounds by shuffling your feet along the bottom instead of walking. The torpedo ray, found on the West Coast of the United States, can generate electricity. This ray can stun a diver, so be able to recognize it, and avoid contact if you encounter one.

Animals That Sting

Many animals sting. Learn to identify and avoid contact with jellyfish, featherlike or whiplike hydroids, and even some sponges. Hydroids have tiny stinging cells, called *nematocysts*, used to kill food. The sting of some hydroids, such as encrusting fire coral, is merely annoying; but the sting of others, such as the Portuguese man-of-war or the box jellyfish, can cause a medical emergency. It is a good practice to wear an exposure suit at all times while diving in the ocean. The suit protects you from stings, but be careful when you remove it. The stinging cells of marine animals remain active even when they are not on the animal. Parts of jellyfish and other animals that are on your equipment may come into contact with your skin when you remove the equipment. Some jellyfish come to the surface at night in tropical waters. Dangerous stinging animals are seasonal in some regions. Check with local divers to find out what to avoid and when to be on the alert.

Avoiding Danger

Many aquatic animals are potentially hazardous. Tropical waters have the most dangerous animals. But serious injuries to divers are not common, because divers avoid animals that can hurt them. Respect animals, but do not be overly concerned about them. Do not panic or flee when you see a dangerous animal; just avoid contact with it. Learn to recognize the dangerous animals in an area, know where to look for them, be alert for them, and keep clear of them. Move slowly and look carefully. Shuffle your feet when wading. Don't touch anything unless you know it is safe to touch.

The biology of the underwater world is so interesting that many divers study it as a hobby. It is fun to learn about animals and plants and then observe them in their natural habitats. Some divers, fascinated with aquatic life, pursue biology as a career.

Conserving and Preserving Life

Life in the waters is beautiful and precious, but pollution from people jeopardizes life in the lakes and seas. Even divers physically ruin beautiful reefs. Unless we take action immediately, there is a real danger that many areas of the underwater world will become barren and lifeless. We must preserve and conserve the resources of our waters.

Because the waters are so vast, people often take them for granted. Lakes and seas seem too big to be harmed, but that is not the case. The underwater environment is fragile; the balance of nature can be upset more easily than many people realize. We think of the seas as great and powerful because we see big waves and pounding surf. People who do not see beneath the surface may not realize the delicate nature of the animals that inhabit the waters. Some living things in the seas grow slowly—only a fraction of an inch (a few centimeters) per year.

As a diver, you can help reduce damage to the underwater world. Every diver should take two actions: (a) Do everything possible personally to preserve the diving environment, and (b) do everything possible to educate others and help them learn to preserve the aquatic environment. You will get closer to the aquatic environment than most of your friends, and you will see firsthand the effects of pollution, litter, and exploitation. You also will see the beauty and abundance that are possible when the environment is clean and unmolested. Your influence in society can make a difference. If you do not become part of the solution to problems in the aquatic environment, you are part of the problem.

Pollution

Stemming pollution is one of the greatest challenges facing the world today. Humans are incredible polluters of the environment; we have polluted the air, the land, and the waters.

People dump billions of gallons and billions of pounds of waste into water every day. People seem to think that when something is out of sight, it no longer is a problem. This is not true of pollutants. Sewage, industrial waste, garbage, and sediment have killed many underwater environments and are continuing to kill. If we stopped all pollution today, the aquatic environment would continue to suffer for decades from the waste materials that are already in the water.

Runoff from land that enters rivers and streams and flows into the ocean also causes pollution. Chemicals used in agriculture, on lawns, and in gardens cause death and destruction in the aquatic environment. Sediment from construction and drilling finds its way into water and blocks out life-giving sunlight and smothers bottom-dwelling creatures.

Lakes and oceans have been viewed as bottomless toilets for waste disposal. There are two problems with this narrow view: (a) Animals and plants live in the water and are killed by the pollution, and (b) the water cannot be replaced because large bodies of water cannot be flushed.

> Name four types of pollutants and describe the effects they have on the diving environment.

Diver Impact

As a diver, you can directly harm the aquatic environment in several ways. You can remove living things from the environment, you can smash and kill life while moving about underwater, and you can stir up clouds of silt on the bottom. The silt can choke and kill some organisms. Good intentions also can cause problems: Handling and feeding animals can kill them.

You can be an effective predator underwater. There are many animals you can hunt and take. A few callous individuals kill animals for "sport," but most people take only what they will eat. Although the impact of divers is of little significance compared to that of commercial fishing, you do have an effect. If you spearfish on a reef, it will not be long before the fish in the area will be unapproachable by divers. If you want to be a predator, do so in a responsible manner. (Conservation and preservation of aquatic resources are discussed later in this section.)

It is difficult to resist touching animals underwater, but you should refrain from doing so until you know what animals may be touched and how to touch them without harming them. Many animals are delicate; rough handling will cause them to die. Predators will eat animals removed from a protected area for viewing. Some animals, including fish, have a protective coating of mucus. If you remove the coating by handling a creature, the animal can develop an infection and die. The stress of being handled by a gigantic, bubble-blowing monster may be more than some aquatic animals can take. Do not be guilty of killing animals for your amusement. After you learn how, you will be able to get extremely close to animals underwater. You can interact with them and enjoy them without handling them.

> Why should divers refrain from touching or feeding underwater animals?

Feeding animals underwater was a popular activity until environmentalists showed that this is harmful (not to mention dangerous). There are several potential problems. Unnatural food fed to animals can interfere with the digestive process. The animals may become dependent on the food fed to them by divers and may not be able to forage if the food supply is discontinued. And feeding can make animals overcome their natural fear of divers. When an animal that would normally take cover at the sight of a diver becomes accustomed to divers providing food, the animal will readily approach a diver who is a hunter.

A diver underwater can be like a bull in a china shop. Overweighted divers plow along the bottom with their fins pointed downward, stirring up great clouds of silt. Buoyancy difficulties cause divers to hold onto and crash into reefs and living things. Divers who rest on the bottom crush life without realizing it. Divers who swim too close to a reef often kick animals to death.

Minimizing Diver Impact

One of the most important reasons for good buoyancy control skills is to prevent damage to the underwater environment. An environmentally responsible diver is properly weighted and in control of buoyancy at all times. Make your diving "no contact" diving. You should be able to hover above a reef, move your mask within inches of an animal, and view the animal without touching anything but water and without stirring up silt. Learn to use your hands to scull into position while your fins remain still. You can do this with short movements of the hands (not the arms). Buoyancy control and sculling are excellent skills for reducing diver impact. Figure 2.6 shows a diver sculling.

> **What are five things you can do to keep from damaging the environment while you're underwater?**

Figure 2.6 Sculling helps reduce diver impact.

Another way to protect the environment is to keep your equipment secured close to you so it does not dangle and drag. Equipment that drags along the bottom for an entire dive can do a great deal of damage. Streamline your equipment.

Moving slowly underwater conserves energy and air and makes you less likely to make contact with things. This helps you avoid injury to both yourself and animals.

If you must hold onto something underwater or push yourself away from something, look before you touch, and avoid touching anything that is living. If you must settle onto the bottom for some reason, select an area where there is no visible life. If you are weightless, keep in mind that one finger may be all you need to provide the leverage to move. Leave no evidence that you ever visited an underwater area.

Conservation

Many animals that once were plentiful are nearly extinct because of a lack of conservation. Buffalo and passenger pigeons are good examples of land creatures. In some areas, this is happening to aquatic animals. Bait fish, which once swarmed in enormous schools in some areas, no longer exist. With no food to eat, larger predatory fish no longer frequent the areas.

Fish and game regulations were designed to conserve natural resources. Rules regarding sizes, seasons, limits, and the means by which game may be taken have been established to help ensure an ongoing supply of a resource. Obey fish and game regulations, and encourage others to abide by them as well. The rules can benefit everyone in the long run.

If you take life from the water, do it in a responsible manner. Avoid taking animals from areas that are popular dive sites. Limit hunting and collecting to remote areas, where the impact of divers is much less. Take only what you need, not what you can get or what you are allowed. The two types of hunters most harmful to the environment are the quantity hunter and the trophy hunter. The quantity hunter seeks to take as much and as many of everything as possible to build an image as a mighty hunter. The trophy hunter seeks the largest animals and destroys the fittest of the breeding stock. If you kill an animal, you have a duty to know how large one must be in order to breed and what the maximum size of the animal is. You should take animals that have had the opportunity to reproduce, but do not take the largest ones. It is difficult at times to be selective, but you should attempt to conserve life.

Nature, left undisturbed, maintains a balance of life. Animals are both predator and prey. An animal eats other animals and is, in turn, eaten by others. If there are too many predators, their population will diminish due to an inadequate food supply. If there is a temporary overpopulation of prey, the number of predators will increase. People upset nature's balance. We are the most efficient predators of all. We disturb the food cycle with pollution, hunting, fishing, boating, and every way in which we impact the aquatic environment. It takes nature longer to recover from our impact than from any natural disaster. It is important today to lessen the effect of people on the environment so that nature will have less interference with the management of the life within the waters.

Preservation

Preserving the diving environment is everyone's business, but it is more of your business now than it was before you became a diver.

How do humans upset the balance of nature?

LET'S RESPECT IT, NOT COLLECT IT

You know more than your friends and neighbors about the aquatic environment. Be an ambassador for preservation, and educate and motivate people to help preserve the diving environment.

What people do above water affects life beneath the surface. What people put down their drains and toilets winds up in the aquatic environment. So do the chemicals they use on their lawns and gardens. Litter in and around the water kills animals, birds, and fish. Think twice about the products you buy, how you use them, and how you dispose of your wastes. Where will the toxic chemicals and waste end up? Be environmentally conscientious; then teach others to be so. A simple act, such as using detergents without phosphates, can make a difference. Phosphates are powerful nutrients that upset the balance of nature in the aquatic environment. Figure 2.7 shows the effects of environmental pollution.

> **Describe several ways you can help preserve the underwater environment.**

Figure 2.7 Litter is ugly, and it kills sea life.

Be involved in your community. Be concerned about issues that affect the aquatic environment, such as sewage treatment, toxic wastes, and construction. Construction and drilling on shorelines or on waterways can be extremely harmful. So are waste products from manufacturing. Help others understand the seriousness of pollution.

Get more informed and keep informed. Join groups that are working to preserve the environment, such as the Center for Marine Conservation, Project Reefkeeper, and the Oceanic Society. These groups provide up-to-date information and specifics on how you can help. Various organizations sponsor underwater cleanups from time to time; these are enjoyable and worthwhile projects. (For a list of environmental organizations you can join, see the appendix.)

There are actions you can and should take when diving. Dispose of trash properly, and encourage others to do the same. If you have a boat for diving, anchor it away from reefs to avoid reef damage caused by the anchor and chain. Retrieve trash you find in the environment, especially plastic, and collect trash while you dive. Collect plastic, monofilament, lead, and stainless steel leaders. Not all trash is bad; bottles and cans provide homes for animals. Report unlawful dumping, and report lost or discarded fishing nets and traps, which continue to catch and kill after abandonment.

Introduction to Aquatic Conditions

The particular state of the environment or the physical situations in which divers find themselves are *conditions*. The conditions of concern to divers include the temperature, visibility, and degree of movement of the water. You need to be familiar with aquatic conditions in general and local aquatic conditions specifically.

The Big Picture

Many factors affect the seas. The sun bears down on the earth at the equator more directly than at other parts of the earth. The climate and waters near the equator are warm; the greater the distance from the equator, the colder the water. The difference in water temperatures in different parts of the world causes the movement of air and water by convection currents. Winds move from areas of high pressure to areas of low pressure, and winds and the turning of the earth move water. On a global scale, water currents move in a clockwise direction in the Northern Hemisphere and in a counter-clockwise direction in the Southern Hemisphere. Weather moves from west to east. The gravitational attraction between the earth and other heavenly bodies produces changes in the water level called tides. Storms at sea produce energy in the form of waves that travel thousands of miles before giving up their energy in the form of surf.

Temperature changes, winds, and storms affect inland bodies of water. Water from snow and rain in the mountains and hills flows into streams, rivers, and lakes. Water seeping into the ground resurfaces in quarries and springs.

Weather, seasons, geography, and other factors affect two categories of diving conditions: surface and underwater. The water may be rough at the surface and calm at depth. There may be a current at the surface, but none on the bottom. The visibility may be good at the surface, but poor on the bottom. The temperature usually is warmer at the surface than it is at depth. You should become familiar with both surface and underwater conditions and their effect on diving.

Perhaps the most important fact to remember about diving conditions is that they vary from place to place. This is why an environmental orientation is important when you dive in a new region. The diving conditions usually dictate the way you dive. What works well in one area may be totally ineffective for another.

An understanding of the effects of diving conditions in an area is important. You should know what conditions to expect, how the conditions affect your approach to diving, and how to manage the effects of the conditions. Chapters 6 and 7 will help you learn this.

General Freshwater Diving Conditions

Fresh water is 2.5% less dense than salt water, so you are less buoyant in fresh water than in salt water. The density of water

How can water conditions vary at surface and at depth?

What implications does a thermocline have for a diver?

What conditions may make spring and fall the best seasons for freshwater diving?

thermocline
The area in water where water temperature changes abruptly with increased depth

overturn
The process of surface water moving to deep water (up to 60 ft or 18 m) as a result of temperature differences and wind movement

reverse thermocline
The area in water where water temperature increases abruptly with decreased depth

upwelling
The replacement of warm water at the surface with colder water flowing up from the depths as a result of a strong wind blowing along a shore for a sustained time

varies with temperature. Fresh water is most dense at a temperature of 39.2 °F (3.99 °C)—the usual temperature of the water at depths greater than 60 ft (18 m) in freshwater lakes and quarries. The water becomes lighter when it is either warmer or cooler than this.

Fresh water often forms layers—a layer of warmer, lighter water on top of a layer of colder, denser water. The **thermocline** is abrupt. When the water is calm, the thermocline appears to have wisps of smoke on top of it when viewed from above. The refraction of light is different when the density of the water is different, so there is a slight visual blurring at the interface of a thermocline. When you dive in fresh water, you must insulate yourself for the water temperature below the thermocline. Although the surface of the lake may be warm, the water at the bottom may be close to freezing.

The best season for diving in a freshwater lake or quarry varies depending on the body of water. Spring and fall are often good times because the water temperature is the same from surface to bottom, there is oxygen for fish at all depths, populations of plankton are low, and visibility usually is good.

In later spring, the sun warms the surface water, and the lack of wind keeps it from mixing with the colder water at depth. The water stratifies, and a thermocline forms that remains until fall. The layer of water below the thermocline stagnates in most lakes during the summer. Decaying matter depletes oxygen and creates toxins. Fish seek refuge above the thermocline. Sunlight and warm water often lead to plankton blooms, which are aggravated by pollution.

In the fall, surface waters in lakes and quarries cool until they equal the temperature of the water at depth. Colder water and reduced sunlight stifle plankton growth, and visibility improves. Winds cause water circulation. The **overturn** carries oxygenated water to the bottom and leads to the spring conditions. Visibility tends to be poor during an overturn.

In the winter, the surface water in a lake or quarry is colder than the water at the bottom. A **reverse thermocline** remains until the surface water temperature warms to that of the water at the bottom. This allows the spring overturn to begin. Water becomes 10% lighter when it freezes. If ice sank when it froze, bodies of water could become solid ice from top to bottom. Ice that forms over water insulates the water beneath it. Figure 2.8 shows the annual cycle of freshwater lakes and the concept of thermoclines.

When a strong wind blows along a shore for a sustained period over a body of water, the surface water is pushed away from shore. This water is replaced by colder water flowing up from the depths. This **upwelling** also can occur in the ocean. If the wind conditions persist, the water temperature can become constant throughout the water column, even in the summer. An upwelling carries nutrients from the depths into shallow water. This brings animals into the area. Following an upwelling, a bloom may occur because of the increase in nutrients in warm, shallow water.

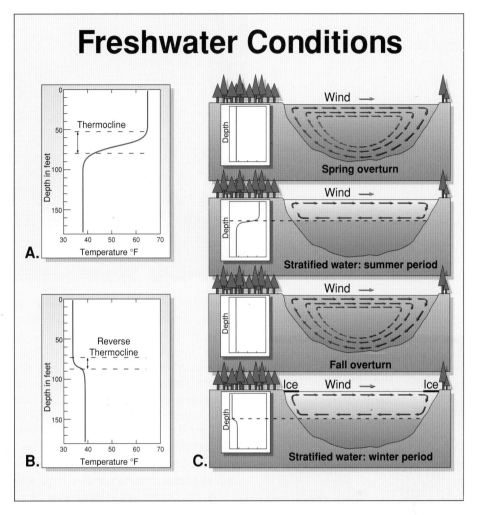

Figure 2.8 Thermocline (a), reverse thermocline (b), and a depiction of the annual cycle of overturn in lakes (c).

eddy
Swirling current

Specific Freshwater Diving Conditions

There are good diving experiences in many kinds of freshwater environments. Springs, low-altitude lakes, and quarries are good sites for divers who don't live near a coast. Other freshwater environments, such as rivers, caverns and caves, high-altitude and frozen lakes, and around submerged wreckage, can be dangerous (see Figure 2.9). Complete specialty courses before diving in any of these areas.

You may encounter strong currents in rivers. The currents are strongest at the surface and on the outside of bends. Countercurrents and **eddies** are common, and entanglements are likely in many rivers. Currents can undercut the bank of a river, so direct access to the surface may be impossible at times. Rivers are especially prone to seasonal changes and are often unpredictable.

Freshwater springs can provide beautiful diving environments. The flow of clean, calm water, which usually is at a moderate temperature (65 °F to 78 °F or 18 °C to 25.6 °C), provides excellent visibility. The water often flows through underground limestone cave systems that extend for thousands of feet. Diving in open-water basins in a spring is appropriate for certified divers, but entering any overhead area that lacks a direct, vertical ascent to

Figure 2.9 Diving in rivers provides unique experiences, but shouldn't be attempted without specific training.

cavern
A large roomlike opening where light from the surface can be seen

cave
Underwater passageways that extend further than caverns where no surface light can be seen

sink
Underground cave system caused by the earth collapsing

syphon
Opening where water is channeled back from a sink into the cave system

What makes cavern and cave diving dangerous?

At what altitude does diving become a specialty activity?

the surface, such as **caverns** and **caves**, is not appropriate. Entering such an environment—even a short distance—without the required training and equipment can lead to your death. It is easy to become disoriented, to stir up thick clouds of silt that instantly reduce visibility to nothing, and to panic and drown. You may dive in spring basins, but stay out of caverns and caves unless you meet the requirements to dive in them. The appendix contains contact information for organizations that offer cavern and cave diving training.

Sometimes the earth collapses into an underground cave system and forms a **sink**. The water flowing into the sink forms a basin, and a **syphon** channels water from a sink back into the system. Diving in syphons can be dangerous. The amount of water moving through a system depends on the amount of rainfall in the area. Under extreme conditions the normal flow of water can reverse.

People dig pits to excavate sand, gravel, and stone. At some depth they encounter the water table, and the pit floods, forming a quarry or sand pit. At some of these sites you may view submerged construction equipment, which was abandoned when the pit flooded. Sand pits and quarries tend to have fair to good visibility, although the disturbance of silt that has settled to the bottom can ruin the visibility quickly. Gravel quarries usually are siltier than other types of quarries, so the water may be turbid.

Lakes can be excellent dive sites. There are freshwater lakes at altitudes above 10,000 ft (3,048 m). Diving at altitudes above 1,000 ft (305 m), a specialty called altitude diving, presents many hazards because the rate of change of pressure is greater when you descend into water from atmospheric pressure that is less than the pressure at sea level. You must follow special procedures to avoid decompression sickness. Problems also can result from the thinner air, which provides less oxygen with each breath taken above water.

When ice forms over water in the winter, diving becomes hazardous. Perils include hypothermia, the freezing of regulator

What hazards make ice diving dangerous?

How can you minimize the hazards of freshwater diving?

continental shelf
Underwater area that extends from land and slopes gradually to a depth of about 600 ft (183 m)

tsunami
Giant waves caused by underwater geological disturbances; erroneously referred to as tidal waves

and buoyancy control valves, and getting lost beneath the ice. Ice diving can be beautiful and adventurous, but it is dangerous to attempt it without the proper training, equipment, and procedures.

Hazards of freshwater diving include loss of body heat; submerged trees; wire; fishing line, hooks, and lures; log jams; debris; currents; rapids; whirlpools; poor visibility; silt; and overhead restrictions. You can minimize these hazards with training, experience, equipment, correct diving techniques, area orientations, and good judgment.

General Saltwater Diving Conditions

There are five oceans on the earth; seas, gulfs, and bays are smaller sections of the oceans. The land beneath the oceans is not flat. Beyond the **continental shelf** are great underwater canyons and mountains as well as hills, valleys, and great plains. In some areas, the tips of some mountains and volcanoes extend above the surface of the ocean from great depths. In other areas, deep canyons sever the continental slope, creating deep-water conditions close to shore.

The saltwater environment varies greatly from one part of the earth to another. The clear waters of the Caribbean, with temperatures that can exceed 85 °F (29.4 °C), feature coral reefs covered with beautiful, lush animals that look like plants. Schools of colorful tropical fish abound. Temperate waters, with temperatures ranging from 55 °F to 70 °F (13 °C to 21 °C), may have great forests of kelp, which contain more life per cubic foot than a tropical rain forest. Cold ocean waters in northern latitudes are nutrient-rich and teem with life. There are beautiful sights and wonders to behold in all the oceans of our planet; Figure 2.10 shows one example.

Oceans always are in motion. Tides, winds, and currents cause water movement. An underwater earthquake can move water by creating **tsunami**. Although these giant waves are sometimes

Figure 2.10 Sights like this are common in the temperate waters of the Caribbean.

called tidal waves, the tide has nothing to do with them. Tsunamis can cause great destruction, but they are rare and can be forecasted.

The energy source for water movement may be local or may originate thousands of miles away. As a diver, you need to understand what causes water to move, how it moves, and how to dive in ocean water that is in motion.

Tides

The gravitational attraction between the moon and the earth pulls water toward the moon, causing an increase in water depth called a high tide. Water pulled away from the sides of the earth in the process produces a decrease in water depth called low tide. A high tide forms on the side of the earth opposite the moon because the attraction of the moon is least at that point and because of centrifugal force created by the rotation of the earth. At any given time, two areas on the earth are experiencing high tides and two areas are experiencing low tides. There is a brief period of time, called a **stand**, when the tide neither rises nor falls; there can be four tidal stands per day, two high and two low. Geographical formations interfere with or enhance the rising and falling of the water in some areas.

The sun also affects the tides, but only about half as much as the moon because the moon is much closer to the earth. When the moon and the sun are aligned with the earth, which happens twice monthly (during the new and full moons), a **spring tide** occurs (see Figure 2.11). When the moon and sun are at right angles to each other in relation to the earth, a **neap tide** occurs.

The moon rotates around the earth in the same direction that the earth spins, and the duration of a lunar day is nearly 25 hours. This causes tides to occur at different times each day and explains why the heights of subsequent tides vary.

stand
Period of time when the tide neither rises nor falls

spring tide
The twice-monthly period of highest tides; occurs when the moon and sun are aligned with the earth

neap tide
The twice-monthly period of lowest tides; occurs when the moon and sun are at right angles to each other in relation to the earth

Why don't high and low tides occur at the same time and same height each day?

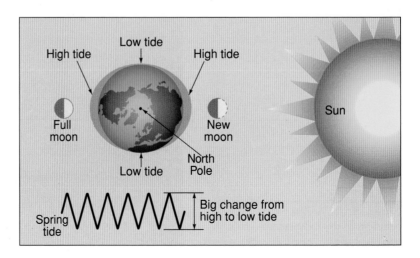

Figure 2.11 The effect of the sun and moon on tidal patterns.

flood
Flow of water into an area because of the high tide

ebb
Flow of water away from an area because of the low tide

slack water
Period of time between the flood and ebb when the water has minimal movement

What effects do tides have on diving activities?

To change the water height during a tidal change, water must flow from one area to another. Between the **flood** and the **ebb** is a period of **slack water**. The water movements caused by the tides are called *tidal currents*, and they vary in velocity between tides. Due to geography, water cannot move instantly in many areas. There usually is a delay between the predicted time of a tide and the time when the water is slack.

Tidal changes affect diving activities and operations. Large differences in the water level between tides affect visibility and other conditions. Water height also affects entries and exits, shoal areas when boating, the mooring of boats, and the loading and unloading of vessels. It is a good idea to know how high the tide will be. Tidal changes are small (less than 2 ft or 0.6 m) in some areas or on some days and large (more than 6 ft or 1.8 m) in other areas or on other days. The greater the difference between high and low tide, the greater the effect of the tides.

Because the earth, moon, and sun follow set courses, the tides are predictable. Tides vary because the distance between the heavenly bodies and their positions relative to one another change constantly. In spite of all the variables, scientists predict with accuracy when the tides will occur and the heights of the tides. The government publishes tide tables, and national weather channels broadcast tidal information continuously. Local correction tables and current tables can provide more precise information. Tide tables refer to the height of the tide in relation to an average of the low tides in an area (see Figure 2.12). Wind and barometric pressure affect the height of tides, aiding or opposing the movement of tidal waters.

November 1986

	Low tide				High tide			
	a.m.	ht.	p.m.	ht.	a.m.	ht.	p.m.	ht.
	Sunrise 6:19		-PST-		Sunset 5:08			
1 Sa	1:35	1.0	2:35	0.5	7:49	6.4	8:46	4.7
2 Su	2:06	1.3	3:17	0.9	8:21	6.7	9:36	4.4
3 M	2:38	1.7	4:06	1.0	8:56	8.8	10:35	4.0
4 Tu	3:14	2.1	5:02	0.9	9:33	6.7	11:44	3.7
5 W	3:50	2.6	6:03	0.7	10:19	6.5	—	—
	Sunrise 6:24		-PST-		Sunset 5:03			
6 Th	4:42	3.0	7:17	0.4	1:14	3.5	(11:15	6.0)
7 F	6:00	3.3	8:36	0.2	2:57	3.8	12:28	5.4
8 Sa	8:23	3.3	9:43	0.1	4:15	4.0	2:03	
9 Su	10:12	2.8	10:42	0.1	5:01	4.4	3:39	
10 M	11:22	2.1	11:27	0.3	5:37	4.9	4:55	
	Sunrise 6:28		-PST-		Sunset 5:00			
11 Tu	—	—	12:14	1.4	6:09	5.3	5:	
12 W	12:06	0.6	12:59	0.8	6:34	5.6	6	
13 Th	12:38	0.9	1:38	0.3	6:59	5.9		
14 F	1:07	1.3	2:13	0.1	7:24	8.1		
15 Sa	1:31	1.6	2:45	0.3	7:47	6.2		
	Sunrise 6:33		-PST-		Sunse			
16 Su	1:56	2.0	3:21	0.4	8:1			
17 M	2:21	2.2	3:53	0.3				
18 Tu	2:40	2.5	4:33	0.				
19 W	3:03	2.7	5:1					
20 Th	3:21	3.0						

Figure 2.12 An example of a tide table.

Generally, it is best to dive at high tide, but you may need to time your diving to coincide with slack water in areas with strong tidal currents. The timing may not be important in areas where tidal changes are small. Consider local knowledge about the effects of tides when planning dives.

fetch
The distance over which wind blows to create waves

swell
A wave with a rounded top that transfers wave energy through water

crest
The top of a wave

trough
The channel between wave crests

wave height
The distance from a wave crest to the trough

wavelength
The distance between waves

period of a wave
The time it takes two waves to pass a given point

wave train
A long series of waves

If you can feel a passing wave at a depth of 30 ft (9 m), what is the minimum wavelength?

Waves and Surf

Ripples form when wind blows across water. You can see this in a puddle on a windy day. When ripples form on a large body of water and the wind continues to blow, the sides of the ripples form a surface against which the wind can push to set the water in motion. The longer and harder the wind blows in a constant direction, the larger the waves that form. As waves move away from the **fetch**, the tops of the waves become rounded, forming **swells**. The water within swells moves in a circular motion but has little forward motion. The effect is similar to the transmission of a waveform along a rope that is tossed up and down at one end. Waves of energy travel along the rope, but the rope itself does not move forward.

Swells can travel thousands of miles and still contain a great deal of energy. The vertical distance from the **crest** to the **trough** is the **wave height**, and the distance between waves is a **wavelength**. The time it takes two waves to pass a given point is the **period of a wave**. The greater the wave height and the greater the wavelength of a **wave train**, the greater the energy contained in the waves. Two wave trains can have phases during which the waves of each train reinforce the other and produce larger waves, called *wave sets*. The formation of larger and smaller waves may occur in phases. By timing the "beat" of the surf, you can make entries and exits easier by moving through the surf zone when the wave sets are small. Figure 2.13 illustrates fundamental concepts of waves and surf.

The water within a passing wave moves in a circular motion. The diameter of the motion equals the wave height at the surface and diminishes with depth. Motion from a passing wave can be felt to a depth equal to half of the wavelength for a series of waves. If it is 100 ft (30 m) between waves, you can feel the effect of a passing wave to a depth of 50 ft (15 m).

When waves enter shallow water, contact with the bottom interrupts the circular motion of the water within the waves. The circular movements flatten and eventually become a back-and-forth subsurface motion called *surge*. Wave contact with the bottom causes waves to slow and steepen. The wave height increases as the water depth decreases. When the water depth is about the same as the wave height, the wave becomes unstable and tumbles forward. At this point the water within the wave moves forward and gives up its energy in breaking waves known as *surf*. In areas with offshore reefs, sandbars, and underwater obstructions, waves can break in shallow water, pass over the obstruction, reform, and break again in shallow water near the shore. Waves that break offshore indicate the presence of shallow water in the area where the waves are breaking.

Waves can break and release their energy all at once, or they can spill forward and expend their energy over a wide area. Plunging breakers build quickly and break suddenly; they occur on steeply sloping shores. Spilling breakers spill forward over some distance to shore and occur on bottoms that slope shallowly. Spilling breakers tend to reduce visibility more than plunging breakers.

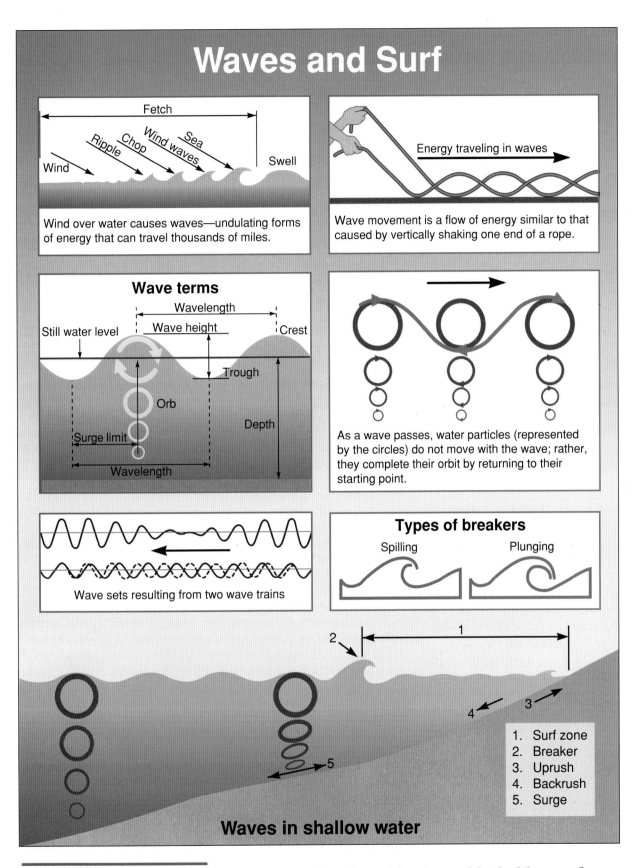

Waves and Surf

Fetch

Wind · Ripple · Chop · Wind waves · Sea · Swell

Wind over water causes waves—undulating forms of energy that can travel thousands of miles.

Energy traveling in waves

Wave movement is a flow of energy similar to that caused by vertically shaking one end of a rope.

Wave terms

Wavelength · Wave height · Crest · Still water level · Trough · Orb · Depth · Surge limit · Wavelength

As a wave passes, water particles (represented by the circles) do not move with the wave; rather, they complete their orbit by returning to their starting point.

Wave sets resulting from two wave trains

Types of breakers

Spilling · Plunging

1. Surf zone
2. Breaker
3. Uprush
4. Backrush
5. Surge

Waves in shallow water

Figure 2.13 Wind speed, the absence or presence of obstacles, and the shape and depth of the ocean floor influence the formation of waves and surf.

What do the following wave actions tell you about the area you're diving in?
a. Waves that break offshore
b. Plunging breakers
c. Spilling breakers
d. Foam in surf zone

The crashing water of surf contains air. The white water and foam in the surf area, called the *surf zone*, do not provide as much buoyancy as water that does not contain air. It can be difficult to remain above water in the foam of surf, but you should not attempt to rise above the breakers, because you can be picked up and tossed forward by the moving water. It is best to remain low in the wave and breathe from your scuba regulator.

Surf rushes up the face of a beach and then flows back again to the still water level. The return flow of water is called the *backrush*. This countercurrent, mistakenly called an undertow by some, does not extend beyond a depth of 3 ft (1 m). Although backrush can be strong when surf is large on a steep beach, there is no undertow that will carry a swimmer out to sea.

The surf's crashing onto the shore moves sand. Gentle summer waves carry sand onto the beach, and large, rough winter waves carry the sand offshore, where it forms sandbars. That's why some beaches are rocky in the winter and smooth in the summer.

Currents

Currents are in water what wind is in air—fluid in motion. Since water is 800 times more dense than air, water poses much more resistance to movement than air. You need to know how and why water moves and how to move with it. The force of water in motion may be too great to resist. You must learn to use the flow of water to your advantage.

Wind, gravity, tides, and convection cause currents; the most common currents are wind-generated surface currents. Due to the rotation of the earth, currents flow at an angle to the wind that generates them. When the wind pushes water away from an area, another current, a compensating current, replaces the water displaced. Overall, the effect on the earth is to produce **gyres** that move clockwise in the Northern Hemisphere and counterclockwise in the Southern Hemisphere.

When wind blows along a coast, a vertical compensating current—an upwelling—occurs. The opposite of an upwelling is a **downwelling**. A strong downwelling current is rare, but it can occur under the right conditions where there is a steep drop-off near shore. It is frightening to be pulled downward in water. Learn if and where a downwelling occurs in an area, and avoid that location. If you should get caught in a downwelling, swim horizontally until you are clear of the current. Trying to swim up may lead to exhaustion and panic.

Water flows in layers. The water at the surface moves quickly with the wind, whereas the water a few feet beneath the surface moves slower. The deeper the depth, the less the effect of a surface current. After 12 hours of a sustained wind in a given direction, the speed of a surface current is approximately 2% that of the wind that drives it. Because water flows in layers, it is possible for a surface current to flow in one direction and for a subsurface current to flow in the opposite direction only a few feet (about 1 m) beneath the surface (see Figure 2.14).

gyre
Large circulating currents
downwelling
A compensating current that occurs when wind blows along a coast where there is a steep drop-off near shore and which pulls the water downward

What should you do if you're caught in a downwelling current?

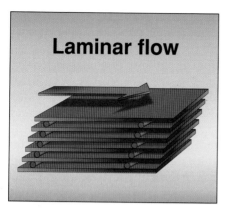

Laminar flow

Figure 2.14 The flow of water is similar to a tipped stack of boards with rollers between them. When the stack is tipped, the top board moves much farther than the bottom board. Surface water moves more than water at depth.

rip current
The narrow, strong current that moves away from shore as a result of water flowing back to sea through a narrow opening in an underwater obstruction

How can you identify a rip current at the surface? How can you escape a rip current?

drift
Speed of a current
set
Direction of a current

Surface water at the equator expands as it is warmed and flows slowly toward the poles of the earth. At the same time, water cooled near the poles increases in density and sinks. Slow-moving convection currents result. These currents do not affect diving procedures, but they greatly affect the oceans by the movement of nutrients and pollution.

Water can move swiftly, and water movement intensifies whenever an amount of water passes through a restriction. When water encounters irregular formations during its movement, turbulence produces dangerous eddies and whirlpools. Swift-water diving is a specialty considered hazardous even with experience and training.

Incoming waves can pass over an underwater obstruction, such as a sandbar, and pile up water on a shore. If the backrush of water flows back to sea through a narrow opening in the obstruction, a **rip current** exists. The current will dissipate shortly after passing through the restricted area. You can identify rips by a fan-shaped area of water on the shore; by muddy, foamy water in the rip area; and by a section of waves that break before the remainder of the waves. Rip currents may be stationary or moving. Recognize and avoid rip currents. If you are unable to swim toward shore, you probably are in a rip current. Swim parallel to the shore for about 60 ft (18 m) to get clear of the rip; then turn and proceed toward shore.

Waves breaking upon a shore at a slight angle move water along the shore. The current, called a *longshore current*, affects diving. On steep beaches, the current can cut a shallow trough in the bottom close to shore. The trough, called a longshore trench, is a sudden drop-off to a wading diver and can cause an unsuspecting diver to fall. Items dropped in the surf zone are moved along the shoreline in the direction of the longshore current. The movement of sand on beaches occurs because of wave action combined with longshore currents.

Two types of currents result from the combined forces of nature: standing currents, which are constant, and transitory currents, which occur briefly. The Gulf Stream that flows around Florida and up the eastern coast of the United States and the Antilles Current that flows through the Caribbean are examples of standing currents. A longshore current is a transitory current. A rip current may be either type. Be familiar with the currents you may encounter in an area. (This is one more reason for encouraging area orientations for diving.)

Currents can flow at a rate of hundreds of feet (meters) per minute. The speed of a current is its **drift**, and the direction assumed by a current is its **set**. A fully equipped diver can swim at a rate of 60 to 100 ft (18 to 30 m) per minute. Attempting to fight even a mild current is futile and a waste of energy. Strong water movement can dislodge equipment, cause regulators to free-flow, and cause rapid heat loss. You must learn to recognize and estimate currents. If the currents are strong, avoid them. Even if they are mild, avoid struggling against them. The primary rule for diving in currents—when you begin and end your dive at the same point—

is to dive along the bottom against the flow of water at the surface. Start a dive by moving along the bottom in a direction opposite the flow at the surface; then use the surface current to aid you when you return at the end of the dive. (See chapter 7 for suggestions on estimating currents.)

There are other general rules for diving in currents. Water movement is minimal at the bottom. Whenever possible, descend along a line from the surface to the bottom. If the current is still strong when you reach the bottom, ascend on the line and abort the dive. When you're unsure of your location during a dive, it may help to surface, determine the direction to the exit point, redescend, and move along the bottom toward your destination.

When there is a surface current, minimize the time spent at the surface. Whenever possible, hold onto a fixed object at the surface to keep from drifting downcurrent at a dive site. When a surface current is mild, swim against it to maintain your position at the surface. Develop the habit of noting your surface position in relation to a fixed reference. If you are caught in a sudden, strong current, swim across it to escape from it.

When diving operations are conducted from a boat, the crew usually extends a long floating line, called a *trail line*, from the stern (back) of the vessel. This line, which has a float attached to the end, may be used by divers to pull themselves to the boat if they surface downcurrent from the vessel (see Figure 2.15). Because an anchored vessel points into the current, you should plan to end your

> **What implications do the following types of currents have for a dive?**
> a. **Strong deep current**
> b. **Mild surface current**
> c. **Strong surface current**

Figure 2.15 Divers may use a trail line to pull themselves to the boat if they surface downcurrent.

If the front of your dive boat is pointing west, in what direction is the surface current moving? Where should you plan to end your dive?

drift dive
A dive made with the flow of current

dives in front of the boat so the surface current will aid your return. If you end a dive downcurrent from a boat, are unable to return to the bottom to move upcurrent, and are unable to swim against the current, you should get buoyant, signal the vessel, and wait to be picked up. This is embarrassing, but it's better than exhausting yourself to no avail.

Simple **drift dives** along a coast are acceptable when planned. You enter the water at one point, move along the shore with the current, and exit at another point downstream. Another type of drift diving, which is a specialty activity, involves diving in currents from a boat. This type of diving is hazardous because the boat must be operated while divers are in the water. Do not attempt drift diving from boats unless you have completed specialty training and have a trained, experienced captain for the vessel.

Potential saltwater diving hazards include loss of body heat, currents, surf, marine life, poor visibility, and fishing nets and equipment. You can minimize the hazards of ocean diving by following the recommendations described in this section.

Summary

The aquatic environment is a vast, wonderful area. We depend upon it for our existence. We need to learn about it, care for it, and respect it. We must protect the environment and encourage others to assist in that effort. Because the environment varies greatly from place to place, divers need area orientations. There are hazards in the underwater world just as there are hazards on land, but you can minimize aquatic hazards with training, experience, planning, proper procedures, and common sense.

3 Diving Science Made Simple

Your body is a marvelous machine. It performs many complex functions automatically. Just as your body is well adapted to an air environment, it can adapt in many ways to the aquatic environment. In this chapter you will become familiar with some of the structures and functions of your body. You will learn about the differences between the air and water environments and how changes in pressure affect your body. Refer to the box on page 36 as you read the chapter to remind yourself of the meanings of the many abbreviations that appear.

Abbreviations

ATA	Atmospheres absolute	g	Gram
ATM	Atmosphere	hr	Hour
CO	Carbon monoxide	kg	Kilogram
CO_2	Carbon dioxide	km	Kilometer
°C	Degrees Celsius	L	Liter
cm	Centimeter	lb	Pound
cm^2	Square centimeter	m	Meter
cm^3	Cubic centimeter	mg	Milligram
°F	Degrees Fahrenheit	O_2	Oxygen
FFW	Feet of fresh water	PP	Partial pressure
FSW	Feet of seawater	psia	Pounds per square inch absolute
ft	Feet	psig	Pounds per square inch gauge
ft^3	Cubic foot		

Anatomy for the Diver

Why are body air spaces of concern to divers?

Inside your body are air-filled spaces that are affected by the changes in pressure divers encounter underwater. The three primary body air spaces of concern to you as a diver are the sinuses, the lungs, and the ears. It also helps you as a diver to understand the function of your throat. Figure 3.1 explains the functions of the sinuses, throat, and lungs.

The Sinuses

The sinuses form air spaces that make the head lighter than it would be if the skull were solid bone. They also help warm and humidify inspired air, and they secrete mucus to help protect the body against airborne germs.

You have four sets of paranasal sinuses. The large sinuses behind your cheekbones are called *maxillary sinuses*. The cavities inside your head above your eyebrows are the *frontal sinuses*. Behind and above the maxillary cavities are two smaller sets of sinuses, the *sphenoidal* and *ethmoidal sinuses*. You do not need to know the names of the sinuses, but you should know their approximate locations.

The sinuses connect to the nasal passage via small airways that normally are open. Congested sinuses pose problems for divers. In chapter 4 you will learn more about sinus problems and how to prevent them.

The Throat

In the back of your throat (pharynx) are two flaps of skin—the soft palate and the epiglottis—that seal the airways to your nasal

Function of the sinuses, throat, and lungs

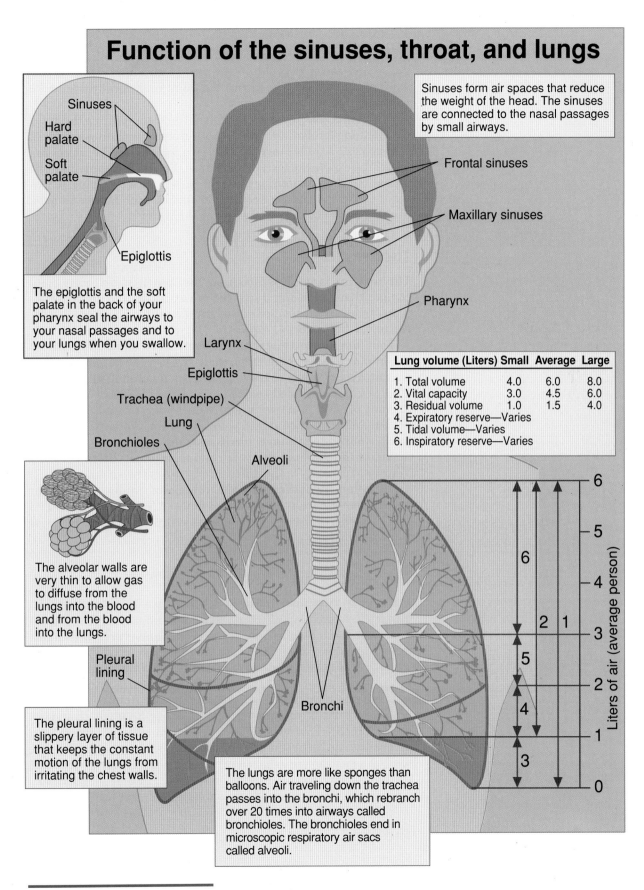

Sinuses form air spaces that reduce the weight of the head. The sinuses are connected to the nasal passages by small airways.

Sinuses
Hard palate
Soft palate
Epiglottis

The epiglottis and the soft palate in the back of your pharynx seal the airways to your nasal passages and to your lungs when you swallow.

Frontal sinuses
Maxillary sinuses
Pharynx
Larynx
Epiglottis
Trachea (windpipe)
Lung
Bronchioles
Alveoli

The alveolar walls are very thin to allow gas to diffuse from the lungs into the blood and from the blood into the lungs.

Pleural lining

The pleural lining is a slippery layer of tissue that keeps the constant motion of the lungs from irritating the chest walls.

Bronchi

The lungs are more like sponges than balloons. Air traveling down the trachea passes into the bronchi, which rebranch over 20 times into airways called bronchioles. The bronchioles end in microscopic respiratory air sacs called alveoli.

Lung volume (Liters)	Small	Average	Large
1. Total volume	4.0	6.0	8.0
2. Vital capacity	3.0	4.5	6.0
3. Residual volume	1.0	1.5	4.0
4. Expiratory reserve—Varies			
5. Tidal volume—Varies			
6. Inspiratory reserve—Varies			

Liters of air (average person)

Figure 3.1 Anatomy for the diver.

passages and to your lungs when you swallow. Beneath the epiglottis is your voice box (larynx), which is the upper end of your windpipe (trachea). The larynx contains your vocal cords and is your organ of voice.

The larynx also prevents foreign matter from entering the lungs. If something foreign, such as food or water, comes into contact with the larynx, a reflex action causes a spasm of the voice box. Coughing expels the foreign substance. You have experienced this sensation when something has gone "down the wrong pipe." Chapter 4 discusses how to keep water out of your larynx to avoid coughing and choking in and under the water.

The Lungs

The lungs are large air sacs contained within the chest cavity. Lung composition is more like a sponge than a balloon. The lungs contain many small air sacs, called *alveoli*. Surfactant, a liquid produced in the lungs, helps alveoli expand.

Your lungs have a maximum capacity and a minimum capacity. When you exhale completely, your lungs are not empty. They contain about 2 pints (1 L) of air. The air remaining in your lungs after you have exhaled completely is your residual volume. The amount of air you move in and out of your lungs is your tidal volume. When you are at rest, your tidal volume is small. When you exert, your tidal volume increases until you reach both your maximum lung volume and your residual volume with each breath. Your vital capacity is the difference between the volume of air for a maximum inhalation and the volume of air for a maximum exhalation—typically about 6 to 8 pints (2.8 to 3.8 L). Chapter 4 explains why your lungs are the most critical air spaces affecting you when diving.

The Teeth

You may be surprised to learn that there are dental concerns for divers. Pressure may affect air pockets in improperly filled teeth and cause tooth pain. If a tooth hurts only under pressure or only following a dive, see your dentist and tell him what you suspect. The roots of some upper molars extend into the sinus cavities. Postpone diving for several weeks after you've had a tooth extracted.

If you bite hard on a mouthpiece with your front teeth only for prolonged periods, your jaws will become sore. Your mouth and jaw are designed for an even bite. A special mouthpiece fitted for a proper bite can help reduce the problem. You should not have to bite hard on a mouthpiece to hold it in place. If you find biting necessary, get lighter equipment. Prolonged improper biting that irritates your jaw can lead to serious inflammation of your jaw and ears.

The Ears

Figure 3.2 illustrates the hearing process. The pressure in the middle ear must equal the pressure in the outer ear, or the eardrum

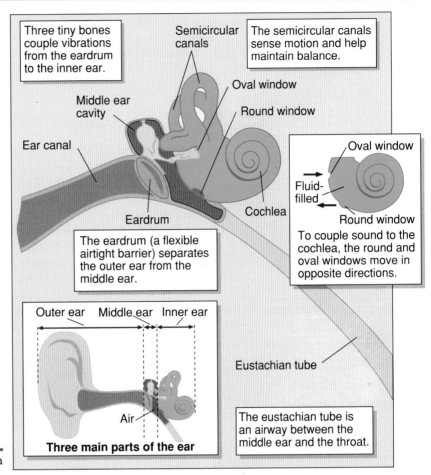

Figure 3.2 Process of hearing in air.

Three tiny bones couple vibrations from the eardrum to the inner ear.

Middle ear cavity

Ear canal

Eardrum

The eardrum (a flexible airtight barrier) separates the outer ear from the middle ear.

Semicircular canals

The semicircular canals sense motion and help maintain balance.

Oval window

Round window

Cochlea

Oval window

Fluid-filled

Round window

To couple sound to the cochlea, the round and oval windows move in opposite directions.

Outer ear   Middle ear   Inner ear

Air

Three main parts of the ear

Eustachian tube

The eustachian tube is an airway between the middle ear and the throat.

Describe the process of hearing in air.

will not move freely. Your eustachian tube allows the equalization of pressure in the middle ear. The liquid-filled cochlea contains hairlike projections called *cilia*. The movement of the oval window—moved by the bones of hearing—moves the cilia back and forth. The oval window movement could not take place except for a second window in the hearing organ—the round window. When the oval window moves inward, the round window moves outward, and vice versa.

If the motion sensed by your semicircular canals and the visual clues received by your eyes are not in harmony, you can get motion sickness. Sudden changes in temperature or pressure in the middle ear can affect your semicircular canals and cause temporary disorientation. (See chapter 4 for a discussion of potential ear problems for divers, how to avoid them, and how to handle them should they happen.)

Respiration and Circulation

It is fascinating how we continually breathe in air and circulate oxygen to the tissues in the body with no conscious effort. As the

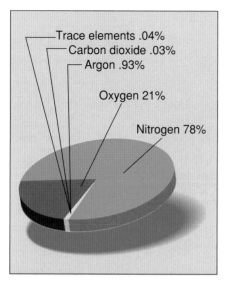

Figure 3.3 Composition of air.

level of exertion increases, the heart and lungs automatically adjust to meet the increased demands for oxygen and nourishment. An understanding of the gases involved in respiration and the basics of respiration and circulation will help you understand the effects and the demands of diving on your lungs and heart.

Gases We Breathe

Several gases affect recreational divers, and you need to know about their effects on your body. Figure 3.3 shows the gas composition of the air. About 80% of air is nitrogen. At sea-level pressures, nitrogen has no effect on your body. At a depth of about 100 ft (about 30 m), the increased pressure of the gas can cause nitrogen narcosis, and excessive nitrogen in your body at the end of a dive can produce DCS, a serious illness. (Nitrogen narcosis and DCS are discussed in more detail in chapter 4.)

Oxygen is the gas that supports life. Any other gas mixed with oxygen serves only as a vehicle for oxygen to be inspired (i.e., inhaled). Approximately 20% of air is oxygen. You need to breathe at least 10% oxygen to remain conscious, but oxygen breathed under high pressure is poisonous and causes convulsions. You must have compressed air—not pure oxygen—in your scuba tanks.

A specialty form of diving uses a nitrogen-oxygen mixture with a higher percentage of oxygen than is found in air. The mixture, which reduces the effects of nitrogen at depth, is called Nitrox. The use of mixed gases, including Nitrox, requires special training, equipment, and procedures.

As your body tissues use oxygen, they produce carbon dioxide (CO_2). CO_2 is the primary stimulus for respiration. The greater the level of CO_2 in your body, the greater the urge to breathe. If the CO_2 level in your body becomes too great, you become unconscious.

Carbon monoxide (CO) is a poisonous gas produced by the incomplete combustion of gas or oil. The exhaust from an internal combustion engine contains CO. An oil-lubricated air compressor that overheats can produce CO. Even a minute amount of CO in your scuba tank can poison you, causing unconsciousness and even death. Air-filling stations must take care to avoid contaminating air with CO.

How do nitrogen, oxygen, carbon dioxide, and carbon monoxide affect divers?

Breathing and Circulation Mechanics

When you need to breathe, sensors at the base of your brain send a signal that stimulates your diaphragm to contract. This draws air into your lungs in the same way as an old-fashioned bellows draws in air when you expand the bellows. Your diaphragm and the muscles of your chest expand your chest cavity to inspire air. Figure 3.4 illustrates how the heart, lungs, and circulatory system work together in respiration.

Blood consists of plasma (a colorless liquid) and a variety of cells. Hemoglobin, a component that makes up about 45% of the blood, is the primary oxygen-carrying mechanism in the blood. The hemoglobin releases the oxygen when it reaches tissues that need oxygen.

How does oxygen circulate through the body?

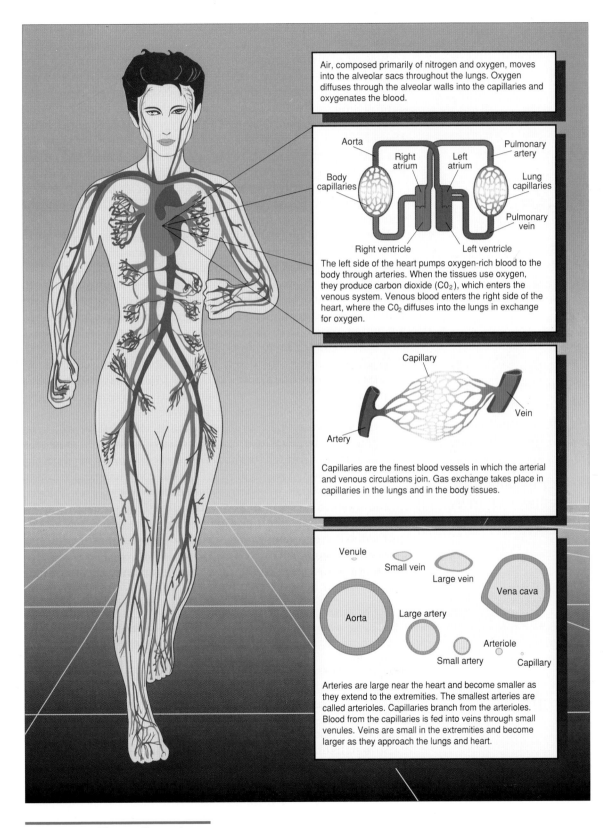

Air, composed primarily of nitrogen and oxygen, moves into the alveolar sacs throughout the lungs. Oxygen diffuses through the alveolar walls into the capillaries and oxygenates the blood.

The left side of the heart pumps oxygen-rich blood to the body through arteries. When the tissues use oxygen, they produce carbon dioxide (CO_2), which enters the venous system. Venous blood enters the right side of the heart, where the CO_2 diffuses into the lungs in exchange for oxygen.

Capillaries are the finest blood vessels in which the arterial and venous circulations join. Gas exchange takes place in capillaries in the lungs and in the body tissues.

Arteries are large near the heart and become smaller as they extend to the extremities. The smallest arteries are called arterioles. Capillaries branch from the arterioles. Blood from the capillaries is fed into veins through small venules. Veins are small in the extremities and become larger as they approach the lungs and heart.

Figure 3.4 The cardiorespiratory system.

When the tissues use oxygen, they produce CO_2. The CO_2 enters the venous system and diffuses into the lungs in exchange for oxygen. This completes a circulatory cycle, which takes about 1/2 minute.

Beware of diving equipment that is tight around your neck. The carotid sinuses—sensors in the arteries in your neck—detect blood pressure within the circulatory system. Excessive pressure on the carotid sinuses during exercise causes the heart to slow when it should be working hard to meet the oxygen demands of the body. Decreased output from the heart can lead to insufficient oxygen for the brain, which can result in unconsciousness. A blackout caused by pressure on the carotid sinuses is a carotid sinus blackout.

Exhalation usually is a passive process. To exhale CO_2-laden air from the lungs, the diaphragm relaxes and the elasticity of the chest cavity forces air from the lungs.

When at rest, you ventilate your lungs approximately 12 to 14 times per minute. Respiration functions automatically. The key to this is the CO_2 level in your circulatory system. When the CO_2 reaches a certain level, your brain stimulates respiration. When you voluntarily hold your breath, the buildup of CO_2 within your body urges you to breathe. Although many people believe the amount of oxygen in the body controls respiration, it is the level of CO_2 that regulates breathing.

You'll need to pay attention to your breathing when you're diving. Limited **hyperventilation**—three to four breaths—enhances breath-holding. But if you hold your breath after excessive hyperventilation, you may lose consciousness before you are stimulated to breathe. There are no warnings. A breath-holding diver who loses consciousness from lack of oxygen usually blacks out near the surface during ascent. The sudden loss of consciousness near the surface is shallow-water blackout. Loss of consciousness while in the water can cause drowning. Avoid excessive hyperventilation.

You should also avoid **hypoventilation**. If you breathe rapidly and shallowly, CO_2 continues to build in your system, but you do not expel it from your lungs. Shallow breathing is dangerous, especially when you exert yourself, because you can lose consciousness from lack of oxygen. You must breathe sufficiently to exchange the air in your lungs.

> **How can you keep from hyperventilating and hypoventilating while diving?**

> **hyperventilation**
> Rapid, deep breathing in excess of the body's needs
>
> **hypoventilation**
> Shallow breathing that doesn't allow CO_2 to be flushed out of the lungs

Contrasting Air and Water Environments

We live immersed in air, which is a fluid. Air has weight and takes up space. We don't pay much attention to our immersion in air because we are adapted to the environment, we have lived in it all our lives, and we cannot see the air. But the weight of the atmosphere does affect us.

Air weighs about 0.08 lb/ft³ (1.28 mg/cm³) at sea level. As altitude increases, air becomes thinner, so its weight per cubic foot (or mg/cm³) is less in the mountains than it is at the seashore. The change in the weight of air upon us with altitude affects the air spaces in our ears when we fly or when we drive in the mountains.

Why does buoyancy differ in air, salt water, and fresh water?

Density

Water is also a fluid, but it is much heavier than air. Seawater weighs about 64 lb/ft³ (1.025 g/cm³), which makes it about 800 times more dense than air. Fresh water, because it does not contain salt, weighs a little less than seawater: 62.4 lb/ft³ (1.0 g/cm³). Temperature also affects the density of water: Cold water is slightly denser than warm water.

Air compresses, but water essentially is incompressible. Whereas air becomes thinner as altitude increases, water density remains constant throughout the water column.

Drag is a force that retards movement. Resistance to movement is much greater in water than in air; it is easier to move something through air than to move it in water. Factors affecting drag include the viscosity of the fluid, the speed of motion, and the size and shape of an object. The denser the fluid, the faster the motion, the larger the object, and the more irregular the surface of the object, the greater the drag.

Due to higher density, the molecules of water are much closer together than those of air, and this affects the transmission of light, sound, and heat. Light travels about 27% slower in water than in air, sound travels about 4 times faster in water than in air, and water conducts heat nearly 25 times faster than air. Water has an enormous capacity for absorbing heat with little change in its temperature. The higher density of water affects you in many ways when you dive. The effects of heat, light, and sound are discussed in more detail at the end of this chapter, and chapter 4 explains how to deal with the effects of water density.

Buoyancy

An object's ability to float in a fluid depends on the density of the object compared to the density of the fluid. Water pressure at any point exerts equally in all directions, even upward. You can feel the upward force when you try to push something underwater. Buoyancy results from the difference in pressures on the upper and lower surfaces of an object. The weight of an object plus the weight of the fluid (air, water, or both) above the object exert a downward force. Fluid pressure pushes upward from below. The difference between these two forces is the buoyancy of the object.

Calculations prove that the force of buoyancy acting on a submerged object equals the weight of the water displaced. A hot-air balloon floats in air because hot air inside the balloon weighs less than the volume of cooler air the balloon occupies. A diver is buoyed upward with a force equal to the weight of the water displaced (see Figure 3.5). If you and your equipment weigh less than the water displaced, you will float and have positive buoyancy. If you and your equipment weigh more than the water displaced, you will sink. An object that sinks has negative buoyancy. An object that weighs exactly the same as the water displaced neither floats nor sinks. Instead it remains at the depth where it is placed because it has neutral buoyancy.

Divers can achieve each of these three states of buoyancy. You can float at the surface, sink to the bottom, or hang suspended

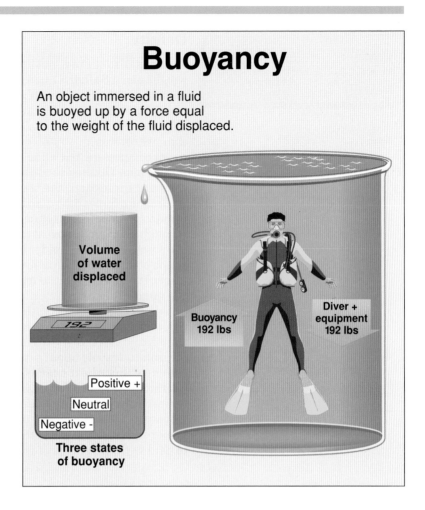

Buoyancy

An object immersed in a fluid
is buoyed up by a force equal
to the weight of the fluid displaced.

Volume
of water
displaced

192

Buoyancy
192 lbs

Diver +
equipment
192 lbs

Positive +
Neutral
Negative -

Three states
of buoyancy

Figure 3.5 Principles of
buoyancy.

How can you increase
buoyancy?

between the bottom and the surface. If the volume of an object increases with very little change in its weight, buoyancy increases. This happens when you add air to an inflatable jacket or vest. (Chapter 4 addresses the factors affecting buoyancy and the principles of buoyancy control.)

Pressure Measurement

The weight of something per unit area, such as pounds per square inch or grams per square centimeter, is pressure. The envelope of air surrounding the earth is the atmosphere. The weight of one square inch of the atmosphere at sea level is 14.7 lb (1.03 g/cm^2), or one *atmosphere* (ATM) of pressure. As you descend in water, the weight of the fluid (the pressure) exerted upon each square inch of your body increases. One square inch of salt water that is 33 ft (10.06 m) in height weighs 14.7 lb (1.03 g/cm^2), or 1 ATM. One square inch of fresh water that is 34 ft (10.36 m) in height also exerts a pressure equivalent to 1 ATM. Water does not compress (for the pressures you will experience in recreational diving), so water pressure increases by 1 ATM for every 33 ft (10.06 m) of salt water (FSW) and for every 34 ft (10.36 m) of fresh water (FFW). Figure 3.6 shows how atmospheric and water pressure are measured.

The reference for pressure is either the atmospheric pressure at sea level or zero pressure (outer space). A pressure gauge that reads zero at sea level displays only the pressure in excess of 1 ATM. Tire gauges and depth gauges are good examples of instruments that indicate pressure in pounds per square inch gauge (psig).

The total pressure exerted is what matters to divers. Both the pressure of the atmosphere and the pressure of the water apply to diving. The reference for this pressure is zero. The total pressure is absolute pressure, which is expressed in pounds per square inch absolute (psia). When we express absolute pressure increments of atmospheres, we measure the pressure in atmospheres absolute (ATA).

> **How do divers determine the total pressure exerted upon them when underwater?**

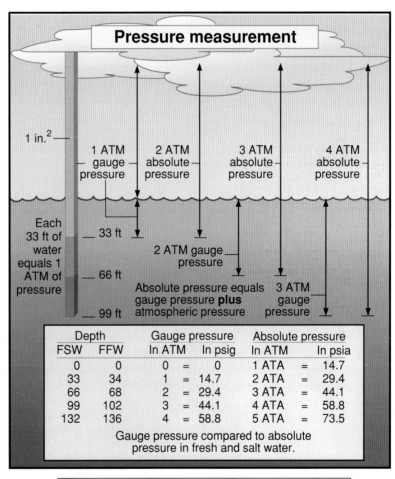

Depth		Gauge pressure		Absolute pressure	
FSW	FFW	In ATM	In psig	In ATM	In psia
0	0	0 =	0	1 ATA =	14.7
33	34	1 =	14.7	2 ATA =	29.4
66	68	2 =	29.4	3 ATA =	44.1
99	102	3 =	44.1	4 ATA =	58.8
132	136	4 =	58.8	5 ATA =	73.5

Gauge pressure compared to absolute pressure in fresh and salt water.

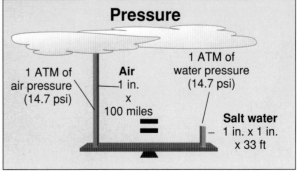

Figure 3.6 Principles of pressure.

You obtain absolute pressure by adding atmospheric pressure to gauge pressure. Be sure you understand the concept because when we deal with the effects of pressure in this and later chapters, we use absolute pressure.

Gas Laws

When you compress a quantity of gas, you reduce its volume and increase its density. **Boyle's law** states, "For any gas at a constant temperature, the volume varies inversely with the absolute pressure while the density varies directly with the absolute pressure."

Effects of Boyle's Law

If you compress a closed, flexible air space, such as a balloon, you reduce its volume in proportion to the increase in pressure. When you double the pressure, a closed, flexible air space occupies only half the volume it did at the surface. No air is lost. The molecules compress into a smaller area. The density of the air is twice as great as it was at the surface.

When you return the compressed air space to the surface, the air inside expands until the object reaches its original volume. You compress your lungs during a breath-hold descent, and they return to normal volume when you return to the surface, provided you do not expel air underwater.

Scuba equipment provides air to you at the exact pressure of the surrounding water. This allows you to expand your lungs to their normal volume regardless of the depth. The density of the air inside the lungs increases so the air pressure equals the water pressure. Figure 3.7 shows the relationships between pressure, volume, and density.

When compressed air equalizes an air space at a pressure greater than sea level, Boyle's law also takes effect when you reduce the surrounding pressure. As outside pressure decreases, compressed air in a closed, flexible container expands in proportion to the reduction in pressure (e.g., if the pressure halves, the volume doubles). If a

> **Boyle's law**
> The pressure of a given quantity of gas whose temperature remains unchanged varies inversely with its volume, while the density varies directly with the absolute pressure.

> Why is it important to vent your lungs as you ascend from a dive?

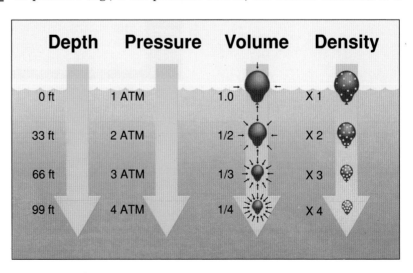

Figure 3.7 Pressure, volume, and density relationships.

container filled with compressed air at depth vents correctly during ascent, expanding air escapes through the vent, and the container remains full throughout the ascent. If the container is not vented, pressure inside increases when the container reaches its maximum volume. If the container is weak, the increase in pressure will rupture the container. This concept is important to scuba divers, who have many air spaces equalized with compressed air. Vented air spaces do not pose a hazard. If your lungs are not vented during ascent, you will suffer life-threatening injuries. If you do not vent air from a flotation jacket during ascent, you will lose control of buoyancy as air expands and the jacket volume increases.

Figure 3.7 shows an interesting point about the rate of change of pressure (and volume) in water. The pressure doubles from 1 ATM to 2 ATM in 33 ft (10 m) of seawater. To double the pressure again requires a depth of 99 FSW (30 m). You must ascend from 99 ft (30 m) to a depth of 33 ft (10 m)—a distance of 66 ft (20 m)—to experience the same rate of change of pressure that you experience when you ascend from 33 ft (10 m) to the surface. In other words, the closer you get to the surface, the greater the rate of change of pressure (and of the volume of an air space). You must be more attentive to compressed air in air spaces the nearer you are to the surface.

Perhaps the most significant challenge for divers is the change in pressure experienced during descents and ascents in water. Changes in pressure have direct, mechanical effects on the body. Pressure imbalance in body air spaces can cause discomfort. You feel pressure changes in air with changes in altitude, although pressure changes in water occur at a much greater rate. You can sustain serious injury unless you keep the pressure in air spaces that are inside and attached to you equalized with the surrounding water pressure. Boyle's law causes **squeezes** and reverse blocks, which Figure 3.8 illustrates. Knowledgeable and experienced divers routinely manage the task of equalization to avoid squeezes and blocks. You will learn how to keep air spaces equalized with the surrounding pressure in chapter 4.

squeeze
Condition that occurs when the pressure inside an air space is less than the surrounding water pressure

Gay-Lussac's Law

Boyle's law begins with "For any gas at a constant temperature . . ." because there are relationships between the temperature, pressure, and volume of a gas. These relationships are expressed by **Gay-Lussac's law**, which states: "For any gas at a constant volume, the pressure of the gas will vary directly with the absolute temperature." Just as absolute pressure must be used for pressure calculations, absolute temperature must be used for temperature computations. The absolute temperature scale for Fahrenheit temperatures is Rankine. To convert a Fahrenheit temperature to Rankine, add 460 degrees. The absolute temperature scale for a Celsius temperature is Kelvin. To convert a Celsius temperature to Kelvin, add 273 degrees.

You can observe the effect of Gay-Lussac's law with a scuba tank, which has a constant volume. When you decrease the temperature of the air in a tank, the pressure decreases. When you increase the temperature of the air in the tank, the pressure increases. A scuba

Gay-Lussac's law
For any gas at a constant volume, the pressure of the gas will vary directly with the absolute temperature.

Squeezes and Blocks

If the pressure inside an air space is less than the surrounding water pressure, the outside pressure attempts to compress the air space. This condition is a "squeeze."

During descent, squeezes may occur in ears, sinuses, the mask, and other air spaces in or attached to the body.

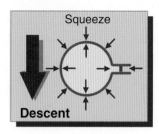

During ascent, the pressure surrounding an air space decreases. If the air inside the space, which was equalized to a higher pressure during descent, cannot escape, a situation that is the reverse of a squeeze occurs. When the pressure inside an air space is greater than the surrounding pressure, the condition is a "reverse block.

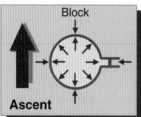

"A "block" describes a situation where·some form of blockage prevents compressed air from escaping along the route by which it entered an air space.

Prevention of both squeezes and blocks involves keeping the pressure within an air space equalized with the surrounding pressure.

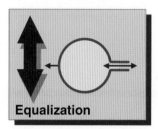

Figure 3.8   Equalizing pressure.

How does temperature affect pressure and volume?

ingassing
The process of gas diffusion into a substance

tank taken from the trunk of a hot car and cooled in water experiences a drop in pressure although you do not release air from the cylinder. Pressure increases or decreases in a standard 80-ft³ (2,266-L) aluminum scuba cylinder at a rate of about 6 psig per degree Fahrenheit temperature change. Pressure increases or decreases in a standard 71.2-ft³ (2,016-L) steel scuba cylinder at a rate of about 5 psig per degree Fahrenheit temperature change.

Dalton's and Henry's Laws

A gas diffuses into or out of a substance. When a gas comes into contact with a liquid, the gas dissolves into the liquid, a process called **ingassing**. The amount of gas that diffuses depends on the temperature of the liquid, the pressure of the gas, and the length of time the gas is in contact with the liquid. The gases you breathe diffuse into your body tissues.

In a mixture of gases, such as air, the percentage of the total pressure exerted by each gas is the partial pressure, which is described by **Dalton's law**. The partial pressure of a gas determines the amount of that gas that dissolves into a liquid. **Henry's law** expresses gas absorption. Table 3.1 shows the partial pressures of gases in the air at 1 ATM.

The *partial pressure* of a gas is the percentage of the gas in the mixture times the absolute pressure of the mixture. The partial

Dalton's law

The partial pressure of a given quantity of gas is the pressure it would exert if it alone occupied the same volume. Also, the total pressure of a mixture of gases is the sum of the partial pressures of the components of the mixture

Henry's law

At a constant temperature, the amount of a gas that dissolves in a liquid with which it is in contact is proportional to the partial pressure of that gas

Table 3.1
Partial Pressures of Gases in Air at 1 ATM

Air composition	Percentage of gas	Partial pressure at 1 ATA	Partial pressure at 1 ATA (metric)
Nitrogen	78%	11.466 psia	.803 kg/cm²
Oxygen	21%	3.087 psia	.2163 kg/cm²
Argon	0.93%	0.137 psia	.0095 kg/cm²
Trace gases	0.04%	0.006 psia	.0004 kg/cm²
Carbon dioxide	0.03%	0.004 psia	.0003 kg/cm²
Totals	100%	14.7 psia	1.03 kg/cm²

pressure of a gas at depth has the same effect as a higher percentage of that gas at the surface. If a mixture of gas contains 2% CO_2 at sea level (14.7 psia or 1.03 kg/cm²), the partial pressure of the CO_2 is 0.294 pounds per square inch (psia) (0.021 mg/cm²). If the absolute pressure of the same mixture of gases increases to the pressure found at a depth of 99 ft (58.8 psia or 4.12 kg/cm²) in the ocean, the partial pressure of the CO_2 is 1.176 psia (0.082 mg/cm²). The amount of CO_2 sensed by the body at 99 ft (30 m) is four times greater than the amount sensed at the surface. Breathing 2% CO_2 at a depth of 99 ft (30 m) is the same as breathing 8% CO_2 at the surface! A high level of CO_2 has a profound effect on respiration. The surface equivalent effect of partial pressures makes minute amounts of contaminants in breathing gases unsafe at depth. Table 3.2 shows the surface equivalent effect of partial pressures at various depths.

Table 3.2
Surface Equivalent Effect of Partial Pressures

Depth	Pressure	O_2[a]	CO[b]	CO_2[c]
0 ft (0 m)	1 ATA	20%	1%	2%
33 ft (10 m)	2 ATA	40%	2%	4%
66 ft (20 m)	3 ATA	60%	3%	6%
99 ft (30 m)	4 ATA	80%	4%	8%
132 ft (40 m)	5 ATA	100%	5%	10%

[a]Breathing air (20% oxygen) at 132 ft (40 m) has the same effect as breathing 100% oxygen at the surface.

[b]Breathing a (toxic) mixture containing 1% CO at 66 ft (20 m) is the same as breathing 3% CO at the surface.

[c]Breathing a mixture containing 2% CO_2 at 99 ft (30 m) is the same as breathing 8% CO_2 at the surface and causes labored breathing.

Additional Information About Gas Laws

The following gas law formulas can be used to make precise mathematical calculations of pressure, volume, and temperature.

Boyle's law: $P_1V_1 = P_2V_2$

P_1 = Initial pressure (psia or ATA)

P_2 = Final pressure (psia or ATA)

V_1 = Initial volume

V_2 = Final volume

Example: A balloon with 2 pints of air floats from 2 ATA to the surface (1 ATA). What is the volume of the balloon at the surface?

P_1 = 2 ATA

P_2 = 1 ATA

V_1 = 2 pints

V_2 = unknown

Rearranging the formula to solve for V_2, we find that

$$V_2 = P_1V_1/P_2 = (2 \times 2)/1 = 4 \text{ pints}$$

Partial Pressure (PP) = psia × percent of gas

Example: What is the partial pressure of oxygen if the gas comprises 20% of a gas mixture that has an absolute pressure of 58.8 psi?

$$PP = 58.8 \times 0.2 = 11.76 \text{ psia}$$

Gay-Lussac's law: $P_1/T_1 = P_2/T_2$

P_1 = Initial pressure (psia or ATA)

P_2 = Final pressure (psia or ATA)

T_1 = Initial temperature (°R or °K)

T_2 = Final temperature (°R or °K)

Example: A scuba tank with a pressure of 2,250 psig and a temperature of 70 °F is heated to a temperature of 150 °F. What is the pressure of the scuba tank at the higher temperature? First, convert readings for pressure and temperature to absolute measures.

P_1 = 2,250 psig + 14.7 psia = 2,265 psia

P_2 = unknown

T_1 = 70 °F + 460 = 530 °R

T_2 = 150 °F + 460 = 610 °R

Rearranging the formula to solve for P_2, we find that

$$P_2 = (P_1T_2)/T_1 = (2,265 \times 610)/530 = 2,607 \text{ psia}$$
$$2,607 \text{ psia} - 14.7 \text{ psia} = 2,592 \text{ psig}$$

> **outgassing**
> **The diffusion of a gas out of a liquid**

When a liquid has absorbed all of a gas that it can, the liquid is saturated. When you reduce the partial pressure of the gas in contact with the liquid, **outgassing** occurs. Ingassing and outgassing provide a foundation for the dive tables used to prevent DCS. These tables are presented in chapter 7.

Air Consumption

The volume of air you breathe per minute during exertion is much more than the volume you breathe at rest—up to 17 times more on land and about 14 times more in the water. Also, pressure on the torso in the water allows only 85% of normal inhalation.

Because the density of the air breathed increases with depth, depth is a significant factor affecting the rate at which you consume air. For a given level of exertion, a supply of air lasts only half as long at a pressure of 2 ATA as it does at a pressure of 1 ATA. With heavy exertion at a pressure of 4 ATA (99 ft or 30 m), you exhaust an air supply more than 40 times faster than you would the same volume of air when at rest at the surface! The rapid depletion of your air supply is one reason you must avoid heavy exertion while diving.

> **What are the two primary factors that affect the air consumption of a diver?**

The rate of air consumption is expressed in cubic feet per minute (or liters per minute) or psig (or ATM) per minute. You need to know your consumption rate for various levels of activity so you can plan your dives. To calculate air consumption, you need three items of information: the depth at which you're diving, the length of time you remain at that depth, and the amount of air you use during that time. Armed with that information, you can complete the following steps:

1. Determine your depth air consumption rate (DACR). This is simply the amount of air used divided by the time at depth. For example, the DACR for a diver who uses 1,000 psig (68 ATM) in 10 minutes is 100 psig (6.8 ATM) per minute.

$$DACR = \frac{Air\ used}{Time\ at\ depth}$$

2. Convert the DACR to the surface air consumption rate (SACR). After you do this, you can apply the air consumption rate to any depth and to a cylinder of a different size than the one used initially to calculate the air consumption rate. Obtain the SACR by multiplying the DACR times the ratio of the pressure at the surface to the pressure at depth. Because you may express pressure in terms of depth, you can use the following formula:

$$SACR = DACR \times \frac{33\ ft\ (or\ 10\ m)}{Diving\ depth + 33\ ft\ (or\ 10\ m)}$$

If, for example, your DACR for a depth of 33 ft (10 m) is 30 psig/min (2 ATM/min), your SACR is 30 (33/66) = 15 psig/min (1.0 ATM/min).

3. Convert the rate to volume, establish a ratio of the tank volume and pressure (when the tank is full) to the breathing rate volume and pressure, and then solve for the breathing rate volume (BRV). You solve for BRV as follows:

If

$$\frac{V_1}{P_1} = \frac{V_2}{P_2}$$

where

   V_1 = Full tank volume
   V_2 = Breathing rate volume
   P_1 = Full tank pressure
   P_2 = Breathing rate pressure

then

$$BRV = \frac{V_1 \times P_2}{P_1}$$

For example, the BRV for a diver with an 80-ft³ (2,266-L), 3,000-psig (204-ATM) tank and an SACR of 30 psig/min (2.04 ATM) is

$$BRV = \frac{80 \text{ ft}^3 \times 30 \text{ psig/min}}{3,000 \text{ psig}} = 0.8 \text{ ft}^3/\text{min}$$

$$\text{Metric BRV} = \frac{2,266 \text{ L} \times 2.04 \text{ ATM/min}}{204 \text{ ATM}} = 22.7 \text{ L/min}$$

4. For the same level of activity, calculate the approximate duration (in minutes) of any amount of air from a tank of any size used at any depth. Here is an example: How long will 1,750 psig (119 ATM) of air from a 71.2-ft³ (2,016-L), 2,475 psig (168 ATM) tank last at a depth of 70 ft (21.3 m) for a diver with a BRV of 0.08 ft³ (22.9 L) per minute?

First, determine the volume of air in the tank at a pressure of 1,750 psig (119 ATM). The formula for determining the volume of air in the tank is

$$V_2 = \frac{V_1 \times P_2}{P_1}$$

where

   V_1 = Full tank volume
   V_2 = Partially filled tank volume
   P_1 = Full tank pressure
   P_2 = Partially filled tank pressure

The air supply volume for the partially filled tank is, therefore,

$$V_2 = \frac{71.2 \text{ ft}^3 \times 1,750 \text{ psig}}{2,475 \text{ psig}} = 50.3 \text{ ft}^3$$

The metric air supply volume for the partially filled tank is

$$V_2 = \frac{2,016 \text{ L} \times 119 \text{ ATM}}{168 \text{ ATM}} = 1,428 \text{ L}$$

The formula for air supply duration (ASD) is

$$ASD = \frac{\text{Air supply volume}}{\text{BRV}} \div \frac{\text{Diving depth} + 33 \text{ ft (or 10 m)}}{33 \text{ ft (or 10 m)}}$$

The ASD for the question posed above is

$$ASD = \frac{50.3 \text{ ft}^3}{0.8 \text{ ft}^3/\text{min}} \div \frac{70 \text{ ft} + 33 \text{ ft}}{33 \text{ ft}} = 20 \text{ min}$$

$$\text{Metric ASD} = \frac{1,428 \text{ L}}{22.7 \text{ L/min}} \div \frac{21.3 \text{ m} + 10 \text{ m}}{10 \text{ m}} = 20 \text{ min}$$

What steps does a diver take to calculate air consumption?

These calculations may seem complicated at first, but the ideas are simple. The calculations become easy with practice. Let's review the four steps of air consumption calculations: (a) Determine your DACR; (b) determine your SACR; (c) determine your BRV; and (d) determine the ASD for a quantity of air. The abbreviated formulas for the calculations are in the sidebar that follows.

Formulas for Air Supply Calculations

$$DACR = \frac{\text{Air used}}{\text{Time at depth}}$$

$$SACR = DACR \times \frac{33 \text{ ft (or 10 m)}}{\text{Diving depth} + 33 \text{ ft (or 10 m)}}$$

$$BRV = \frac{V_1 \times P_2}{P_1}$$

$$ASD = \frac{\text{Air supply volume}}{\text{BRV}} \div \frac{\text{Diving depth} + 33 \text{ ft (or 10 m)}}{33 \text{ ft (or 10 m)}}$$

Heat, Humidity, Light, and Sound

You experience many changes when you enter water. You lose body heat faster, you lose body moisture when you use scuba equipment, what you see is deceiving, and what you hear may cause confusion. When you understand what happens to you and why, you can manage the differences between the water and air environments.

How is heat lost from divers' bodies, and how can this heat loss be minimized?

The Transfer of Heat

You can chill quickly when diving. You can lose heat by radiation, convection, conduction, or evaporation. Heat waves radiate from exposed surfaces, heat travels through fluids by convection, and heat is transferred directly through substances in contact with each other via conduction. Metals are good conductors. Water is a poor conductor compared to metal but conducts heat 25 times faster than air. Conduction and convection are the primary means by which heat transfers from a diver to the surrounding water. Heat rises from the skin and water carries the heat away. You lose body heat through evaporation. Moisture evaporates from your lungs when breathing underwater and from the surface of your skin when you perspire in air. Scuba equipment expands high-pressure air and cools it. Your body heat warms the air you breathe, and you lose the heat energy with each exhalation.

You can slow the transfer of heat by insulating yourself with a material that is a poor conductor of heat. Exposure suits help insulate you from the environment, but insulation does not help reduce heat lost through respiration. (Chapters 4 and 5 present ways to manage the problems of heat loss.)

Humidity

Scuba divers must guard against the effects of humidity, or the amount of water vapor present in a gas. The temperature of the gas determines the amount of water vapor a gas can absorb and retain. The warmer the gas, the more humidity the gas can contain.

You humidify inspired air. The process of compressing the air that is put into scuba tanks dehumidifies the air in the cylinder. When you humidify dry scuba air during respiration you draw moisture from body tissues, which can cause partial dehydration, an undesirable condition, especially for a scuba diver. In chapter 4 you will learn how to avoid the problems of dehydration.

Diving poses other humidity problems. Moisture in the air inside your mask condenses on the faceplate of the mask as the air cools. Unless you thoroughly clean your mask lens in advance so that the condensation runs off in a thin sheet, foggy beads of condensation form and blur your vision. Chapter 5 presents the process for cleaning, or **defogging**, your mask.

In freezing temperatures, moisture from your exhaled breath may cause a scuba regulator to freeze. Water in other items of diving equipment also may freeze. If you intend to dive in a cold environment, you should complete special training and know how to prepare and use your equipment in those conditions.

Light and Vision

The density of water makes it challenging to interpret what we see and hear. Light travels slower in water than in air. When rays of light traveling in water pass through the lens of your mask, they accelerate and bend (refract). The effect is that what you see underwater is magnified. Objects appear three fourths of their actual distance (25% closer) and one third larger (four thirds of their actual size). The visual distortion requires adjustments, and

What causes a mask to fog?

defogging
Cleaning a mask to reduce the surface tension of water and keep the water from forming droplets on the mask lens

How is underwater vision affected by the way light travels? What implications does this effect have on divers?

you will learn to make these with experience. An object 12 ft (3.7 m) away appears to be only 9 ft (2.7 m) away. A fish that appears about 2 ft (0.6 m) long actually is only 1-1/2 ft (0.5 m) in length. Many new divers discover that items they take from under the water are much smaller than they had perceived them to be when the objects were underwater. Figure 3.9 illustrates how light is perceived differently in water.

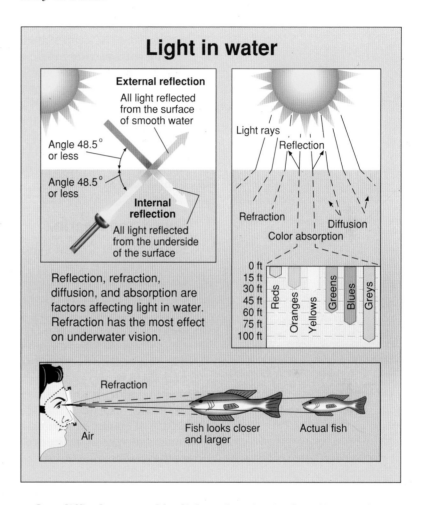

Figure 3.9 Vision underwater.

One difficulty caused by light refraction is that distant objects appear closer than they are. This can create a hazard in clear water when you look downward on a drop-off. You may be tempted to go to a point that appears close, but if you go there, you will exceed your planned maximum depth. You must realize that distance perception is inaccurate; rely on your depth gauge instead of your vision.

You have two types of vision: day vision and night vision. You use different parts of your eyes for each type. When you move from a brightly lit area into a dimly lit area, it takes 15 to 30 minutes for your vision to adapt to the lower level of light. Even after the adaptation, your ability to see fine details is much less than your ability with day vision. In addition, particles in water diffuse, scatter, and attenuate light. The deeper you go, the less light there is. The amount of light decreases very quickly with depth in turbid water. A dive in turbid water involves a change from day vision to night vision.

Water affects light in many ways. The surface of water reflects light. When light strikes the surface of calm water at an angle less than 48°, the water reflects all of the light. Early morning and late afternoon sunlight do not penetrate calm water. Light rays going toward the surface from underwater also reflect from the interface, making the underside of the surface appear as a mirror when the viewer is at the proper angle.

Objects you view underwater often lack their natural colors. White light, such as sunlight, comprises all the colors of the spectrum. Increasing depth absorbs various colors. The water absorbs warm colors, such as red and orange, at only 33 ft (10 m) of depth. Cooler colors, such as blue, penetrate deepest. This is why deep, clear water is blue. The underwater scene appears drab at depths below 99 ft (30 m). Fortunately, you can restore all the colors of the spectrum underwater by using an artificial light at close range.

Sound and Hearing

Sound travels well in water. You will hear many sounds while diving. On land you can determine the direction of a sound by the time difference between a sound reaching one ear and then the other. The delay interval is brief, but it is sufficient for your brain to discern. Underwater you hear when sound conducts through water and the bones of your head to your inner ears. Sound travels more than four times faster in water than in air. The time delay for sound to reach the hearing organ in one ear and then in the other one is so small that directional discernment is difficult underwater.

Sound also does not transfer well from air to water. Only 0.01% of sound can travel directly between air and water. You must use special devices to make voice communications effective underwater.

> How does sound travel differently in water than on land? What do these differences mean to divers?

Summary

The aquatic environment affects your body in several ways. Pressure affects your air spaces—your sinuses, lungs, and ears. The rate of change of pressure in water is many times greater than in air and increases as you approach the surface during ascent. Changing pressures also affect the diffusion of gas into and out of liquids, such as the level of CO_2 in your body, which controls your respiration. The difference in density between air and water affects your buoyancy, mobility, heat loss, vision, and hearing. Divers need to be aware that temperature affects the pressure of a constant volume of gas and that depth and activity have the greatest effect on air consumption. Water absorbs heat from the body, so divers need insulation to help prevent excessive heat loss. Finally, humidity can cause several problems for scuba divers. Now that you are aware of the effects of the aquatic environment upon your body, you are prepared to learn to adapt to the underwater environment.

4 Adapting to the Aquatic Environment

In chapter 3 you learned about the effects of water on your body. In this chapter you learn how to deal with those effects. Most people with average intelligence and normal health can make aquatic environment adaptations, such as in buoyancy control and the equalization of pressure. Many adaptations you will make automatically, but some you must make consciously. Learning to make the transition from an air environment to the underwater environment requires professional instruction and guidance. You need to learn what to do, then do what you have learned.

To function effectively underwater, you need specific attitudes, equipment, and knowledge. This chapter provides the fundamental knowledge and begins teaching the attitudes required to minimize the risk of injury. You will learn to apply the basic aspects of anatomy, physiology, and physics you have learned to a typical person descending into the depths and ascending back to the surface.

Temperature

Maintaining body core temperature within a few degrees of normal is challenging in water. When you are immersed in water, you lose body heat. A water temperature of 50 °F (10 °C) can incapacitate an unprotected diver within 15 minutes. Even water at 80 °F (27 °C), which feels relatively warm, can chill a diver quickly. Wearing only a bathing suit in 80 °F (27 °C) water is the same as being without any clothing in air that is 42 °F (6 °C).

Your brain regulates your body functions to maintain your body temperature. If your core temperature goes below 95 °F (35 °C), you will suffer from **hypothermia**. You need to understand the effects of excessive heat loss and take measures to prevent it.

If your core temperature is higher than normal, you experience **hyperthermia**. You need to guard against two types of hyperthermia, both of which can be dangerous.

Heat Loss

Your body has a variety of physiological responses to the loss of heat. Respiration increases automatically when you get chilled, which is undesirable because as you heat and moisturize inspired air, you lose the heat and moisture with each exhalation. The more you breathe, the more heat and moisture you lose to the surrounding environment. Depth compounds the problem because the greater the surrounding pressure, the greater the density of the air you breathe. Dense air requires more heat than less dense air. The deeper you dive, the quicker you get cold.

Anything that affects the function of your body—excitement, fear, seasickness, and other forms of illness—may increase heat loss. This is why good health and a confident state of mind are important for safety.

One way your body responds to cold is to shunt blood from the extremities through **vasoconstriction**. The circulatory shunting reduces heat loss because it keeps warm blood from losing heat when it passes through areas of the body that have little insulation.

Your head, underarms and sides, groin, and hands and feet are the areas of your body most prone to heat loss underwater. Fortunately, you can insulate these areas easily. You can lose considerable heat from your head in cold water because the head receives a large supply of warm blood and lacks natural insulation.

hypothermia
Lower than normal body core temperature

hyperthermia
Higher than normal body core temperature

vasoconstriction
Narrowing of the blood vessels

What areas of the body lose heat most rapidly?

Your body does not shunt blood from your head the way it does from other body extremities. In water at a temperature of 70 °F (21 °C) or less, it is important to insulate your head.

Hands have large surface areas compared to their volume. To prevent losing excessive heat through your hands when you get cold, your body shunts blood from them. Hands quickly lose to the water any warmth supplied to them. If you dive in cold water without hand protection, you lose body heat through your hands. Although your hands may become numb when they get cold, you should insulate them to conserve body heat.

Failure to wear adequate insulation leads to hypothermia. So does repeated or prolonged exposure until you lose a large amount of body heat. Slow chilling of your body is undesirable. You lose muscle strength and feeling, and your muscles may cramp. Severe heat loss also affects your ability to reason.

Another body response to heat loss is shivering, which restores heat through muscular activity. Shivering generates about five times as much heat as your body produces at rest. Shivering is helpful on land, but it is not beneficial in water. Water conducts away the heat you produce by shivering, and you get colder. Uncontrollable shivering indicates that you have lost too much heat from the core of your body and that you cannot rewarm yourself without getting out of the water. When you are shivering, terminate the dive. Rewarm yourself thoroughly before making any additional dives. Warm, dry clothes, warm surroundings, and warm nonalcoholic drinks help to return your body temperature to normal.

There is a difference between warming the surface of your body and warming the core of your body. You may feel rewarmed, but your deep core temperature may remain below normal. If you return to the water in this condition, you quickly will become chilled. The only way to be sure that you are thoroughly rewarmed is to keep warming yourself until you begin to perspire. Perspiration occurs when the core temperature begins to rise above normal body temperature.

> **What should you do if you begin to shiver during a dive?**

Overheating

You can prevent excessive loss of body heat by insulating your body with an exposure suit, but insulation can cause another problem. When you insulate your body to reduce heat loss in water, you reduce your body's ability to rid itself of excess heat above water. The evaporation of perspiration helps cool your body, but if you cover your body, perspiration cannot evaporate. You may become overheated in warm climates when you are preparing to dive. It is a challenge to maintain your body temperature within acceptable limits before, during, and after dives. Figure 4.1 shows the effects of overheating.

When a person is unable to stop the rise of core temperature, *heat exhaustion* occurs. This condition is serious. A person affected by heat exhaustion becomes weak and may collapse. He or she looks pale and feels sweaty. Place the person with this condition in a cool place and take steps to lower his or her body temperature.

> **What are the signs of heat exhaustion and heatstroke, and what are the first aid procedures for these conditions?**

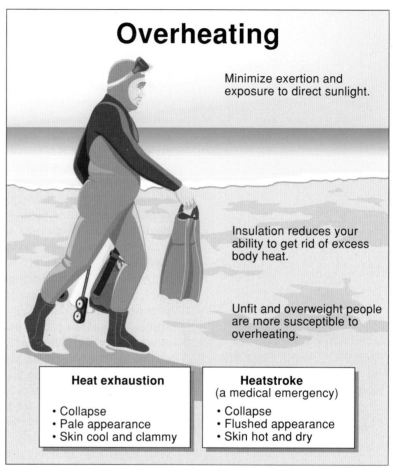

Figure 4.1 Don't allow yourself to become overheated when preparing to dive.

A more serious form of hyperthermia is *heatstroke*, which occurs when the body temperature becomes so high the body's temperature-regulating ability shuts down. A victim of heatstroke looks flushed and has hot, dry skin. This condition is extremely serious. Cool the person's body immediately and summon medical assistance.

It is much better to prevent hyperthermia than to treat it. Avoid prolonged exposure to warm temperatures when wearing insulation. If the air temperature is warm, douse yourself with water after donning your exposure suit and before donning the remainder of your diving equipment. Stay out of direct sunlight, if possible. All thermal considerations for diving are especially important for divers whose physical fitness is marginal.

Buoyancy

Exposure suits and other equipment affect your buoyancy. You must adapt your weight to blend weightlessly into the aquatic environment. When you are buoyant, you must fight to remain submerged; when you are overweighted, you must work hard to keep from sinking or to stay off the bottom. You need to maintain the weightless state of neutral buoyancy underwater and a state of positive buoyancy at the surface. In chapter 3 you learned the principle of buoyancy and the three states of buoyancy. You will learn in chapter 6 how to determine your correct initial weighting and how to control your buoyancy. Here, you will learn some practical applications of buoyancy.

Your body, composed of solids, liquids, and air spaces, has an average density nearly the same as water. A typical human body immersed and relaxed in water has a positive buoyancy of a few pounds when the lungs are filled with air and a negative buoyancy of a couple of pounds when the lungs contain the minimum amount of air.

Factors Affecting Buoyancy

Usually you wear an exposure suit when you dive. Most exposure suits increase buoyancy, so you wear weights to offset the buoyancy of the suit and achieve neutral buoyancy. The weights you use are made of lead, which is about 12 times denser than water.

Your initial state of buoyancy in water depends on the weight of the volume of water you and your equipment displace. You can vary your volume—with a negligible increase or decrease in your weight—by adding air to or venting air from an inflatable device, called a *buoyancy compensator* (BC). A BC is standard equipment for divers. Increasing BC volume increases buoyancy, and decreasing BC volume decreases buoyancy.

Your buoyancy is affected by your physical size, your lung capacity, the equipment you wear, and the items you carry. Exposure suits use air or small bubbles of gas for insulation. When you wear an exposure suit and descend, pressure compresses your suit and reduces its volume, so you become less buoyant. You must add air to your BC to compensate for buoyancy lost from suit compression. On the other hand, buoyancy increases as you consume air from your scuba cylinder. Remember that air weighs 0.08 lb (36 g) per cubic foot. A typical scuba tank contains 80 ft^3 (2,266 L) of air. A full tank of air weighs over 6 lb (2.9 kg) more than an empty tank. As you consume air from your scuba tank, you can vent air you added to your BC to compensate for suit compression. The trade-off helps you keep buoyancy constant during a dive.

Inflating your lungs increases your buoyancy, and deflating them reduces buoyancy. A high average lung volume makes you float; a low average volume makes you sink. When you become excited or begin moving quickly, your respiration increases and this affects your buoyancy. For optimum control of buoyancy, maintain a calm, relaxed state.

The density of the water also affects buoyancy. Salt water is denser than fresh water, so you are more buoyant in the ocean than in a lake. This means if you are weighted for neutral buoyancy in the ocean, you must remove some weight to achieve neutral buoyancy for freshwater diving. The amount of weight you remove is about 3% of the combined dry weight of you and

Determine the amount of weight you would have to remove if you are neutrally weighted in salt water and want to dive in fresh water. Use your body weight and equipment weight.

your equipment. For example, if a neutrally weighted 160-lb (73-kg) diver with 60 lb (27 kg) of equipment, including 16 lb (7.2 kg) of weights, wants to dive in fresh water instead of seawater, the diver must remove about 7 lb (3 kg) to be weighted correctly.

Ways to Control Buoyancy

> **What are the coarse, medium, and fine adjustments you can use to control buoyancy?**

You control buoyancy three ways: (a) by the amount of weight you wear, (b) by the amount of air in your BC, and (c) by the amount of air in your lungs. These means of control are coarse, medium, and fine adjustments, respectively. The skills you need to learn to adapt to the aquatic environment include determining the correct amount of weight to be worn, regulating the amount of air in your BC, and varying your breathing for minor buoyancy adjustments. Chapter 6 addresses these skills.

Pressure

One of the most important adaptations you must learn is how to handle the effects of pressure changes in water. Pressure changes rapidly as you descend and ascend. You must keep air spaces inside and on your body equalized to avoid discomfort and injury. In this section you will learn the procedures for pressure equalization.

Equalizing the Sinuses

Your sinuses equalize pressure automatically as long as they are healthy. But when you have a cold or respiratory illness, the membranes lining your sinuses become swollen. The swelling can close the narrow air passages leading to the sinuses. If you descend with swollen sinus membranes, a sinus squeeze will result. Because the sinuses are formed with bone, they do not compress as a flexible container does. When the pressure inside the sinuses is less than the surrounding pressure, the reduced pressure draws fluids into the cavities to reduce their volume and to equalize the pressure by compressing the air that is there. Do not attempt this painful method of equalization because your problems are not over after you descend. When you ascend in the condition just described, the compressed air in the sinuses expands to its original volume. The expansion can force the fluid in your sinuses out through the openings, which are swollen shut. Avoid this painful process; don't dive unless your head is clear and normal. Figure 4.2 shows how healthy and congested sinuses handle changes in pressure.

Do not use medications to relieve stuffiness and congestion caused by an illness and then dive. Increased pressure may alter the medication's effects and reduce the duration of its effectiveness. Decongestants do not cure an illness; they simply mask its symptoms. When medication taken to open swollen airways wears

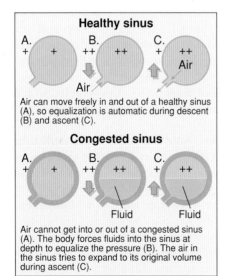

Healthy sinus

Air can move freely in and out of a healthy sinus (A), so equalization is automatic during descent (B) and ascent (C).

Congested sinus

Air cannot get into or out of a congested sinus (A). The body forces fluids into the sinus at depth to equalize the pressure (B). The air in the sinus tries to expand to its original volume during ascent (C).

Figure 4.2 How pressure is equalized in the sinuses.

What implications does the rebound effect have for divers?

off, a rebound effect occurs. The airways become more swollen than they were before you took the medication. If the rebound occurs while you are diving, you can trap high-pressure air in your sinuses. If you are not well enough to dive without medications, do not dive.

Equalizing the Ears

You are likely to be more involved with the equalization of pressure in your ears than any other air space. Whereas the air passages to your sinuses normally are open, the eustachian tubes leading to your ears normally are closed. You need to learn how to open the tubes at will to allow air to pass through them and equalize pressure in the air spaces of your middle ears.

There are several movements you can make that will open the ends where the eustachian tubes connect with the throat. Swallowing, yawning, lifting the base of your tongue, or jutting the jaw forward (individually or in combination) should produce a "cracking" sound in your ears. The opening of the tubes causes the sound. Some divers are able to use simple movements to equalize pressure in their ears during descent, but most people require a more forceful means of equalization. Many divers use a technique known as the **Toynbee maneuver**; a more forceful technique yet is the **Valsalva maneuver**.

You must avoid excessive force when you use the Valsalva maneuver or you can damage your ears permanently by rupturing the round window. When pressure in the outer ear increases, the eardrum bulges inward. The bones of hearing in the middle ear transmit the movement to the oval window in the inner ear. When you attempt to exhale against closed airways, you create an internal pressure that your body transmits to the inner ears. The attempted exhalation pressure in conjunction with the water pressure on the oval window can cause the round window to rupture, a serious injury that can result in a permanent high-frequency hearing loss and constant ringing in the ear. Because you control how hard you attempt to exhale in a Valsalva maneuver, you can prevent this injury. Be careful!

You must equalize your middle-ear air spaces frequently. If you delay equalization during descent, increasing pressure holds your eustachian tubes closed, and attempting to force air through them only closes them tighter. This is the **trapdoor effect**, a difficulty you can avoid by keeping the pressure in your middle ears and your throat equal. You can then open your eustachian tubes and allow air to pass through them.

Equalize pressure in your ears before descending and then about every 2 ft (0.6 m) for the first 15 ft (4.6 m) of descent, every 3 ft (0.9 m) from 15 to 30 ft (4.6 to 9.2 m), and as needed thereafter. You will feel and hear air enter your ears when you "clear" them of any difference in pressure. If you attempt to equalize and cannot get air into your ears, ascend a couple of feet to reduce the pressure on your eustachian tubes and try again. If that works, continue your descent. If that does not work, ascend a few more feet and try again.

Toynbee maneuver
A method of opening the eustachian tubes by blocking the nostrils, closing the mouth, and swallowing

Valsalva maneuver
A method of opening the eustachian tubes by blocking the nostrils, closing the mouth, and gently trying to exhale

trapdoor effect
The tight closing of the eustachian tubes as a result of trying to force air through them when pressure is holding them shut

How often should you equalize the pressure in your ears as you descend? What should you do if the pressure doesn't equalize?

Your initial descents may be somewhat jerky until you become accustomed to equalization techniques.

Failing to equalize pressure in your middle ears is as bad as trying to equalize forcefully. Pressure bows the eardrum inward in an unequalized middle ear. If the squeeze continues, pressure forces blood and fluid into the middle ear to reduce the volume. This process takes time and usually, but not always, is painful. It does, however, damage your ear. If you feel discomfort or pressure in your ears during descent, reascend until the pain is gone, then ascend another couple of feet before trying to equalize.

If you ignore an ear squeeze and continue your descent, the pressure differential can rupture your eardrum. The rupture instantly equalizes the pressure in your middle ear, but it damages your ear in the process. A rupture of your eardrum causes a temporary loss of hearing and a feeling of "fullness" in the ear. If you suspect an ear injury, see a physician; prompt treatment can minimize the risk of permanent injury.

You can cause an outward rupture of the eardrum if you block the ear canal with a plug or cover your ears with a watertight covering. When you obstruct an ear canal, the air in the outer ear remains at surface pressure while the pressure in the middle ear increases with equalization during descent. The difference in pressure between the middle and outer ear pushes the eardrum outward until it breaks. You can and must prevent such an injury. Do not wear ear plugs while diving, and avoid waterproof seals over your ears.

It is easier to equalize when you descend in an upright position than in a head-down position. Membranes line the airways in your head. When you are upside down, the membranes of your air passages swell and narrow.

Ear equalization difficulties during ascent are uncommon. Air expanding inside the middle ear escapes through the eustachian tube. Air passes out through the tube much more easily than it goes in; you do not have to do maneuvers to open your tubes so the air can escape. But if a plug of mucus happens to block a tube, pressure will build up in the middle ear and cause a **reverse block**. This can cause discomfort. If you feel pain or pressure in an ear during ascent, stop the ascent. Pressure inside the ear usually will work its way out, if given time. If you are forced to surface, the pain will increase and an injury may result. Have the ear examined by a physician, especially if you have recurring reverse blocks.

reverse block
The inability of expanding air in a body air space to vent during ascent

How can you prevent a mask squeeze?

Equalizing the Mask

Inside the mask is an air space affected by changes in pressure. If you descend without increasing the amount of air inside your mask, pressure pulls your face and eyes into the mask slightly. The pulling sensation, if ignored, ruptures capillaries in your eyes and on your face and causes a *mask squeeze*. Following a dive with a mask squeeze, the whites of your eyes will be red, and your face will be red and puffy. You can prevent a mask squeeze by exhaling through your nose as needed during descent to keep the pressure inside your mask equal to the surrounding pressure.

Breathing

Breathing while in water differs from breathing while on land in several ways. You cannot breathe as freely in water as you can on land. Also, it is not as easy to get large quantities of air from a scuba system as it is to breathe deeply above water. When you ascend, compressed air in your lungs expands, which can cause your lungs to rupture unless you allow the excess air to escape. And when you breathe under the water, you might inhale some, which will cause you to choke and gasp when the water strikes your vocal cords. You need to learn the correct methods for breathing in and under the water.

Lung Overexpansion

The most important aquatic breathing adaptation you'll make is overcoming the instinct to hold your breath underwater. When you breathe compressed air at depth, the density of the air in your lungs is greater than it is at the surface. When you ascend, the air in your lungs expands as the surrounding pressure decreases. If you hold your breath, your lungs expand until they reach their maximum volume and then rupture with an ascent of as little as 4 ft (1.2 m). It is imperative that you avoid breath-holding when breathing compressed air underwater. You may breathe continuously or may exhale a small amount of air continuously, but never hold your breath during ascent after breathing compressed air. Figure 4.3 illustrates why you must breathe continuously. Table 4.1 describes the possible consequences of breath-holding while ascending with compressed air in your lungs.

Why is it essential that you never hold your breath during a dive?

Skip Breathing

Some divers attempt to extend their air supplies by holding each breath for several seconds. This dangerous practice is called *skip breathing*. When you hold your breath, you increase the amount of CO_2 in your circulatory system. A high CO_2 level reduces your ability to cope with a difficulty, should one arise. And if you skip breathe, you may forget to exhale while ascending. It is important to breathe continuously when breathing compressed air.

THE MOST IMPORTANT RULE OF SCUBA DIVING:

ALWAYS KEEP BREATHING. DO NOT HOLD YOUR BREATH.

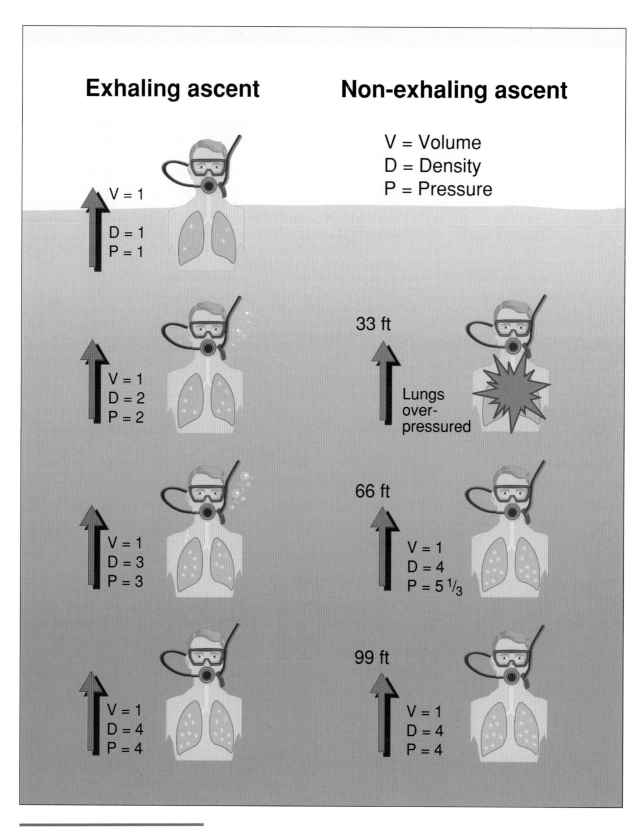

Figure 4.3 A breath-holding ascent after breathing compressed air can cause lung rupture. Breathe continuously while ascending.

Table 4.1
Potential Lung Injuries

Pulmonary Barotrauma

Barotrauma is trauma or injury caused by pressure. *Pulmonary barotrauma* is any lung injury caused by pressure. Failure to allow expanding air to escape from the lungs during ascent can cause several forms of pulmonary barotrauma, either singularly or in combination.

Arterial Gas Embolism

An *embolism* is a blockage of circulation. An embolism resulting from an air bubble blocking the arterial circulation is an *arterial gas embolism* (AGE). This occurs when air expanding in the lungs forces bubbles of air into the circulation. Air bubbles enter the capillary beds of the lungs and pass through the heart, which pumps the bubbles into arteries supplying blood to the body. The diameter of an artery decreases as the distance from the heart increases. At some point a bubble lodges in an artery and becomes an embolus (plug). It is common for an arterial gas embolism to occur in an artery leading to the brain. The embolus has the effect of a stroke, causes unconsciousness, and is an extremely serious injury. Anytime a diver loses consciousness after a dive, you should suspect AGE. The temporary obstruction of an airway, such as that caused by a cold, increases the risk of AGE. Healthy lungs are a prerequisite for diving.

Mediastinal Emphysema

If a rupture of the lung does not force air into the circulation, the air may travel along the bronchi and enter the middle area of the chest, called the *mediastinum*. This results in a *mediastinal emphysema*, which means air in the tissues in the middle of the chest. The injury causes a dull ache or tightness that worsens with coughing, swallowing, or taking a deep breath. Expanding air may interfere with the circulation of the heart and can cause fainting.

Subcutaneous Emphysema

Expanding air in the mediastinum may migrate upward along the breastbone. The air will then swell the tissues around the neck, producing an injury known as *subcutaneous emphysema*, which is air in the tissues under the skin. The injury can cause changes in the voice, crackling of the skin, and a feeling of fullness in the neck.

Pneumothorax

If a lung rupture forces air into the space between the lungs and the lining of the chest wall, a condition known as a *pneumothorax* occurs. The term means air trapped in the chest cavity. As air trapped in the pleural space expands during ascent, it collapses the lung and may affect the action of the heart. Symptoms are severe pain and breathing difficulty.

Lung injuries are serious and can be life-threatening. Life support may be required. This is one reason why you should complete a course in cardiopulmonary (heart and lung) resuscitation (CPR). You may have to administer first aid until professional medical treatment (which all lung injuries require) is available.

Failing to allow excess air to escape causes nearly all lung overexpansion injuries. You can prevent injuries by breathing continuously. If you remove the scuba regulator from your mouth for any reason, exhale lightly and continuously to avoid breath-holding.

Breathing Problems

Divers may encounter respiratory difficulties if they overexert themselves, breathe contaminated air, inhale water, or run out of air. Fortunately, you can (and should) prevent all of these problems.

Overexertion.   Scuba equipment allows you to breathe underwater. A regulator delivers air with little respiratory effort, but breathing underwater requires more effort than breathing above water. If you do not maintain your scuba equipment properly, the effort required to inhale and exhale can be excessive and may cause respiratory distress.

Scuba regulators have a limited capacity to supply air. Regulators are not designed nor are they intended to be used for activities involving heavy exertion. Commercial divers use helmets with air hoses to supply the large amounts of air they need to meet their requirements while working underwater. You must avoid strenuous activities underwater because you can overbreathe your equipment and experience *air starvation*, a suffocating feeling of not being able to get enough air.

Make your breaths while diving longer, slower, and deeper than your breaths on land. Pace your activity to keep respiration at a slow, controlled rate. If breathing becomes rapid or labored, cease all activity immediately and breathe deeply until your respiration returns to a controlled rate.

Contaminated Air.   If the compressed air in your tank comes from an air compressor that is not operated or maintained properly, your tank will contain contaminated air. The contamination is likely to be CO (carbon monoxide), a gas produced by incomplete combustion. CO in the body impedes the blood's ability to transport oxygen. Blood hemoglobin's affinity for CO is 210 times greater than its affinity for oxygen. Hemoglobin normally exchanges oxygen for CO_2 about every half-minute, but when CO attaches to hemoglobin, the contaminant remains bonded to the hemoglobin for hours. Breathing contaminated air under pressure can make you ill and render you unconscious. Avoid contaminated air by having your tank filled only with pure air. CO is an odorless, tasteless gas, but usually other gases that have a foul taste and odor accompany it. If the air from a scuba tank smells or tastes foul, do not use it. Report the situation immediately to the facility that filled the cylinder. Good air stations have their air tested regularly to ensure purity.

Water Inspiration.   If you inhale water, your larynx goes into a spasm as a reflex action to keep the liquid out of your lungs. Avoid coughing and choking in water; not only are these reflexes unpleasant, but they may cause you to inspire more water and lose buoyancy. You need to breathe differently underwater than you do on land. Avoid quick inhalations. Begin a breath with a light, slow inhalation to ensure you are inhaling air and not water. Once air begins flowing, the remainder of your inhalation can be normal.

> How should you adapt your on-land breathing pattern when you're breathing underwater with a scuba regulator?

You also can prevent droplets of water from going down your throat by placing the tip of your tongue on the roof of your mouth behind your upper teeth to form a splashboard. If, in spite of all you do to avoid it, you inhale some water and start coughing, try swallowing hard three times in rapid succession. The swallowing helps you overcome your reflex.

If water does enter your lungs, it interferes with respiration. If an extensive area of the lungs is irritated by water, you can drown. This is a risk you face in any aquatic pastime. The purpose of your training is to allow you to enjoy the aquatic environment with the minimum risk of injury—especially drowning. When you follow the rules and practices you learn, your risk of injury while diving will be negligible.

An automatic response to the inhalation of water is to swallow it to keep your airways dry. When you swallow salt water, you may experience illness, nausea, or diarrhea. If you swallow several mouthfuls of salt water while diving, terminate the dive.

Running Out of Air. You must have air to breathe while submerged. This is obvious, but some divers do not monitor their air supplies and run out of air at depth. There is no more excuse for running out of air underwater than there is for running out of gas on the freeway when you have a working gauge. There are ways to manage an out-of-air situation, but it is much better to avoid the problem.

Heart and Lungs

Water temperature alters the rate and rhythm of your heart, and physical and emotional stress compound the situation. The combined effects of water pressure, exercise, cold, and stress can cause serious problems if your heart is not healthy. If you have heart problems and wish to dive, you should first obtain medical approval from a diving physician. Even minor heart problems can cause you to suddenly lose consciousness in the water, and you could drown. Fitness for diving is an important safety issue.

Trying to work hard underwater will lead to overexertion and a frightening sensation of suffocation. To adapt to your cardio-pulmonary limitations, you must learn to limit your activities and pace yourself.

Equilibrium

vertigo
A feeling of dizziness and disorientation

If you rupture an eardrum, water colder than body temperature may enter the ear and cool the semicircular canals of your inner ear. The canals—your center of equilibrium—are sensitive to temperature and pressure changes. Cold water cooling the semicircular canals can cause **vertigo**, a feeling that passes when the water in the middle ear warms to body temperature. Obviously, it's better to prevent vertigo than to deal with it.

A sudden change in pressure in the middle-ear air space of one ear also can produce a dizziness called *alternobaric vertigo* by affecting your semicircular canals. The disorientation from alternobaric vertigo passes quickly when the inner ear recovers.

What can you do to help yourself recover from severe disorientation or dizziness?

There are many causes of vertigo. Fortunately, instances of severe disorientation are rare in diving. If you experience disorientation underwater, grasp a solid object for a point of reference until the feeling passes. If suspended in water, close your eyes and hug yourself to reduce the effects of the vertigo. Avoid panic by telling yourself that the sensation will not last long.

Motions detected in your inner ears, visual references, and joint pressures on your limbs all affect your equilibrium. When your brain receives mixed signals from your inner ears, eyes, and body, you may experience motion sickness. You must avoid seasickness because vomiting under the water is hazardous.

Medications can help reduce the tendency to be seasick. The medicine dulls the senses of the organs of balance in your ears. Unfortunately, the medications can have other, undesirable effects. If you are prone to seasickness, consult a diving physician regarding the type of medication you should try. Take some of the medicine several days before you plan to dive, and note the effects, if any. If the medication produces drowsiness or blurred vision, do not use it while diving. Seek an alternative that does not produce side effects. Medications that cause dizziness, drowsiness, changes in heart rhythm, or blurred vision may cause you to lose consciousness under pressure. Many divers do successfully use medications to prevent seasickness; you need to find a type that works for you. Take motion-sickness medication at least 30 minutes before you are exposed to motion.

What steps can you take to avoid or minimize seasickness?

If you do not want to use medication, there are other techniques you can use to reduce the tendency to become seasick. Eat a good, non-spicy meal in advance. An empty, acid-filled stomach becomes upset more easily than a full one. People whose breakfast before diving consists of coffee and orange juice are good candidates for motion sickness. When aboard a vessel, position yourself as near the center of the boat as possible. Avoid the front end of the boat, breathing engine fumes, and reading. You can also hasten your adaptation to motion, described as getting your "sea legs," by lying down for awhile with your eyes closed. Being still allows your inner ears to adapt to the motion without visual signals confusing your brain.

You may become disoriented when you are weightless in a dimly lit environment. Under some conditions it can be difficult to tell which way is up if you rely on your sense of balance. To prevent disorientation, learn to recognize clues about your orientation in the water. Water in your mask settles to the lowest point, bubbles ascend, and heavy objects you hold (such as your weight belt) orient themselves up and down.

Vision

Experience will help you adapt to magnified vision underwater. You can adapt so quickly to distance corrections in water that you will have to readapt when you surface from a dive. At the end of a dive, the distance to a boat or to the shore may look much greater than it is. You may be surprised to find that you require less time than you think to swim to a destination.

You also will compensate for color differences. When you know the color something is supposed to appear, it looks more like that color. The use of artificial light at close range makes it easier to view the rich and magnificent colors in the underwater world.

Your vision adapts to low light levels, but the process takes time. Short, deep dives in turbid water will not allow you to complete your adaptation, and details will not be clear. You will not be able to see well without artificial light. You can improve your ability to see while diving by avoiding bright light and glare before a dive. Wear good, dark sunglasses above water during the day. When you complete training for night diving, you will learn other techniques to help adapt your eyes for diving at night.

Ingassing and Outgassing

There are limits to the amount of nitrogen you can absorb while diving and to the rate at which you can eliminate excess gas at the end of a dive. If you exceed these limits, you may be injured.

Decompression Theory

Gases diffuse by moving from areas of greater concentration to areas of lesser concentration. When pressure increases, gases diffuse from your lungs into your blood and then from your blood into your tissues. When the ambient (surrounding) pressure decreases, diffusion occurs in the reverse sequence.

Two factors affecting diffusion are time and **perfusion**. The greater the circulation in a tissue, the sooner the pressures of the gases in that tissue come into balance with the pressures of the gases you breathe. Reaching this state of equilibrium takes time. The amount of time it takes a tissue to accumulate half of the gas it can hold for a given pressure is a **half time**. A tissue is saturated (holds all of the gas it can for a given pressure) after 6 half times. If perfusion permits 50% of a gas to diffuse into a tissue in 5 minutes, the tissue saturates in 30 minutes. Outgassing also occurs in 6 half times.

Air is primarily nitrogen and oxygen. The oxygen in the air you breathe is of no consequence to you within the limits of recreational diving (130 ft or 39.6 m maximum) because you use the oxygen. Nitrogen, the primary component of air, is inert. Your body cannot use the nitrogen, so when you ascend you must eliminate the excess nitrogen you absorb at depth. Since nitrogen diffuses from your

perfusion
The movement of a fluid through a tissue

half time
The amount of time it takes a tissue to accumulate half of the gas it can hold for a given pressure

Why is the rate of nitrogen diffusion important to divers?

Figure 4.4 When you reduce the pressure on a liquid rapidly and there is sufficient gas dissolved in the liquid, the gas forms bubbles.

controlling compartment
The area of the body that determines how long a diver can remain at a given depth. The determination is made by how quickly a gas diffuses from that compartment.

body, there is no problem unless the reduction in pressure is so rapid that the nitrogen cannot diffuse fast enough. When you reduce the pressure on a liquid rapidly and there is sufficient gas dissolved in the liquid, the gas forms bubbles. An excellent example of this is CO_2 dissolved in carbonated beverages (see Figure 4.4). The gas remains dissolved in a sealed, pressurized container. When you reduce the pressure suddenly by opening the container, the gas forms bubbles because it cannot diffuse out of solution slowly. If a beverage container has a tiny leak, however, the CO_2 comes out of solution slowly without bubbling. There is no bubbling when you open a container that has a slow leak because the gas has diffused out of solution.

You must be concerned about the amount of nitrogen in solution in your body and the rate at which you eliminate it. If you absorb too much nitrogen while diving and do not ascend in a manner that allows the excess nitrogen to be eliminated without forming bubbles, the bubbles are likely to cause DCS, a serious diving illness.

Mathematical models provide estimates of the amount of nitrogen in different parts of your body. Since perfusion varies, tissues absorb nitrogen at differing rates. Decompression experts use mathematical models, called compartments, to estimate gas absorption and elimination by various areas of the body. A compartment is identified by its half time; one with a half time of 5 minutes is a 5-minute compartment. Experts use compartments ranging from 5 minutes to as long as 960 minutes when calculating gas absorption and elimination.

A compartment that has absorbed gas will withstand some lowering of pressure before bubbling occurs. Originally scientists believed that a reduction in pressure by a ratio greater than two to one (2:1) would cause bubbling to occur in divers who were saturated for a particular depth. This was the surfacing ratio that could not be exceeded. Then scientists discovered that due to differences in perfusion, the surfacing ratios are different for various compartments. Those that eliminate gas quickly have a higher surfacing ratio than compartments that eliminate gas slowly. The difference in ratios posed an interesting and complex problem for divers because one tissue controlled how long a diver could remain at one depth, and another tissue controlled how long the diver could remain at another depth. The **controlling compartment** eventually was used to establish our modern time limits for diving. Do not remain at any depth longer than the time it takes the controlling compartment to exceed its surfacing ratio. If you do, you must prevent bubble formation by stopping during the ascent and eliminating the excess gas. The time limits for various depths have been conveniently arranged into tables and included in dive computer software to help you keep the amount of nitrogen in solution in the various tissues of your body within the surfacing ratio of each and every compartment.

It takes time to eliminate excess gas from tissues. The rate at which you reduce pressure (ascend) is important. The dive tables explained in chapter 7 use a pressure reduction rate no greater than 1 ft/s (0.3 m/s). Some dive computer mathematical models use rates two and three times slower than the dive tables. It is important to ascend slowly to prevent the formation of bubbles in your body tissues.

Decompression Sickness

Explain why the rate of ascent and the amount of time spent at depth need to be regulated.

Commonly known as the *bends*, decompression sickness (DCS), is the result of a reduction in pressure (decompression) that is too rapid for the amount of gas in solution in body tissues. The gas forms bubbles in the tissues or in the blood before it can be diffused into the lungs and eliminated.

Scientists do not fully understand what occurs when DCS strikes. The symptoms may appear immediately after surfacing from a dive or days after diving. About half of all DCS cases occur within 1 hour after diving. The symptoms vary, depending on the amount and location of the bubbles. Serious cases of DCS can have severe neurological effects and produce permanent paralysis.

What causes the bends? What are some symptoms?

Common Symptoms of DCS	*Factors That Increase the Chances of DCS*
• A mottled skin rash	• Lack of sleep
• Joint pain	• Alcohol and its aftereffects
• Numbness	• Dehydration
• Tingling	• Illness
• Weakness	• Age
• Paralysis	• Cold water
	• Exercise during and after diving
	• Altitude after diving

Some experts believe you should avoid postdive activities that stimulate circulation because increased perfusion may contribute to DCS. Specific activities to avoid include physical exercise, drinking alcoholic beverages, and taking hot showers or baths. Reduced pressure at altitude is an additional factor because flying in a plane or driving into the mountains too soon after diving can cause the bends. Shun all activities that increase the likelihood of DCS.

A person who has DCS requires prompt first aid and medical treatment. The illness worsens with time. The best first aid measure is to administer oxygen in the highest concentration possible. Breathing oxygen eliminates nitrogen in inspired air and enhances the diffusion of nitrogen from the body. The patient should remain still and sip water. Make arrangements to have the patient transported to the nearest hyperbaric (high-pressure) facility for treatment. The medical staff will place the patient inside a large, pressurized chamber (called a recompression chamber), increase the pressure inside the chamber to reduce the symptoms, administer medications, and slowly decompress the patient. Recompression must be done in a chamber (Figure 4.5 shows an example of a recompression chamber). Never attempt the in-water decompression of a victim of the bends.

Figure 4.5 Symptoms of decompression can be reduced by increasing pressure inside a recompression chamber.

DCS is extremely serious; you must prevent it because it can cause permanent injury. To reduce the likelihood of DCS, remain well within the established time and depth limits for diving. Surface at a rate no greater than that specified for the dive-planning device you use (see Figure 4.6). Stop during every ascent

Figure 4.6 Be sure to complete all necessary precautionary decompression stops when ascending after a dive.

for 2 to 3 minutes at a depth between 10 and 30 ft (3 and 9 m) to eliminate excess nitrogen before surfacing. The processes of ascending and stopping are forms of decompression that reduce the likelihood of DCS. The final way to avoid DCS is to delay excursions to altitude after diving. The details of the time delays are contained in chapter 7.

Decompression Illness

When a patient has symptoms of both AGE and DCS, the medical diagnosis is **decompression illness** (DCI). This relatively new term describes a unique condition. Seek medical attention immediately for any diver who has neurological symptoms following a dive.

Nitrogen Narcosis

The increased partial pressure of nitrogen can cause **nitrogen narcosis**, or "rapture of the deep," at depths of about 100 ft (30 m) and deeper. Scientists do not know exactly what causes narcosis, but its effects are similar to those of anesthetic gases. Narcosis impairs thinking and affects judgment, reasoning, memory, and the ability to do physical tasks. Nitrogen narcosis is hazardous; it reduces your awareness and ability to respond to an emergency. Susceptibility to narcosis varies from person to person and within an individual from day to day.

Narcosis begins suddenly at depth. You can relieve its symptoms rapidly by ascending to a shallower depth to reduce the narcotic effect.

decompression illness (DCI)
Condition with symptoms of both AGE and DCS, where a diver has minor symptoms of AGE upon surfacing, recovers, and then develops a severe case of DCS

nitrogen narcosis
Condition characterized by feelings ranging from fear to overconfidence to euphoria as a result of the increased partial pressure of nitrogen at depths of about 100 ft (30 m) and deeper

The following factors predispose a person to narcosis:

- A high level of system CO_2 caused by exertion
- Alcohol or its aftereffects
- Anxiety
- Low body temperature
- Medications
- Social drugs

Experience, frequent diving, and concentration reduce susceptibility to narcosis, but it is better to prevent narcosis than to attempt to cope with it.

Dehydration

You need to preserve body fluids underwater to prevent dehydration. Getting cold makes you produce more urine than normal. You receive air underwater by creating an inhalation pressure that opens valves in an air delivery system. The inhalation pressure is slight, but it is greater than normal. Inhaling harder than normal is negative-pressure breathing, which also has the physiological effect of increasing urine production. Breathing underwater compounds the problem of dehydration.

Some types of diuretic beverages (such as coffee and alcohol) and medications cause increased urine production. Before diving, avoid ingesting anything that makes you urinate more than normal.

You must prevent excessive dehydration because the condition predisposes you to diving injuries. Do the following to prevent dehydration.

- Insulate yourself to stay as warm as possible.
- Keep your regulator well maintained so it breathes as easily as possible.
- Avoid diuretic drinks and medications.
- Replenish body fluids frequently; drink fluids before and between dives.

Mobility

The equipment you wear for diving limits your mobility. It reduces your range of motion and makes it difficult to walk. The colder the water or the thicker your exposure suit, the less your range of movement.

Diving equipment is fairly heavy and is challenging to lift and move. Improper lifting techniques can cause back injuries. Squat down and lift with your legs to pick up a tank or weight belt instead of bending over.

The weight of the equipment changes your center of gravity and affects your balance. This is challenging on a rocking boat or an uneven bottom during entries and exits. Move carefully and hold onto something or someone for support when you move around out of the water.

You wear fins so that you can use the large muscles of your legs for propulsion. To adapt to diving, you need to learn to use your legs for swimming and your body angle to control direction. These actions free your hands for other uses underwater. Do not use your hands for propulsion. Fins make it difficult for you to walk. Shuffle your feet while moving backward or sideways, keep your knees bent, and be careful not to fall.

Drag retards your ability to move in the water. One factor affecting drag is the speed of motion. The greater the speed, the greater the resistance to movement. The average diver can sustain a speed of a little more than 1 mph (1.6 km/hr). Doubling the speed increases the energy requirement fourfold. Trying to move in water as if it were air causes exhaustion quickly. Use a slow, steady pace and slow, deliberate motions to reduce the effects of drag.

Another factor affecting drag is the size of the object in motion. The larger the surface area exposed, the greater the resistance. A swimming diver is under the influence of four forces: Weight pulls the diver downward, lift pulls the diver upward, thrust moves the diver forward, and drag retards forward progress (see Figure 4.7). Divers usually wear weight around the waist, which pulls the lower half of the body downward. Because air in a BC rises to the top, lift from the BC lifts the upper half of the body. The effect of these forces increases the surface area of the diver and, therefore, the drag. Adjust the amount of weight you wear so your body is as horizontal as possible in the water. Correct weighting minimizes drag and the effort required to swim.

Water flows smoothly across a smooth and rounded surface but flows turbulently across an irregular surface. When the surface is irregular, the turbulent flow increases drag. Just as vehicles designed to travel through fluids are streamlined to reduce drag caused by turbulent flow, you can choose and configure your equipment so it presents the smoothest surface possible to the flow of water.

| What factors increase drag and impede a diver's forward motion? |

Summary

You have to make many changes to adapt to the underwater environment. The way you breathe is the most important adaptation: You must breathe continuously and deeply, and you must avoid breath-holding when you use scuba equipment. You must also limit your activity and pace yourself so you do not overexert. Managing the mechanical and physiological effects of pressure requires major adaptations. You must keep pressure equalized in your air spaces and limit depth and time at depth to avoid nitrogen narcosis and DCS. Being in the underwater environment seems strange at first, but you can adapt to weightlessness and other strange feelings. The sensations of diving become exhilarating as you gain experience in the new world beneath the surface.

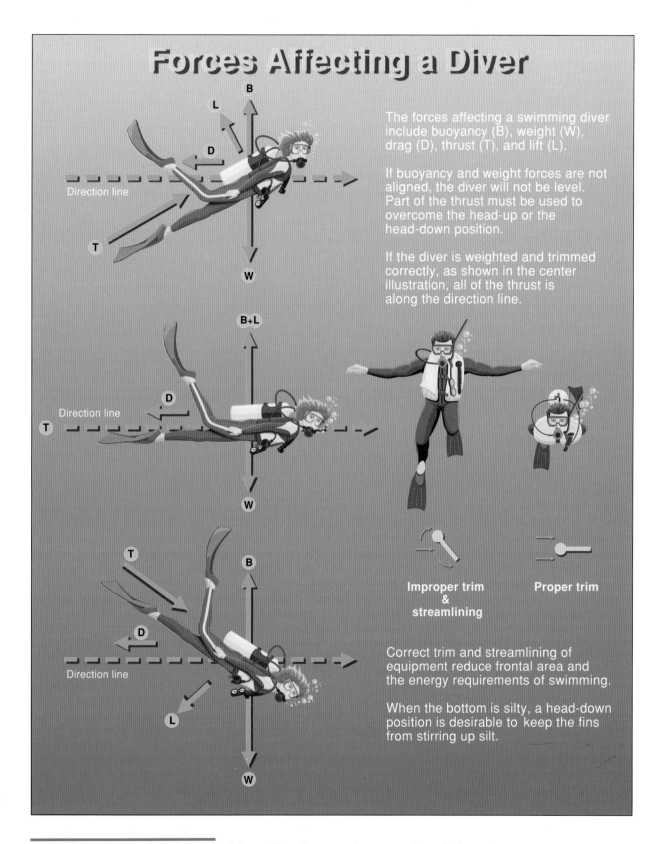

Forces Affecting a Diver

The forces affecting a swimming diver include buoyancy (B), weight (W), drag (D), thrust (T), and lift (L).

If buoyancy and weight forces are not aligned, the diver will not be level. Part of the thrust must be used to overcome the head-up or the head-down position.

If the diver is weighted and trimmed correctly, as shown in the center illustration, all of the thrust is along the direction line.

Improper trim & streamlining

Proper trim

Correct trim and streamlining of equipment reduce frontal area and the energy requirements of swimming.

When the bottom is silty, a head-down position is desirable to keep the fins from stirring up silt.

Figure 4.7 Weight, lift, thrust, and drag affect divers as they move through the water.

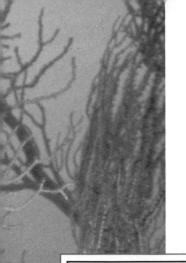

5 Diving Equipment

Equipment helps people adapt to the underwater environment; it allows them to see, breathe, move, and rest. Diving is an equipment-intensive activity. In this chapter you will learn what equipment you need, how to select the best equipment for your needs, and how to care for your equipment. You will become familiar with the following equipment:

- Masks
- Snorkels
- Fins
- Skin diving vests
- Exposure suits
- Weighting systems
- Buoyancy compensators

- Scuba cylinders
- Cylinder valves
- Scuba regulators
- Alternate air sources
- Instrumentation
- Dive knives and accessory equipment

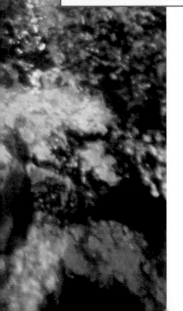

You need to be equipped properly to dive in open water. A snorkeler (a diver who remains at the surface) should wear a mask, a snorkel, fins, and a skin diving vest. A skin diver (a breath-holding diver who dives beneath the surface) uses snorkeling equipment and may wear an exposure suit and a weight belt (if the suit requires weights). Complete scuba equipment includes, at a minimum, a mask, snorkel, fins, an exposure suit, a weighting system (if needed), a BC, a scuba unit (cylinder, valve, regulator, alternate air source), instrumentation, and a dive knife. For cold water, a diver also needs a hood, boots, and gloves. Figure 5.1 shows fully equipped divers.

Snorkeling Equipment

A snorkeler can move about the surface of the water and view the underwater world while breathing easily through a snorkel, a tube that extends from the mouth into the atmosphere. The mask, snorkel, fins, and some type of flotation device are basic equipment for all types of recreational diving: snorkeling, skin diving, and scuba diving.

Masks

The eyes require an air space in front of them to focus sharply. Your mask provides an air space and a window to another world. There are many styles of masks but only two basic recreational types: purge and nonpurge. A purge is a one-way valve through which you can expel water that enters the mask. As you will learn in chapter 6, you can remove water from a mask without a valve, so many masks do not feature a purge valve. A third type of mask, a full-face mask, is for commercial and specialty applications only. Figure 5.2 shows the most common types of masks.

The type of mask you choose is not nearly as important as the fit of the mask on your face. The mask must fit your facial contours perfectly so it will fit comfortably and remain watertight throughout a dive. Fit and comfort are the most important features to consider when you select a mask. To test the fit, choose a mask and remove the strap or position it on the front of the mask. Tilt your head back and lay the mask (do not push it) on your face. Make sure your hair is not under the sealing edge of the mask; then inhale gently. If the mask pulls onto your face snugly from the partial vacuum created by your inhalation, the mask fits. If you have to push the mask to get it to seal on your face, the mask probably will leak when you use it underwater.

Figure 5.1 Fully equipped cold-water (left) and warm-water (right) divers.

What are the two most important considerations for choosing a mask? How can you tell if a mask fits?

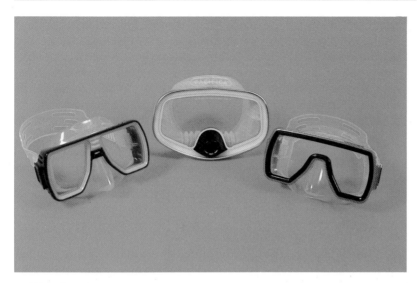

Figure 5.2 Many different masks are available for divers including purge (center) and nonpurge types.

Some features of a mask affect its fit and comfort. Consider the style, type of material, and type of sealing edge. The best masks are made from silicone, which is soft, pliable, and nonallergenic and resists deterioration better than rubber compounds.

The buoyancy of smaller masks poses no problems, but the tug of buoyancy of masks with larger volumes may affect the seal. Low-volume masks are easier to clear of water and provide excellent visibility. A wide, double-edged seal does a better job of excluding water than a single-edged seal.

The configuration of the strap is important. The strap should be easily adjustable, and the adjustment should lock securely with the adjusting locks. A split strap helps the mask seal evenly on the face. Wide neoprene straps are popular in tropical waters (where divers do not wear head coverings) because the straps do not tangle hair as a standard strap does.

A diving mask must provide a means for you to seal your nostrils so you can equalize the pressure in your ears. For example, a pocket for the nose or finger wells allow you to place your fingers on either side of your nose. Your nose must be included in the mask for another reason. During descent, pressure tries to squeeze the mask, and you exhale air through your nose into the mask to prevent the squeeze. Swimming goggles, which have no means for equalization, are not acceptable for diving.

Wide-angle vision is a desirable feature because a mask limits peripheral vision. A design that places the lens (or lenses) close to your eyes enhances your field of vision. Some large masks that position the lens away from your face offer wide-angle vision, but their larger volume requires more air and more time to clear water from them when they flood. Larger masks also are more buoyant.

The lens or lenses of a diving mask are made of tempered glass, which is scratch-resistant. Plastic lenses are unacceptable because they scratch and fog badly. There is a film of oil from production on the surfaces of the glass lenses of new masks. You must remove the film completely or the mask will fog continuously underwater. Clean your mask thoroughly with scouring powder. The glass is too hard to be scratched by the abrasive, so do not be timid when cleaning your mask. Commercial defogging solutions help keep your mask clear while you dive. If a clean mask fogs slightly during use, you can allow a small amount of water into the mask and wash it across the fogged area to resolve the problem.

Divers who wear corrective lenses have several options. If you wear soft contact lenses, you may use them for diving after you complete your training, but you should not use them during training because you may lose them when you are learning how to clear water from your mask. Some contact lens wearers prefer a mask with a small purge valve because they can expel water from the mask with little risk of losing a contact lens. Several companies prepare and bond corrective lenses into any diving mask. If you require only a simple correction, you may be able to use interchangeable corrective lenses that are available for some masks. You may be able to obtain corrective lenses for your mask when you purchase it.

Store your mask in a mask box when you are not using it. The box helps keep the mask from getting damaged and helps prevent discoloration of silicone.

Snorkels

A human head weighs about as much as a bowling ball. If you had to swim while holding a bowling ball out of water, you would become exhausted quickly. If you try to swim while holding your head above water, you will tire rapidly. But if you allow buoyancy to support your head in the water, you can relax and swim for hours. A snorkel allows you to breathe while water supports your head—allowing you to conserve energy and enjoy continuous underwater viewing.

In its simplest form, a snorkel is nothing more than a breathing tube that extends from a diver's mouth to a point above the waterline. A basic diving snorkel is a J-shaped tube with a mouthpiece on one end. Just as with masks, there are two types of snorkels: purge and nonpurge (see Figure 5.3). A purge snorkel has a one-way valve through which you may expel water that enters the tube. As you will learn in chapter 6, you can clear water from a snorkel without a purge valve, so some snorkels do not have a valve. Some types of purge snorkels are self-draining: Gravity drains water from the tube automatically when you are at the surface of the water.

There are additional snorkel features, such as a swivel mouthpiece. Another is a flexible hose for the lower half of the tube so the lower part that usually is curved hangs straight down when you are not using your snorkel. A flex-hose snorkel also reduces interference between the snorkel and your scuba regulator. Also, there are special mouthpieces to maximize comfort and devices to prevent water from entering the top end of the snorkel, although water-exclusion devices are not essential.

The fit of your snorkel is the most important consideration, much more important than the type. The mouthpiece must not irritate your mouth, gums, or jaw when in place for extended periods. The angle of the mouthpiece in the mouth must not require you to bite hard to hold the mouthpiece in place. A snorkel that fits poorly may cause sore gums or jaws.

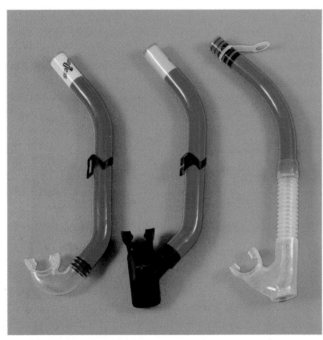

Figure 5.3 The two common types of snorkels are nonpurge (left) and purge (center and right).

How can you tell if your snorkel fits?

It is difficult to breathe through a soda straw. A snorkel tube should have an inside diameter of approximately 3/4 in. (1.9 cm) so that resistance to airflow through the tube will not make breathing difficult.

Attach the snorkel to your mask strap on the left side using a snorkel keeper. There are several types of keepers. Popular keepers are the simple ones depicted in Figure 5.4. The adjustment is correct if the snorkel mouthpiece remains in your mouth when you open your mouth widely.

Figure 5.4 Two types of snorkel keepers.

Fins

Diving would be much less enjoyable without fins. They increase your ability to move in the water and free your hands for many activities. You move in water by pushing against the water. Fins increase your ability to move by increasing the size of the area you move against the water; fins present a larger surface area than your hands. Your leg muscles are much larger and stronger than your arm muscles. Your arms would tire quickly if fins were attached to your hands, but your legs are strong enough to handle the load. Fins help stabilize you in water by providing a surface of resistance to movement, which provides leverage for countermovement and directional control.

The two basic types of fins are shoe fins and open-heel fins. Shoe fins slip onto bare feet, so they are good snorkeling fins for tropical climates. You wear open-heel fins with foot coverings called boots. Open-heel fins, generally used for scuba diving, usually are larger and stiffer than shoe fins. Small, flexible snorkeling fins may be inadequate for the harder work of scuba diving. Figure 5.5 shows examples of different types of fins.

Special materials and designs for fins abound. The fundamental features of a fin are the size and stiffness of the blade. The larger and stiffer the blade, the greater the physical demand when you move the fin through the water. A blade that is too stiff can cause you to cramp and become fatigued. It's best to begin with fins of a

How can you tell if your fins fit properly?

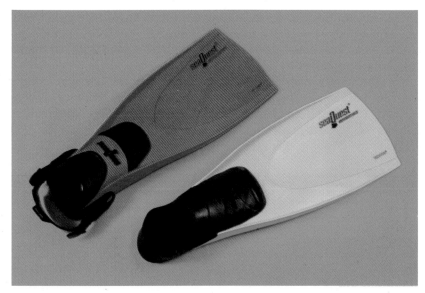

Figure 5.5 Open-heel fins (left) and shoe fins (right) provide alternatives for different diving needs.

moderate size and stiffness. When you can use those fins for extended periods without difficulty, you may then consider fins that can provide greater propulsion.

The most important criteria for the selection of any item of diving equipment are fit and comfort, and this is especially true of fins. To help ensure proper fit, sit down and try on a fin. Wear a boot if trying an open-heel fin. Hold your foot in the air and wiggle it up and down and from side to side. The fin and your foot should move as a single unit. If your foot moves inside the foot pocket, the fin is too large. Diving equipment should fit snugly but not tightly. A fin that is too tight can cause your foot to cramp. The foot pocket of the fin should fit but should not exert pressure on your foot. Select your fins using fit, comfort, and blade size and stiffness as your primary criteria. Features, fashion, and cost should be secondary considerations.

Skin Diving Vests

Positive buoyancy can be invaluable when you want to rest at the surface or carry items you have collected while diving. Wear a buoyancy vest whenever you dive.

There is only one basic type of skin diving vest, and it fits around your neck and secures at your waist (see Figure 5.6). A standard feature of a skin diving vest is an oral inflation tube, which comes in various sizes. It is easier to use larger tubes with mouthpieces than smaller tubes without mouthpieces. Some vests feature a CO_2 detonator. You must care

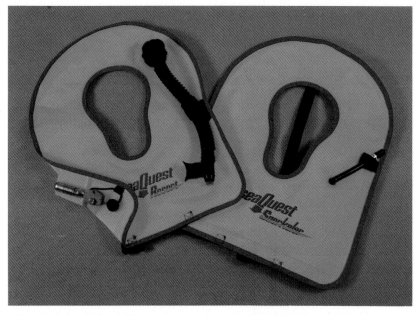

Figure 5.6 Skin diving vests.

for the detonator at the end of every day of diving or it will not function reliably.

Care and Maintenance

Your skin diving equipment will provide years of service if you take care of it properly. Rinse the equipment with clean, fresh water

How do you properly clean skin diving equipment? How often should you do so?

after use, dry it in the shade, and store it in a cool, dark, smog-free location. Prolonged sunlight, smog, salt crystals, and swimming pool chlorine harm your equipment. Fill a skin diving vest partially with fresh water after use, and swish the water inside. Drain the vest completely, and then inflate it for drying and storage. If the vest has a CO_2 detonator, remove the CO_2 cartridge, rinse the cartridge and assembly thoroughly, and lubricate the cartridge threads. Screw the cartridge back into the assembly only after the vest has dried thoroughly. Periodically inspect the straps on your mask and fins for drying and cracking, and replace straps when they begin to deteriorate. After your mask has dried, rub a drop of defogging solution on the lens to help keep the lens clean during storage.

Exposure Suits

You should use some type of exposure protection when diving, regardless of the water temperature. An exposure suit provides protection against scrapes and stings as well as insulation.

There are two basic types of exposure suits: wet suits and dry suits. Generally speaking, the colder the water, the thicker your suit and the more of your body you cover with the suit. There are many suit configurations, but most are one piece or a combination of a jacket and pants. Vests are accessories that help conserve heat in vital organs. Hoods, boots, and gloves help reduce heat loss from the head, feet, and hands, respectively.

Wet Suits

Describe the features of the three types of wet suit materials.

A wet suit is a good exposure suit for water temperatures ranging from 60 °F to 85 °F (15.6 °C to 29.4 °C). A wet suit allows water inside, but any water that enters can also exit and carry heat with it. The better the fit of the suit, the less water inside and the warmer the suit. Table 5.1 provides a comparison of wet suit types. The descriptions in the text that follows provide some additional information.

Spandex suits are thin, stretchy, attractive, full-body garments that are popular for diving in tropical waters. The garments, made from a special nylon material called spandex, provide 45% more insulation than bare skin and provide protection against stings, scrapes, and sunshine. Spandex suits also make it easier to slip into a heavier suit. If you live in a temperate climate, you can use a spandex body suit beneath a neoprene wet suit for local diving and use the spandex suit by itself for vacation diving in the tropics.

Thermoplastic, sandwiched between two layers of spandex, is another type of wet suit material. Suits made from this three-ply material are thin (1.2 to 1.4 mm) and designed for use in tropical waters (75 °F to 85 °F or 23.9 °C to 29.4 °C). Some suits feature a soft, plush lining for extra warmth. You can also wear a thermoplastic suit beneath a neoprene wet suit for extra warmth in colder water.

A third type of wet suit material is foam neoprene. The foam consists of tiny bubbles of inert gas, which provide insulation. The thicker the wet suit material, the greater the insulation quality of

Table 5.1
Wet Suits

Type	Warmth	Features	Temperature range
Spandex	45% more than bare skin	Light, compact; useful as undergarments for thicker suits	78 °F (25.6 °C) +
Thermoplastic	30% warmer than spandex	Neutrally buoyant; no weights required; wicks perspiration; windproof	76 °F (24.4 °C) +
Plush-lined thermoplastic	10% warmer than unlined	Same as thermoplastic	72 °F (22.2 °C) +
Foam neoprene • 1/8 in. (2-3 mm) • 3/16 in. (4 mm) • 1/4 in. (5-6.5 mm) • Titanium (4-6 mm)	20-100% warmer than plush-lined thermoplastic	Buoyant; weights required; long drying time; evaporation chills wearer; minor repairs easy to do	Down to 60 °F (15.6 °C)
Hoods, vests, boots, and gloves or mitts	16-66% more warmth	Reduces water circulation; layering allows flexibility for various temperatures	Down to 60 °F (15.6 °C)

the suit. A 1/8-in. (2- to 3-mm) neoprene wet suit is about 20% warmer than a plush thermoplastic suit.

Wet suit material ranges from 1/8 in. (2 to 3 mm) for warm-water diving to 3/8 in. (9 mm) for extreme cold-water diving. The most common wet suit thicknesses are 1/8 in. (2 to 3 mm), 3/16 in. (4 mm), and 1/4 in. (5 to 6.5 mm). You can layer wet suit material on critical areas of your body to reduce heat loss, but the thicker the insulation you wear, the more difficult it is for you to control buoyancy. Select the thickness of wet suit material used by experienced divers in the area where you plan to dive.

Nylon usually covers both sides of the neoprene used for wet suits. The nylon increases the strength and durability of the suit, which is glued and sewed together. You can make minor repairs with wet suit cement, but you should have a wet suit manufacturer do repairs that are extensive.

Neoprene wet suits require weights to achieve neutral buoyancy. The suit provides immediate buoyancy when you release the weights, but the buoyancy of the suit can be either a benefit or a hazard. Neoprene is not windproof, and the evaporation of water from the suit between dives may cause you to chill. You can get wet suit overgarments to retain warmth between dives. Wear an overgarment between dives in colder climates. Neoprene suits require longer to dry than other types of wet suits. Mobility is good with thin neoprene wet suits but decreases as the thickness of the material increases.

There are numerous wet suit designs, including the **shorty**, the **jumpsuit**, and **Farmer Johns** (see Figure 5.7).

You should consider several features when selecting a wet suit design. The more zippers a suit has, the more water circulates inside

shorty
A one-piece wet suit with short legs and sleeves

jumpsuit
A one-piece wet suit that covers nearly all of the body

Farmer Johns
Wet suit pants that extend all the way up the body and over the shoulders

Figure 5.7 Common styles of cold-water wet suits.

the suit and the greater the loss of heat. You can get zipperless suits for cold-water diving. Good wet suits feature a spine pad to minimize water circulation along the channel formed by your spine, and some suits for cold-water diving have attached hoods to minimize water circulation at the neck of the suit. You may spend time kneeling around and in the water, so many suits have knee pads.

Heat packs are available for wet suits. These packs contain a nontoxic, reusable chemical that heats to about 130 °F (54.4 °C) for a half hour or more, depending on conditions. The packs fit into heat pack pockets, an optional suit feature.

You can buy wet suits in standard sizes, or you can have a suit tailored for a custom fit. The fit of a wet suit is its most important feature. The suit must fit snugly all over, but it must not be so tight that it hampers your breathing and circulation. A suit that fits well may feel slightly restrictive out of the water. The true test of the fit of a suit is to dive with it. You may be able to rent a wet suit identical to one you would like to purchase.

Wet Suit Accessories

Scuba divers usually wear foot protection. There are several types of footwear for various needs (see Figure 5.8). Foot coverings, usually made from neoprene, may cover only the foot or both the foot and the ankle. Diving footwear, called *boots* or *booties*, ranges from inexpensive neoprene socks to sturdy footwear with durable, molded soles. Boots may or may not have zippers. Zippered boots are easier to don and remove, but zipperless boots are warmer.

You should wear hand coverings when the water temperature is less than 70 °F (21.1 °C). Some divers wear gloves for protection, such as when catching lobsters. Types of hand coverings include gloves and mitts (see Figure 5.9), and gauntlets. Wear mitts in cold water because they are thicker and have less surface area for heat dissipation than gloves have. Wear gauntlets (neoprene mitts with long cuffs) when the water is extremely cold. Thin neoprene gloves provide sufficient insulation in temperate water. Do not wear gloves in tropical areas. You are more likely to touch things when you wear gloves, and grabbing delicate coral reefs and marine animals while wearing gloves harms the animals.

A hood is an important warmth accessory that can reduce your heat loss from 20% to 50%, depending on the water temperature. Two basic types of hoods, attached hoods and separate hoods, are

> When should you wear mitts? Gauntlets? Gloves? When should you not wear gloves?

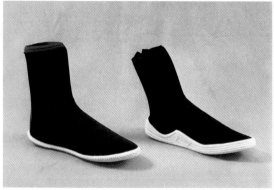

Figure 5.8 Various types of footwear.

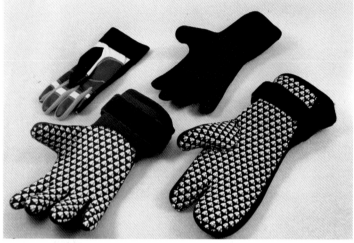

Figure 5.9 Glove and mitts provide protection for divers' hands.

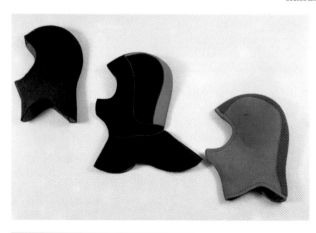

Figure 5.10 Hoods conserve warmth.

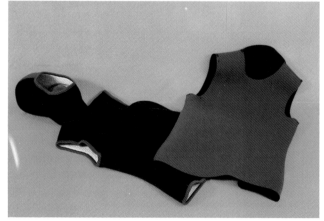

Figure 5.11 The addition of a vest can increase the warmth of your wet suit by as much as 16%.

available for wet suits (see Figure 5.10). Cold-water divers like attached hoods because they restrict water circulation in a suit more than separate hoods do. Some separate hoods have skirts that end at the base of the neck, and other, cold-water hoods have large bibs that cover the neck and shoulder area. There are thin hoods for protection in warm water and thicker hoods for insulation and protection in cold water.

You can increase the warmth of your wet suit by as much as 16% by wearing a vest. Wet suit vests come in all types of material to add warmth with layers of insulation (see Figure 5.11). Layering is an effective technique for reducing water circulation while increasing insulation. Some vests have attached hoods.

Wet Suit Care and Maintenance

With proper care, wet suits can provide years of service. Soak your wet suit in clean, fresh, warm water. If you can't soak your suit, rinse it. Hang your suit on a specially designed, wide, wet suit hanger; dry the suit in the shade; and store it on the hanger in a cool, dark, smog-free location. A garage is a poor environment for storing equipment. Do not fold your wet suit for storage because folds can form permanent creases, which insulate poorly. Inspect your suit regularly for seam integrity and tears. Make repairs or have them made as needed.

> What is the proper way to clean and store your wet suit?

Dry Suits

When the water temperature is less than 60 °F (15.6 °C), you should consider using a dry suit, an exposure suit that excludes water. Dry suits are much warmer than wet suits for three reasons:

- There is air in contact with your skin instead of water. Since air conducts heat less than water, you lose less heat via conduction.
- You wear undergarments beneath a dry suit. The undergarments provide a layer of air, which is a good insulator.
- Suit compression affects two of the three types of dry suits only slightly, so the insulating ability of those types of dry suits remains nearly constant with depth.

> What are the advantages of foam neoprene dry suits? Of crushed neoprene? Of shell suits?

The material from which the dry suit is made denotes the type of suit. Table 5.2 compares the three most common types of dry suits. The foam neoprene dry suit is made of the same material as the wet suit, but the dry suit has seals at the wrists and neck, attached dry boots, and a waterproof zipper. Figure 5.12 shows what the three types look like.

Dry suits can cost two to five times as much as wet suits, but with proper care and maintenance, a good dry suit will last many times longer than a wet suit. If you dive primarily in cold water, a dry suit is a good investment.

A dry suit is a closed air space subject to squeezes. A low-pressure inflator valve, a standard feature, allows you to add air to the suit during descent to prevent suit squeeze. Since air

Table 5.2
Dry Suits

Type	Advantages	Disadvantages
Foam neoprene	Form-fitting and streamlined	Long drying time; hard to locate and repair leaks; buoyancy control difficult
Crushed neoprene	Durable; easy to repair; long-lasting; less buoyant than foam neoprene	Less insulation than foam neoprene; expensive; somewhat bulky
Shell (two kinds) • Coated nylon • Rubberized fabric	Fast drying; easy to repair; nylon suits inexpensive; rubberized suits long-lasting	Easily punctured; bulky; nylon suits do not last long; rubberized suits expensive

expands during ascent, an exhaust valve is another standard feature. Get a dry suit that has a constant volume exhaust valve that automatically maintains a constant state of buoyancy during ascent.

Diving is a diuretic activity—it increases the amount of urine you produce. Urination in a wet suit is a regular practice by divers in open water, but the problem is more complex when you wear a dry suit. An optional feature for a dry suit is a relief zipper, which is useful only when you are out of the water. Dry suit divers must exit the water to urinate, and those without a relief zipper must disrobe.

There are several types of undergarments for dry suits. Some are inexpensive but compress with depth and lose insulating ability when wet. More expensive undergarments are highly resistant to compression and retain most of their insulating quality even if wet. Many dry suit divers prefer to wear two layers of undergarments: a thin garment against the skin to carry perspiration away from the body and a thicker overgarment for the bulk of the insulation. Moisture conducts heat, so you are warmer when you wick perspiration away from your body.

Dry suits have several drawbacks. Controlling buoyancy is more difficult with a dry suit than with a wet suit. Rapid, uncontrolled ascents can occur unless you control the suit. You should complete a dry suit training course before attempting to dive in a dry suit.

Figure 5.12 Dry suits can be made from foam neoprene (left), crushed neoprene (center), or nylon (right).

Dry suits are bulkier than wet suits. It is easier to don and remove a dry suit than a wet suit, but the bulkiness of a dry suit makes surface swimming difficult, and a dry suit restricts your mobility more than a wet suit. The inconveniences of a dry suit are of little consequence, however, when warmth is your primary concern.

Dry Suit Accessories

Most dry suits have attached boots, a desirable feature for a dry suit. The boots may be thin latex booties on less expensive suits or hard-soled boots on more expensive suits. With latex booties, you must wear heavy socks for insulation and wet suit boots over the latex booties to protect them, so dry suit divers usually need fins with large foot pockets.

You can wear neoprene gloves or mitts with a dry suit. If the water is extremely cold, you can get dry gloves with insulating liners that attach to some dry suits. An attached latex dry hood is an option for some models, but most dry suit divers use a separate neoprene dry suit hood. Figure 5.13 shows examples of dry suit accessories.

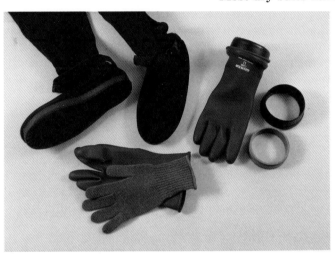

Figure 5.13 Dry suit boots and gloves help keep divers warm.

Dry Suit Care and Maintenance

Dry suits require more care than wet suits. The zipper is expensive to replace, as are the control valves, so do not allow salt crystals to form in the zipper or in the valves. Soak and rinse the zipper and valves in clean, fresh water as soon as possible following a saltwater dive. Wash the neck and wrist seals with soapy water, and then rinse them. Coat latex seals with pure talc after they dry. The talc helps protect the rubber against the elements. Fold dry suits in half over a wide hanger for drying. Lubricate the suit zipper according to the manufacturer's instructions; then store the suit with the zipper open. If the suit needs to be repaired, have an authorized dealer make the repairs.

> What is the proper way to clean and store your dry suit?

Exposure Suit Selection

There are many factors to consider when selecting an exposure suit and accessories: your physical characteristics, where you intend to dive, how you intend to dive, how much diving you intend to do, and what you intend to do while diving. The amount of money you invest also is a factor, but keep in mind that buying an inexpensive suit may be false economy. If the suit does not meet your needs, you will have to spend more money for another suit.

The amount of diving you intend to do is also important. If you plan to make only one dive per day, your insulation requirements are not as great as if you plan to dive several times per day. The

> Considering your circumstances, determine the type of exposure suit you should get.

more time you plan to spend in the water, the warmer the suit you should have.

If you are a thin person who chills easily, you need more insulation than the average person for a given water temperature. People with above-average body fat may not need as much insulation as those with average body fat; natural fat is a good insulator. Thermal comfort is essential for diving safety and enjoyment.

If you intend to do most of your diving in the local area, the most popular type of suit in the area probably is the best type for you. If the local waters are cold, you will have to choose between a wet suit and a dry suit. If you choose a wet suit for your first exposure suit for cold-water diving, a layered design with Farmer John pants, a vest, and a step-in jacket or a jacket with an attached hood retains more warmth than high-waisted pants, a regular jacket, and a separate hood. A custom fit retains more warmth than a suit of a standard size.

Dry suits are not desirable for long surface swims because you can overheat, and the drag caused by the bulkiness of some dry suits may cause you to tire or cramp. On the other hand, dry suits retain much more warmth at depth than wet suits. If you believe most of your diving will be deeper than 40 ft (12 m), the water will be 60 °F (15.6 °C) or colder, and you can avoid long surface swims, a dry suit is a good choice as long as you complete training before using the suit.

If you plan to dive in a variety of climates, a spandex or thermoplastic suit combined with a neoprene wet suit may be a good option. You can wear different parts of the suits to meet different warmth requirements. Your diving activity affects your needs. An underwater hunter looking for game generates more body heat than an underwater photographer whose movements are minimal. The less active you are while diving, the more insulation you need.

The accessories you choose for your suit depend on the type of suit you choose, the water temperature, the activity you intend to pursue, and your budget. A hood may be thin and short for warmer water, thick with a long skirt for colder water, or a dry suit type. Foot coverings may be low-cut, ankle-high, or attached to the suit. The soles may be soft or rugged. Hand coverings may range from nothing to thick mitts, gauntlets, or dry gloves.

Local diving professionals can help you select an exposure suit and accessories. No matter what type of suit you choose, keep in mind that it is an investment in your enjoyment of diving. Diving is not fun if you get cold.

Weighting Systems

Exposure suits increase your buoyancy. You need weights for ballast so you can achieve neutral buoyancy. One type of weighting system is a weight belt; another type integrates the weights into the scuba unit. Figure 5.14 shows examples of weighting systems.

Figure 5.14 Weight belts or integrated weighting systems are two options for divers.

Why is a quick-release feature an essential part of a weighting system?

Weight Belts

You can attach weights to or insert them into a belt that you wear around your waist. The belt is heavy nylon webbing 2 in. (5 cm) wide. You can thread the belt through lead weights, wrap pouches of lead shot around the belt, or put weights or pouches of lead shot into pockets on pocket-type belts. A hollow fabric belt that can be filled with lead shot is more comfortable on your hips than hard weights. Lead shot, which comes in various sizes, causes less damage than hard lead weights if you drop a belt accidentally. Smaller diameter shot allows more weight per volume than larger shot, so the more weight you need, the smaller the shot you should use.

Because exposure suits compress with pressure, a weight belt around your waist loosens unless it has a means of compensating for the suit compression. A compensator is a desirable feature for a weight belt; you can select from a variety of designs.

Secure the weights on your weight belt so they will not shift position. Pocket-type belts are good in this respect. When you thread separate weights onto a belt, secure the first and last weights with retainers (which are an accessory item).

The most important feature of any weighting system is the quick release. In an emergency, you must discard weights quickly to establish positive buoyancy. No matter what system you choose, an easily located and easily operated quick release is essential.

Types of Weights

There are several types of weights. Large, curved hip weights help offset the buoyancy of cold-water exposure suits. Smaller, rectangular weights find widespread use because they are economical. Coated weights are attractive and practical. Manufacturers mold weights into various shapes and offer a heavy vinyl coating as an option. The coating reduces pollution from lead, improves appearance, makes the weights easier to see in the water, and reduces exposure suit abrasion. Fabric mesh packets filled with lead shot are popular. You can get bulk lead shot for hollow fabric belts. Coated lead shot, although slightly more expensive, is better than uncoated shot. There are also shot-filled tubular ankle weights, although some diving experts believe ankle weights are unnecessary.

Integrated Weighting Systems

An integrated weighting system eliminates the need for a weight belt by holding lead weight in the backpack that holds the scuba cylinder or in the BC. An integrated weighting system makes the scuba unit heavier, but it also allows better distribution of weight in the water than a separate system can provide. Some divers consider an integrated weighting system advantageous because weights are less likely to shift, there is no need for a suit compression compensator, and having the weight above the waist improves the diver's trim in the water and reduces strain on the lower back. But when you raise your center of gravity, you are more likely to lose your balance and fall when you are out of the water. You need strength, good balance, and caution to use an integrated weighting system. The type of weight used in integrated systems usually is lead shot, either in bulk or in pouches.

Care and Maintenance

Weighting systems do not require as much care and maintenance as other items of diving equipment. Do not soak or rinse raw lead after use because lead in the runoff will pollute the environment. If "gray water" seeps from your weighting system, replace the lead with new, coated lead. (You can recycle old lead, so do not throw it away.) Pocket-type weighting systems allow you to remove the weights and rinse the remainder of the system.

Inspect the functional aspects, such as the quick release and the compensator, regularly. If you use a belt, inspect the weight retainers to make sure they are not broken, and make sure the end of the belt is clean and neat for easy insertion into the buckle. If the end of your belt is frayed, trim and singe it. Be careful when you fix a frayed end that you do not cut or burn yourself.

Weighting System Selection

When selecting a weighting system, consider your physical characteristics, the amount of weight you need, and how frequently you will need to change the amount of weight you use.

Lead shot is more comfortable to wear than hard lead. Women usually prefer a lead shot system. If your waist is larger than your hips, a weight belt may not work well—especially if you need more than 30 lb (13.6 kg) of weight. What local divers with your physical characteristics use for a weighting system can aid you with selection.

If you require more than 30 lb (13.6 kg) of weight, you may need weights on a weight belt plus an integrated system. If you require only a small amount of weight, nearly any system is acceptable.

If the type of diving you do varies, the amount of weight you need also varies. If you dive in fresh water and in salt water, you need to adjust your weights. When you vary your exposure suit configuration, you also need to vary the amount of weight you wear. The more you need to change weights, the more you need a weighting system that allows changes to be made easily.

Based on your body type and the kind of diving you plan to do, what is the best weighting system for you?

Buoyancy Compensators

A buoyancy compensator helps you control buoyancy. You can inflate your BC at the surface to increase buoyancy, deflate it to reduce buoyancy for descent, and add air to it to achieve neutral buoyancy underwater. Most BCs also contain a backpack to hold your scuba cylinder.

Types of BCs

The three types of BCs are jacket-style, back-mounted, and front-mounted. Figure 5.15 shows examples of the types, and Table 5.3 compares them. Most BCs used in diving today have a wraparound jacket design, which provides front and rear buoyancy. There are two basic jacket designs: One style has inflation tubes over the shoulders, and a newer style has straps over the shoulders. The straps have convenient, adjustable releases.

Figure 5.15 Buoyancy compensators come front-mounted (left), jacket-style (center), or back-mounted (right).

Back-mounted BCs place buoyancy chambers behind you. These systems are useful for underwater modeling and for specialty diving activities. Models look better without bulky BCs covering them.

Front-mounted BCs fit around your neck and cover your chest area. This was the first type of BC, but few divers use front-mounted BCs today. You can use a front-mounted BC for both skin diving and scuba diving. BC jackets and back-mounted BCs are not suitable for skin diving because much of the flotation is above the waterline when the BC is inflated. Most divers believe a jacket BC is superior to a front-mounted one.

Table 5.3
Buoyancy Compensators

Type	Location of buoyancy chamber	Advantages	Disadvantages
Jacket	Front and rear	Even lift; diver can remain upright	Not suitable for skin diving.
Back-mounted	Rear	Doesn't interfere with dry suit valve operation	Pushes diver forward; difficult for diver to remain upright
Front-mounted	Front	Suitable for skin diving; allows diver to remain upright	Need separate backpack for cylinders; requires disconnection of inflator hose before removal; doesn't provide as much lift as jacket

BC Features

In its simplest form, a BC is a bladder with attachments. The bladder may be coated material that comprises the BC itself or a separate bladder inside a fabric shell. The seams of a BC bladder may be glued or electronically welded depending on the material used.

Each bladder design has advantages and disadvantages. If there is a cut or a puncture, a repairman can install a new bladder in a separate-bladder BC. Because the outer shell containing the bladder does not hold air, various attachments—such as pockets and fasteners—are made quite easily. But separate-bladder BCs are bulky. Also, water gets between the fabric shell and the bladder while you're diving, and it takes time for the water to drain when you exit from a dive. In contrast, BCs without a separate bladder are less bulky and retain little water when you exit from a dive. Although BC material is tough and durable, a cut in a BC without a separate bladder may pose an expensive problem. Because the fabric itself forms the bladder, attachments to a BC without a separate bladder must be made in a way that does not affect the BC's ability to hold air.

All BCs feature a means to inflate and deflate the bladder. You inflate a BC through an inflator-deflator valve attached to a large-diameter hose connected to the top, left side of the BC. There are two types of inflator-deflator valves: manual and low-pressure. Depressing a button on a manual inflator valve allows you to blow air into the bladder orally or to vent it. A low-pressure inflator assembly has a manual inflator-deflator valve and a low-pressure valve. The low-pressure valve inflates the BC with air from your scuba tank when you depress the valve; this desirable feature is standard on modern BCs. On some BCs a cable inside the inflator-deflator hose runs from the control valve assembly to a dump valve located where the hose connects to the BC. By pulling on the valve assembly, you can dump air from the BC. Without this feature, you have to open the manual deflator valve and raise the valve higher than the point where the inflator-deflator hose connects to the BC.

A pressure-relief valve, a standard BC feature, prevents excessive internal pressure from rupturing the bladder. Some pressure-relief valves also function as a dump valve. Dual-purpose valves usually have a pendant attached that you may pull to vent the BC.

Nearly all modern BCs incorporate a backpack for the scuba tank. The pack may be rigid or soft, and the tank retaining band also may be rigid or soft. Soft packs and bands are desirable for travel and for warm-water diving because they are compact and comfortable.

Most modern BC jackets feature a cummerbund waistband. The wide band helps prevent the BC from riding up when you inflate it. Some cummerbunds have elastic sections to compensate for wet suit compression.

Other BC features for convenience include pockets, attachment rings, retainers for scuba hoses, adjustable straps, elastic shoulder straps to permit more mobility, shoulder releases, and size adjustments. Some models feature integrated weighting systems. CO_2 inflator assemblies (see the discussion on skin diving vests earlier in this chapter) are optional with some BCs. Few divers opt for CO_2 mechanisms, because the detonators are not essential and increase maintenance requirements.

BC Selection

When selecting a BC, consider your physical characteristics, where you plan to dive, and the type of diving you plan to do. Some BCs provide more buoyancy than others. A cold-water wet suit diver needs more lift than a warm-water diver wearing a thin exposure suit. A large amount of lift is not necessarily desirable.

If you are a large, strong individual, the size and bulk of a BC may not be much of a consideration; but if you are short, you may be wise to choose a small, compact BC. The length of the BC is important. One that extends downward too far makes donning and removing your weight belt difficult. If you are short-waisted, consider an integrated weighting system.

The fit is important because a BC needs to support you in the water. The BC should fit snugly and should not ride up on your body. Models that allow adjustment for a custom fit are desirable.

Renting and using different types of BCs will aid you in making a selection. Talk to experienced divers and diving professionals and observe BC trends in your area.

How can you determine the most appropriate BC for your needs?

Care and Maintenance

An investment in a BC is not modest. But, like most diving equipment, your BC will provide years of service if you take care of it. You need to rinse your BC inside and out after use, especially after use in a swimming pool or in the ocean. Chlorine in pool water and salt crystals that form from seawater are harmful to your BC. Drain the water from your BC after use, fill the BC about one-third full with fresh water, swish the water around, and then drain the bladder. Rinse the inflator assembly thoroughly and leave the BC fully inflated until it dries. Inflation tests the airtight integrity of the bladder and valves. If the BC does not remain firm for at least an hour, take it to a professional repair facility. Anytime your BC fails to function properly, obtain the services of a professional repair person. It is hazardous to attempt BC repairs without special training, tools, and parts.

What is one sign that your BC needs to be repaired?

Scuba Cylinders

A scuba cylinder stores compressed air at high pressure. The container must be strong and free of corrosion. Scuba cylinders (also called tanks) are made of either steel or aluminum. Each type

Figure 5.16 Scuba cylinders are made from steel or aluminum.

has advantages and disadvantages. Figure 5.16 shows examples of various steel and aluminum tanks.

Steel Cylinders

Steel scuba cylinders come in various sizes and pressure ratings. Common sizes are 50, 71.2, and 94.6 ft³ (1,416, 2,016, and 2,679 L). The pressure to which the cylinders may be filled, or the *working pressure*, ranges from 1,800 to more than 4,000 psi (122 to 272 ATM).

Some compressors pump air to only 2,500 psi (169 ATM). When you cannot get air at a pressure higher than 2,500 psi (169 ATM) a steel tank may be more desirable than an aluminum tank. A steel 71.2-ft³ (2,016-L) scuba tank filled to 2,250 psi (153 ATM) contains about 5 ft³ (141.6 L) more air than an 80-ft³ (2,265-L) aluminum tank filled to the same pressure. This is because the aluminum tank must be filled to 3,000 psi (203 ATM) to obtain 80 ft³ (2,265 L).

The main disadvantage of a steel cylinder is that it can rust, which can render a tank unsafe and unusable. Do not allow water inside a cylinder. The high-pressure atmosphere has a large amount of oxygen to fuel corrosion. You can keep the inside of a steel scuba tank dry, but the outside is exposed to moisture. Galvanizing inhibits rust on the outside of steel tanks, but the inside should not be galvanized because it affects air purity. Painting a galvanized finish may improve the appearance of a cylinder, but paint alone is an inadequate finish because cracks or chips in the paint allow moisture to reach the steel. The tank will begin to rust unless there is a galvanized coating beneath the paint.

Another disadvantage of a steel scuba tank is that it has a rounded bottom because of the process used to manufacture the cylinder. The tank will not stand by itself unless you place a rubber or plastic boot, called a tank boot, on the end of the cylinder. The boot makes the base of the tank flat so it will stand. Some boots also have flat sides to help keep a tank from rolling when you lay the cylinder on its side. Moisture and salt trapped between the tank boot and the cylinder can cause corrosion. Boots with internal ridges—the preferred type of boot—are self-draining.

Aluminum Cylinders

Aluminum alloy cylinders also come in various sizes and pressure ratings. Common sizes are 50, 63, and 80 ft³ (1,416, 1,784, and 2,265 L). The working pressure for aluminum cylinders is 3,000 psi (203 ATM).

Aluminum corrodes, but the oxide that forms arrests the corrosion process—a significant advantage over the corrosive process of rust in steel tanks. Rust is an accelerating process, but corrosion in an aluminum cylinder is a self-arresting process.

The bottom of an aluminum cylinder is flat. You do not need a tank boot on the cylinder to allow it to stand by itself, but many divers put boots on aluminum tanks to protect both the tanks and objects struck by the bottoms of the cylinders.

Aluminum cylinders also have drawbacks. Because aluminum is softer than steel, aluminum tanks dent and gouge more easily than steel tanks. Also, brass cylinder valves control the flow of air, and an electrolytic action between the dissimilar metals of a cylinder and a valve can cause the valve to seize in the aluminum cylinder threads unless you have the valve removed periodically and coated with a special compound. Valve seizing is seldom a problem with steel cylinders.

Aluminum cylinders do not need to be galvanized. You may paint them to improve appearance, but do not bake the paint finish. Temperatures hotter than 180 °F (82.2 °C) reduce the strength of an aluminum cylinder and can cause the tank to explode when filled. If you would like your cylinder painted, have it done by a professional tank painting service.

Cylinder Markings

There are several rows of markings on the neck of a scuba cylinder; the markings provide useful information about the cylinder. You should be able to determine the meaning of several of the marks. Figure 5.17 shows an example of cylinder neck markings.

The first row of marks on U.S.-manufactured tanks discloses the government agency sanctioning the manufacture of the tank, the type of metal from which the tank was made, and the working pressure. The first letters in the row identify the government agency, such as DOT (the Department of Transportation), CTC/DOT (the Canadian Transportation Commission and the Department of Transportation), or ICC (the old Interstate Commerce Commission). The next letters in the first row identify the type of metal from which the tank was made. The designations 3A and 3AA are for steel cylinders, and 3AL, E6498, and SP6498 are designations for aluminum cylinders. The next figures in the first row—the important ones for you to remember—are numbers indicating the working pressure of the cylinder in psi.

The second row of markings includes the serial number of the tank (which you should record for identification purposes), letters or numbers identifying the manufacturer of the cylinder, and the date (month and year) of the tank's first pressure test.

United States regulations require compressed gas cylinders to be pressure-tested before being put into service and every 5 years thereafter. The date of the first pressure test is part of the second

> **What do the markings on the neck of a tank mean?**

Figure 5.17 The markings on the necks of cylinders provide useful information.

row of cylinder markings, but subsequent test dates may be stamped anywhere on the neck of the tank. A registered symbol between the date and year of a pressure test identifies the facility that did the testing.

When you take your scuba tank to an air station to have it filled, the facility personnel will examine the tank markings to determine if the cylinder test date is current and note the pressure to which the tank may be filled.

Cylinder Selection

The main criteria for selecting diving equipment—fit and comfort—apply to scuba tanks as well. A small person should use a small tank. Larger divers may use and require larger tanks because they have larger lungs and use more air.

The material from which a tank is made affects its capacity, size, and working pressure. Although steel is heavier than aluminum, aluminum tanks are larger and heavier than steel tanks with similar capacities. Because aluminum is not as strong as steel, the walls of an aluminum tank are thicker than the walls of a steel tank of about the same capacity.

The higher the pressure rating, the greater the capacity of a tank of a given size. Modern high-pressure steel scuba tanks are high-capacity cylinders, but they are quite heavy. Good sizes for female divers to consider for an initial scuba tank are 50 ft³ and 63 ft³ (1,416 and 1,784 L). Popular sizes for male divers are 71.2 and 80 ft³ (2,016 and 2,266 L).

Another important factor you should consider when selecting a scuba tank is the buoyancy of the cylinder, which is determined by the volume and weight of the tank. Aluminum tanks are more buoyant than steel tanks. High-capacity tanks have a greater change in buoyancy than smaller cylinders as you use air from them. The change in buoyancy between a full and an empty tank can vary by more than 8 lb (3.6 kg) (see Table 5.4). Some tanks are negatively buoyant whether full or empty, but most tanks sink

> Which tank is better for a 120-lb (54.4-kg) diver?
> a. 80-ft³ (2,266 L) aluminum
> b. 50-ft³ (1,416 L) steel

Table 5.4

Cylinder Size, Working Pressure, and Buoyancy

Capacity (ft³)	Working pressure (psi)	Buoyancy (lb) from full to empty
Aluminum 50	3,000	−2.7 to +1.3
Aluminum 63	3,000	−2.3 to +2.7
Steel 71.2	2,250	−2.0 to +3.5
Aluminum 80	3,000	−2.0 to +3.8
Steel 76	2,400	−6.5 to −0.1
Steel 80	3,500	−7.4 to −1.0
Steel 102	3,500	−7.6 to +0.5

when full and float when empty. Buoyancy for tanks varies so much that you should select one of the tanks most often used for diving in your area or try diving with several different tanks to determine which one is easiest to manage.

Multiple-tank scuba units are for specialty applications. As a beginning diver, you do not need double or triple scuba tanks. A single tank is adequate for most diving activities.

Cylinder Accessories

Fabric or plastic sleeves can help protect the exterior of your scuba cylinder. Some sleeves have places to attach various items so the wearer can reach the items easily.

Tank bands vary. Some allow you to attach a small, backup scuba cylinder to your main cylinder. There are additional accessories to help you carry or transport your scuba cylinders. Tank boots, which were discussed earlier in this chapter, are a desirable cylinder accessory.

Care and Maintenance

Scuba tanks are high-pressure vessels. They are strong, but you should handle them with care. Exterior damage can render your tank useless. Avoid throwing scuba tanks or allowing them to roll about on the deck of a boat or in the trunk of your car. Secure cylinders for transportation or storage. Unless you are holding a scuba cylinder, do not leave it standing in an upright position, especially at a dive site. But do store your scuba tanks in an upright position, because any moisture inside will settle to the bottom where inspectors can detect it with relative ease. Rinse the outside of your cylinder with clean, fresh water after use, and pay special attention to the tank boot area of steel tanks.

Moisture in a scuba tank causes corrosion. Corrosion can ruin a cylinder rapidly, and pieces of corrosion can damage a tank valve or scuba regulator. One way to prevent moisture from entering a tank is to have air in the tank. Water can get into an empty scuba cylinder while diving, so avoid using all of the air in your tank. Moisture may also enter an empty tank if you store it with the valve open. Store your scuba cylinder with a few hundred pounds (about 20 ATM) of pressure inside. A low pressure keeps moisture out but provides little oxygen to aid corrosion if there is moisture in the tank.

The filling process can force water into the tank. A water trap in an air compressor is supposed to remove moisture from air, but if the moisture-removal system does not function properly, water may be pumped into your tank along with air. The filling hose attachments for scuba tanks can get wet, and water inside the filling attachments may be forced into your cylinder. It is important to use a quality air station.

The diving industry requires an annual visual inspection of scuba cylinders. The examination consists of an external inspection, the removal of the valve from a cylinder, an internal inspection

> **Why should you store a tank with low pressure in it?**

using a special light, the replacement of the valve, and the attachment of a decal indicating the inspection date. Most air stations require a current visual cylinder-inspection sticker on a tank before they will fill it. When you handle your scuba tank, listen for sounds of anything moving inside the cylinder. If you hear anything, have the tank visually inspected.

Government regulations specify that compressed gas cylinders must be pressure-tested every 5 years in the United States. Some countries require pressure testing every year or two. The test is a hydrostatic test because it takes place in water. An inspector fills a scuba tank with water and submerges it in a closed container that is completely filled with water. The inspector applies pressure to the scuba tank hydraulically, and the tank expands slightly from the pressure. The expansion displaces water from the container holding the scuba tank. The inspector measures the expansion and then releases the pressure. The tank must return to within 10% of its original volume within a specified period of time to pass the pressure test. If the tank is too brittle to expand and contract correctly, the inspector condemns it.

You may transport a scuba tank on airplanes only if it is completely empty and the valve is open—a situation that is not good for scuba tanks. Do not transport your cylinder by air. Diving destinations have tanks readily available, so there is no need to take a tank on a dive trip.

Cylinder Valves

Cylinder valves control the flow of a liquid or gas. Three types of valves are available for scuba tanks: the simple valve, the reserve valve, and the multiple-cylinder valve. Because multiple tanks are for advanced specialty diving activities, this section addresses only the simple valve and the reserve valve. Figure 5.18 shows examples of valves.

The Simple Valve

A simple valve is an on-off valve that operates like a faucet. You turn the valve handle counterclockwise to open it and clockwise to close it. The first catalog of diving equipment listed this type of valve as Item K, and the valve has been identified as a **K-valve** ever since.

The **valve seat** is a soft sealing surface. You can damage it with excessive pressure, so when you close a tank valve, be careful that you don't damage the valve seat.

Valves for scuba tanks have several features, one of which is a snorkel tube that extends from the bottom of the valve into the scuba cylinder. The valve snorkel prevents moisture or par-

Figure 5.18 K-valves (left) and J-valves (center) control the flow of air from the cylinder. DIN valves (right) withstand greater pressure than other types of valves.

K-valve
Simple type of cylinder valve that operates like a faucet

valve seat
The portion of the valve that closes and stops the flow of air

burst disk
Thin metal disk designed to rupture when the tank pressure becomes excessive

O-ring
A soft circular ring that forms a high-pressure seal

DIN outlet
A new type of outlet for a scuba tank valve that is threaded and has a recessed O-ring seal

J-valve
A reserve valve that restricts the flow of air at a specified tank pressure

ticles from entering the valve when you invert the tank. Another standard feature of tank valves is a **burst disk**. If a tank is overfilled, or if the heat from a fire causes the tank pressure to increase to a hazardous level, the disk will burst and vent the tank to prevent an explosion. The disks corrode over time, and occasionally a burst disk will rupture. The failure makes a loud noise and the tank hisses loudly, but the situation is not dangerous. If the burst disk in your tank valve ruptures, you need to have the valve serviced professionally. Manufacturers rate burst disks for various pressures, and the correct disk must be used. Keep the burst disk pressure rating in mind if you want to change a valve from one scuba tank to another. A valve for a low-pressure burst disk will rupture if you use it on a tank with a higher pressure rating.

There are two types of outlets for scuba tank valves. The traditional outlet is nearly flush with the surface of the valve and is surrounded by an **O-ring**. The ring must be clean and free of nicks or cuts. A newer type of outlet, called a **DIN outlet**, withstands higher pressures than an O-ring valve does. Tank pressures in excess of 3,000 psi (203 ATM) require a DIN fitting.

The Reserve Valve

A **J-valve** (the valve was listed as Item J in the first equipment catalog) maintains a reserve of air to permit a normal ascent. The need for a reserve valve was much more important years ago than it is today. Until the introduction of submersible pressure gauges (SPGs) for scuba tanks, it was difficult to estimate how much air remained in a cylinder. Divers ran out of air at depth unless they had and used a J-valve. All divers today use SPGs to monitor the amount of air in their tanks.

A J-valve is a spring-loaded reserve valve. Pressure in the tank holds the spring-loaded valve open so air can flow through the valve until the tank pressure is insufficient to overcome the force of the reserve valve spring. At this point, a pressure of 300 to 600 psi (20 to 40 ATM), the spring begins to close the reserve valve and restricts the flow of air. The diver senses the increased breathing resistance and must open the spring-loaded valve manually by turning the reserve lever on the valve. Activation of the lever removes the restriction to airflow.

The reserve lever on a J-valve can create problems. If the lever is in the incorrect position (down), the valve will not maintain a reserve. If you fail to put the reserve lever in the up position before a dive, or if the lever is bumped during your dive, you might rely on a reserve of air that will not be available.

During the filling process, the reserve lever of a tank with a J-valve must be in the reserve position (down). If the lever is in the up position when the operator applies high-pressure air to the tank valve, the seat of the reserve valve will be damaged.

Because J-valves cost more than K-valves to purchase and service, and because of the problems just mentioned, the J-valve's popularity has declined steadily over the years.

Valve Protectors

A protective cap is a desirable accessory for a tank valve. The cap helps prevent loss of the O-ring, helps keep dirt out of the valve, and can help prevent physical damage to the high-pressure sealing surface around the valve opening.

Care and Maintenance

Cylinder valves are made of soft metal and have thin areas, so physical abuse can ruin them. Protection of the valve is one reason why you should secure scuba tanks when you store them and why you should not leave them standing unattended. A tank that rolls about or falls over can damage the valve and render it inoperable.

When you open a tank valve, turn it slowly, open it all the way, and then close it one half turn. If you use the tank with the valve fully open and something strikes the valve handle, the valve seat will be damaged more than it would if the valve were closed slightly. When you close the valve, avoid excessive force, which shortens the life of the valve seat.

It is good to rinse your tank valve after use, but soaking the valve by inverting your scuba tank in a container of warm water is even better. Water remains in the valve opening after rinsing or soaking. Open the valve momentarily to blow the water from the opening. If you leave the water in the opening and have the tank filled before the water evaporates, moisture will be forced into the tank.

> **How often should you have your tank valve serviced?**

Have your tank valve serviced annually by a professional. Also have your valve professionally serviced any time it fails to operate easily or when the burst disk needs to be replaced. Valves receive partial servicing (lubrication) during the annual visual cylinder inspection of your scuba tank. The large O-ring that seals the valve to the scuba tank may be replaced at the time of the visual inspection. But the partial servicing of your valve during a tank inspection is not the annual servicing of the valve. In a complete valve servicing, a qualified repair technician completely disassembles the valve, cleans the parts, replaces various parts, and then reassembles and tests the unit.

Scuba Regulators

The function of a regulator is to reduce high-pressure air to a breathable level. Most scuba regulators use two stages of pressure reduction. The first stage attaches to the valve of a scuba cylinder and reduces the high pressure to an intermediate pressure of about 140 psi (9.3 ATM). The first stage of the regulator connects via a hose to the second stage, which contains the mouthpiece. The second stage reduces the pressure from the intermediate level to the surrounding pressure. A scuba regulator is a demand system; it delivers air only when you demand it by inhaling. A demand system differs from a constant-delivery free-flow system, which

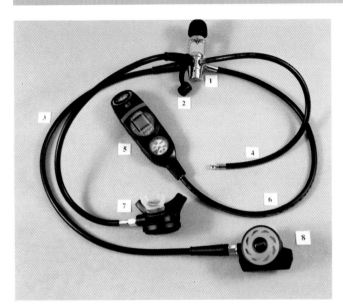

Figure 5.19 Scuba regulator nomenclature: 1—first stage, 2—dust cover, 3—low-pressure hose, 4—low-pressure inflator hose, 5—console, 6—high-pressure hose, 7—primary second stage, 8—extra second stage.

commercial divers use. Scuba regulators are highly reliable and have a fail-safe design, which turns a demand system into a free-flow system in the event of a component failure. Figure 5.19 provides more information about scuba regulator nomenclature.

First Stages

The first stages for scuba regulators are either balanced or unbalanced. Changes in tank pressure affect the performance of a balanced first stage only slightly. With an unbalanced first stage, the performance of the regulator changes as tank pressure changes, so a balanced first stage is desirable.

The two main types of regulator first stage valves are diaphragm and piston. A diaphragm first stage has a diaphragm that excludes water and dirt from the working parts inside. A bias spring combined with water pressure pushes the valve open. Tank pressure closes the valve when the first stage pressure equals intermediate pressure plus water pressure. A diaphragm valve has more parts than a piston first stage, so it is more expensive to manufacture and service. The diaphragm valve's exclusion of water and dirt from the mechanics allows high performance for longer periods of time than a piston valve.

Piston first stages have an open, simple design with few moving parts. Water pressure in direct contact with the piston combines with the force of a bias spring to open the piston valve. Tank pressure causes the piston to move and the valve to close when the first stage pressure equals intermediate pressure plus water pressure. Piston first stages are easier and less expensive to service than diaphragm first stages. But dirt, salt crystals, and mineral deposits that accumulate inside a piston regulator can affect its performance. Each type of first stage has advantages and disadvantages, so either type is acceptable. A diaphragm-piston regulator combines the two concepts. The diaphragm excludes water and dirt and transfers pressure to a piston.

A first stage must have a means of attachment to the tank valve. A typical regulator has a yoke that surrounds the valve and mates the regulator to the tank valve. The regulator inlet, which has an inlet filter, secures to a tank with a yoke screw. Scuba regulators that operate at above-average pressures use a DIN fitting instead of a yoke screw. A DIN fitting screws directly into a DIN valve and does not have a yoke.

There are multiple openings, called **ports**, in first stages. One port is for high-pressure air measurement with an SPG. The remaining ports are for low-pressure air. A regulator should have several low-pressure ports to supply air to the primary second stage, an alternate second stage, a BC inflator, and possibly a dry suit inflator. The sizes of ports vary. The high-pressure port usually is larger than the low-pressure openings because a

---

port
Opening in regulator first stages for hose attachment

low-pressure hose inadvertently connected to the high-pressure port would rupture.

Some regulators feature environmental shielding by sealing special fluid inside a flexible chamber attached to the first stage. The sealed, flexible chamber transmits water pressure to the regulator, but no water, salt, or dirt can enter the first stage. Extremely cold water can cause an unshielded regulator to freeze, but the fluid in an environmental chamber will not freeze.

Second Stages

The most common second stage is shaped like a cup lying on one side. Imagine a pliable diaphragm across the top of the cup, a mouthpiece attached to the bottom of the cup, and a purge valve attached to the lower side. A lever that activates a valve inside the container is in contact with a static diaphragm. An inhalation through the mouthpiece creates a partial vacuum inside the second stage. The pressure reduction pulls in the diaphragm, moving the lever and opening the valve, allowing air to flow from the first stage of the regulator into the second stage. When you stop inhaling, the buildup of pressure returns the diaphragm and lever to their normal positions, closing the valve and stopping the flow of air. When you begin to exhale, increased pressure inside the second stage opens the purge valve, allowing air to escape.

There are two types of scuba regulator second stage valves: the downstream valve and the pilot valve. With a downstream-valve regulator, a small bias spring holds a valve closed. Inhalation moves the diaphragm, which moves a lever. The lever movement overcomes the resistance of the bias spring and opens a valve, allowing intermediate-pressure air to enter the second stage. After the inhalation, air flows until the diaphragm moves outward, allowing the bias spring to close the valve. Downstream second stage valves are simple and inexpensive and tolerate more sand and dirt than pilot valves do.

In a pilot-valve regulator, the movement of the diaphragm in the second stage opens a small valve that, in turn, opens a larger valve. When you stop inhaling from the regulator, the diaphragm returns to its normal position, and the valves close. A pilot valve delivers air up to four times more easily than a downstream valve. But pilot valves are more expensive to manufacture and service than downstream valves, and you may experience a shuddering effect of air movement with a pilot-valve regulator in shallow water.

All regulators have a purge, a button or area on the regulator that you depress to manually open the second stage valve. Use the purge to test the regulator, expel water and debris from inside the second stage, and relieve the pressure in the regulator after you close the tank valve.

The location of the exhaust varies. Some regulators have the exhaust valve at the bottom of the second stage, some have it at the side, and some have it in the front. The position of the exhaust affects the bubble pattern and the clearing of water from the regulator when it has water inside and you place it in your mouth.

Figure 5.20 Scuba regulators have different configurations.

Some regulators direct exhaust bubbles by means of an exhaust tee. You will learn more about regulator positioning for clearing in chapter 6.

A regulator may be right-handed, left-handed, or bidirectional, depending on the direction from which the regulator hose must come when the regulator is in your mouth. For example, the hose must come from the right side when you are using a right-handed regulator. The hose may come from either side when using a bidirectional regulator. The directional configuration is important only for knowing how to orient the regulator when you place it in your mouth. Figure 5.20 shows directional configurations.

Some second stage casings feature strong, light, durable materials that do not bend or corrode as metal does. Several types and styles of mouthpieces are available. Use a soft, comfortable mouthpiece that does not cause jaw fatigue. A repair technician can replace mouthpieces quickly and easily.

Regulator Accessories

A regulator hose is flexible but has rigid metal connectors crimped onto the ends. The points where the hose and the metal meet are stress points because the hose fibers strain against an unyielding surface. To prevent the breakdown of the hose fibers at the stress points, use hose protector sleeves. At a minimum, equip all regulator hoses with hose protectors at the first stage end.

Padded regulator bags help provide protection when you are transporting or storing your regulator. The bag should be large enough to accommodate the regulator and all of its hoses without bending the hoses sharply.

Adapters allow you to use DIN-fitting regulators on standard cylinder valves. Use protective covers for the threads on DIN fittings.

Purge depressors are a feature on some regulators and an accessory for regulators that do not have them. A purge depressor depresses the purge partially to remove bias spring pressure from the second stage valve when you are not using the regulator, thus extending the life of the valve seat.

Colored second stage covers allow you to color-coordinate your regulator with your other equipment. Other, previously mentioned accessories include mouthpieces and hose adapters.

Regulator Selection

It takes effort to inhale and exhale through a scuba regulator. The effort is needed to overcome a resistance to breathing; good regulators have minimal breathing resistance. Compare the performance data for various regulators, and select one that breathes easily over

Where are hose protector sleeves vital?

a wide range of tank pressures. A wide range of performance implies a balanced first stage.

Choose a widely used and easily serviced regulator. You want a regulator that can be serviced by facilities anywhere you happen to be and that uses readily available parts.

The type of diving you do should affect your selection. If you plan to do most of your diving from shore, avoid a pilot-valve second stage, which sand and dirt can affect adversely. Diaphragm first stages may be a better choice if most of your diving will be from shore.

If you do not have a scuba tank, consider purchasing the tank and regulator at the same time so you can match the fittings of the regulator and the cylinder valve. If you will be diving in water that is near freezing, select an environmentally shielded regulator.

Care and Maintenance

Your regulator is a precision instrument; it requires care and maintenance to ensure the best possible performance. Keep sand and dirt out of your regulator, and do not allow salt crystals to form inside. Soak your regulator in clean, fresh, warm water as soon as possible after diving in the ocean. You need to remove salt before it dries. If you cannot soak your regulator, at least rinse it. A combination of soaking and rinsing is best. Follow these rules when rinsing or soaking a regulator:

• *Keep the inside of the first stage dry*. The purpose of the dust cover on the first stage is to exclude water and dust. Develop the habit of replacing the dust cover and securing it in place with the yoke screw any time you do not have the regulator attached to a tank. Make certain the dust cover is in place before you rinse or soak a regulator.

• *Allow low-pressure water to flow gently through the second stage and into the appropriate first stage openings*. High-pressure water can force dirt and grit into crevices where they will cause damage. Gentle pressure washes the dirt away.

• *Do not depress the purge button when you rinse the second stage unless you have the regulator pressurized*. If you do not pressurize the regulator and you depress the purge valve with water inside the second stage, you open the second stage valve and allow water to flow through the hose into the first stage.

When the regulator has dried thoroughly, lay it flat for storage. For prolonged storage, place the regulator in a plastic bag to help protect it against the harmful effects of smog. Do not bend the hoses sharply because the bending damages hose fibers. Replace hoses that are cut, bulging, or leaking.

You can avoid most problems with your regulator by having it serviced annually. Have your regulator serviced even if it seems to be functioning properly. Failure to invest in regular service can affect your safety and can shorten the life of your regulator.

What are the best choices for first and second stage regulators if you do most of your diving from shore? Why?

What three rules should you follow when rinsing or soaking a regulator?

Alternate Air Sources

Several equipment options can help if you run out of air underwater. (But remember, running out of air when you have a working pressure gauge is due only to sheer negligence.) Your best option is an alternate air source (AAS), which is a source of compressed air other than your primary scuba regulator. An AAS also is valuable if your primary source of air begins free-flowing or leaking during a dive because you can switch to the AAS and make a normal ascent. The two primary types of AASs are extra second stages and backup scuba units. Extra second stages allow two divers to share air without passing a single mouthpiece back and forth. Backup scuba units are fully redundant scuba systems that provide an independent source of air in an emergency. You are not dependent on a buddy to provide air when you are equipped with a backup system. Extra second stages are less expensive than backup scuba units but do not provide the benefits of an independent scuba system.

Extra Second Stages

There are two types of extra second stages: an extra second stage for your regulator or a BC low-pressure inflator that has an integrated regulator second stage (see Figure 5.21). An extra second stage, or **octopus**, should meet the following criteria:

octopus
An extra regulator second stage

- The first stage of the regulator should be capable of meeting the airflow demands of two second stages.
- The hose on the extra second stage should be several inches (7 to 10 cm) longer than the primary second stage hose.
- The extra second stage should attach to your chest area in such a way that your buddy can remove it quickly and easily. Do not allow the extra second stage to dangle.
- The attachment device should cover the extra second stage mouthpiece opening to prevent the regulator from free-flowing and to keep dirt and debris from getting inside.
- The extra second stage should be brightly colored for easy identification.

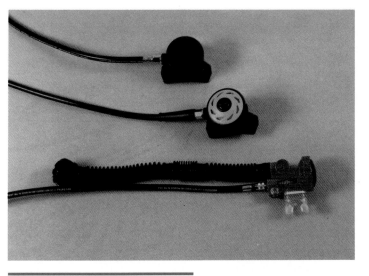

Figure 5.21 A primary second stage (top), an extra second stage (center), and an integrated second stage (bottom).

There are two ways to integrate a regulator second stage into the low-pressure inflator of a BC. Quick-release hose fittings on the regulator second stage can allow it to be fitted in series in the low-pressure hose leading to the inflator assembly, or the BC inflator mechanism can have a built-in regulator second stage. Both types of extra second stages have advantages and disadvantages. An integrated

What are the advantages and disadvantages of having an extra second stage integrated into a BC inflator?

second stage requires one less hose on your regulator because a single hose provides air for both the extra second stage and the BC inflator. When you must share air and you have an integrated second stage, you must breathe from the integrated second stage because the hose is too short for your buddy to use. With an extra second stage, you or your buddy may use either air source. Extra second stages integrated into the BC inflator may leak air. To stop a leak, you must disconnect the low-pressure air, thereby losing the functions of the low-pressure inflator and the extra second stage.

Backup Scuba Units

There are two types of backup scuba units. A *pony tank* is a small (13- to 20-ft³ or 368- to 567-L) scuba cylinder that you clamp to the side of your main scuba cylinder. A *Spare Air® unit* is much smaller (2 to 4 ft³ or 57 to 113 L). A pony tank provides an adequate air supply for many situations, but a Spare Air® unit provides only enough air to permit an ascent. On the other hand, a Spare Air® unit is small and light, whereas a pony tank is bulky and heavy.

Care and Maintenance

AAS equipment should receive the same care and maintenance as your primary scuba equipment. Some divers attempt to save money by having only their primary scuba equipment serviced annually. This is false economy. AAS equipment needs servicing just as much as primary scuba equipment.

CAUTION:

DO NOT ATTEMPT TO LUBRICATE OR SERVICE SCUBA EQUIPMENT. IMPROPER LUBRICATING OR SERVICING CAN CAUSE EQUIPMENT FAILURE.

Instrumentation

You move in three dimensions in water the way a pilot does in air. Instruments are important safety requirements for flying. A pilot needs information about altitude, direction, time, and the amount of fuel remaining. Similarly, you need information about depth, direction, time, and the amount of air remaining. The minimum instrumentation you need includes a depth gauge, an underwater timer, a dive compass, and a submersible pressure gauge (SPG). You may also find it helpful to have a dive computer.

Depth Gauges

To tell you how deep you have descended, you can use one of four types of depth gauges: capillary, Bourdon tube, diaphragm, and electronic. Manufacturers calibrate depth gauges in FSW (feet of salt water). The gauges do not indicate the correct depth in fresh water, but they indicate the equivalent seawater depth if you use them starting at sea level in fresh water or if they are designed to adjust for altitude pressure changes. The FSW reading of gauges in fresh water is acceptable because tables for time limits at various depths are based on sea-level depths. Table 5.5 compares the four types of depth gauges.

Table 5.5
Depth Gauges

Type	Accuracy	Advantages	Disadvantages
Capillary	Accurate only to depth of about 40 ft (12 m)	Rugged, inexpensive	Can clog with debris or air bubbles
Bourdon tube	Plus or minus 1% to 2% of full scale	Accurate	Can be damaged by reduced pressure at altitude
Diaphragm	Very accurate	Can adjust zero setting for pressure changes at altitude	Expensive
Electronic	Reading accurate within ±6 in. (15 cm)	Gauge may zero itself to compensate for changes in atmospheric pressure	Must have sufficient battery power; expensive

A capillary depth gauge is a simple instrument. It is a hollow, air-filled, transparent plastic tube sealed at one end and placed around a circular dial. The open end of the tube aligns with zero on the gauge dial. A capillary gauge uses the principle of Boyle's law. Water pressure compresses the air inside the tube during descent. The position of the air-water interface inside the tube relative to markings on the dial indicates the depth. At 2 ATM of pressure, the air in the tube compresses to one-half its original volume.

A Bourdon tube is a thin, metal tube formed into a spiral. The tube may be open to the water, or it may be closed and placed inside a housing filled with oil. Oil-filled Bourdon gauges are more popular than open-tube gauges. Pressure on an open-tube gauge tries to straighten the tube and increases the coil diameter. The straightening produces a spiral movement of the tube, which is linked mechanically to a needle to indicate the depth. Water pressure causes the coil of a closed-tube gauge to decrease in diameter. The coil movement, linked mechanically to a needle, indicates the amount of pressure exerted on the gauge.

The accurate but expensive diaphragm gauge uses elaborate mechanics to connect a thin, movable diaphragm to an indicating needle. Electronic depth gauges, also accurate and expensive, use a pressure sensor (transducer), electrical circuitry, a display, and a battery to indicate depth.

A maximum-depth indicator is a desirable feature for all depth gauges. As you will learn in chapter 7, you must know the depth of a dive for planning purposes. A digital depth gauge retains the maximum depth you attain. The instrument displays the information until the next dive or for 12 or more hours following a dive, then resets automatically. Many modern depth gauges with needle displays have a thin indicating wire that the gauge needle pushes along the dial face. When the needle retreats, the wire remains at the highest point reached on the dial. You can reset the indicating wire by turning a screw on the dial face. You must remember to reset the maximum-depth indicator before each dive when you use a needle-display gauge.

Underwater Timers

You can use either automatic or manual underwater timers to keep track of time during a dive. Either type may indicate time with hands on a dial or with a digital display. Pressure activates automatic timers, which start timing at a depth of about 3 to 5 ft (1 to 1.5 m) and stop timing when the depth is less than that. Automatic timers are better because you do not have to remember to start or stop the timing of your dive, although you have to reset some watch-type automatic timers before a dive. Waterproof watches that you may use as underwater timers usually feature a rotating bezel, a movable ring that you can set to indicate elapsed time. Digital watches are accurate, but they have small buttons that can make them difficult to operate. The best timers are electronic automatic timers, which can keep track of how long you dive, how long you are at the surface between dives, and how many dives you make. You do not have to remember to reset or activate anything when you use an electronic automatic timer.

If you wear a timer on your wrist, use a fabric band that passes under both watchband pins of the instrument. If you wear a timer with a band that attaches to each pin, you can lose the timer if one of the band pins comes loose or breaks.

Dive Compasses

Rarely can you see more than 100 ft (30 m) underwater, so a navigational aid can be valuable. If you dive without a directional reference, you can end a dive a long distance from your exit point. A dive compass can help you avoid long surface swims or swims through thick surface canopies of underwater plants. You can use a compass to navigate beneath the canopies, where there are passages through the plants. A compass also is useful for relocating a precise area underwater and as a surface navigation device if fog arises.

Two types of compasses are card types and needle types. Both are mechanical. Magnetic deposits in the earth near the North Pole attract either a magnetized disk or a magnetized needle to provide

What is the preferred type of underwater timer?

What factors can affect the accuracy of a compass card or needle alignment?

a directional reference. Metal and magnetic forces—ferrous metal, magnets, or electrical motors—can deviate the compass card or needle from its correct alignment if the influence is in close proximity to a compass.

Diving compasses have liquid inside to lessen the swinging of the needle or disk. To be useful for diving, a compass needs a **lubber line**. A rotating bezel with bracketing index marks that allow you to mark the needle position for a specific direction is also desirable.

You view some compasses from the top and some from the side. Side-reading compasses display a selected course in a window on the side of the instrument. You look across a top-reading compass. You will learn how to read and use a compass in chapter 6.

Submersible Pressure Gauges

An SPG is equivalent to the gas gauge for a car and is just as essential. You can use either a mechanical or an electronic SPG to measure cylinder pressure. A mechanical SPG is a high-pressure Bourdon tube. High-pressure air from the cylinder passes through the regulator first stage, through a high-pressure hose, and into a Bourdon tube inside a housing at the end of the high-pressure hose. The pressure tries to straighten the spiral tube, which moves a needle on a dial to indicate the tank pressure. Physical shock can damage a mechanical SPG.

An electronic SPG has a pressure sensor (transducer), circuitry, a battery, and a display. It is a form of a high-pressure depth gauge. The display may be digital or graphic. Either a symbol or psi (or ATM) in numbers may indicate the amount of air in your tank. If the electronics get wet, or if the battery dies, an electronic SPG will not function.

You should retain at least 300 to 500 psi (20.4 to 34 ATM) in your tank at the end of a dive. Mechanical SPGs typically have a red area on the dial for the last 500 psi (34 ATM). When you dive, you should monitor your air supply and make sure that you surface before the needle gets into the red area. Electronic depth gauges usually warn of a low supply of air by blinking the display.

An SPG has a *blowout plug* to relieve pressure in the housing in the event of a high-pressure leak. Identify the blowout plug on your SPG, and do not place anything over the plug that will prevent it from functioning. If the plug cannot come out to release high pressure inside the SPG housing, the face of the instrument could explode.

Instrument Consoles

You can purchase diving instruments individually or in combination. It is convenient to combine several gauges into a display unit called a *console*. An instrument console attaches to the high-pressure hose coming from your regulator first stage. When you have your instruments in a console, your arms are free of gauges and dive preparations are quicker.

---

lubber line
A reference line on a compass that indicates the direction of travel

What is the minimum amount of air you should surface with?

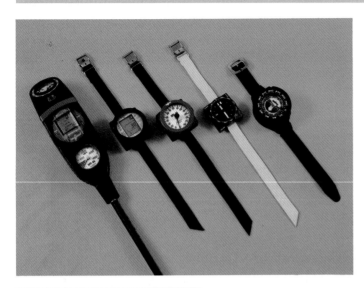

Figure 5.22 Divers use many instruments to monitor their activity underwater.

ceiling
The minimum depth that a diver cannot rise above without risk of DCS

The two types of instrument consoles are mechanical and electronic. A mechanical console contains an SPG and a depth gauge. Some also contain an underwater timer, a compass, and a thermometer. The instruments usually feature luminous displays, which are easy to read when it is dark.

With an electronic console, all instrument information except direction is in a single display (there are no electronic underwater compasses). If one gauge fails in a mechanical console, the remainder can still function; but when an electronic console fails, all of the information provided by the unit is lost. Electronic displays are difficult to read in the dark unless they feature some type of illumination. Figure 5.22 shows various diving instruments.

Dive Computers

A dive computer is an electronic instrument with a pressure sensor, electronic circuitry, a battery, and a display. A programmed computer inside the instrument uses pressure and time information to continuously calculate the uptake of nitrogen by various compartments that have different half times. When the absorption by any one of the compartments reaches a selected level, the device indicates that you are approaching a time limit, after which a direct ascent to the surface will no longer be possible. Upon reaching a time limit, the computer indicates a minimum depth, or **ceiling**, that you cannot exceed during ascent. You risk DCS unless you wait until the computer indicates sufficient outgassing has occurred to allow you to continue your ascent. A dive computer provides extremely accurate time and depth information. Other common features are a low-battery warning, a rapid-ascent warning, a dive-log mode, a dive-planning mode, and flying-after-diving information. Additional information about dive computers is presented in chapter 7.

Care and Maintenance

Physical abuse can damage instruments, so protect your instruments from shock. Secure your console instead of allowing it to swing freely.

Heat or prolonged exposure to the hot sun can cause oil in a liquid-filled gauge to expand and break the seal on the housing encasing the instrument. If you break the seal, you must have the gauge repaired. Hot water in a Jacuzzi or a shower may cause an underwater timer to expand, break a seal, and allow water inside. Do not subject diving instruments to high temperatures.

Have air leaks in SPGs repaired at the first opportunity. Have your depth gauge tested for accuracy from time to time by a professional repair facility, or compare your gauge to an extremely accurate instrument, such as a digital depth gauge. Follow all manufacturer recommendations.

Reduced pressure at elevations above sea level can damage some instruments. Unless an instrument is designed for use at altitude, pack it in an airtight container for flying.

Soak and rinse instruments with clean, fresh water after use. Give special attention to pressure-sensing areas to prevent them from becoming clogged with dirt or salt crystals.

Dive Knives and Accessory Equipment

This section describes some additional equipment you should have and some you may want to have. Figure 5.23 shows examples of dive knives and some dive accessories.

Dive Knives

A dive knife is mandatory. Do not consider a knife optional equipment or an accessory. Lines and cords in water can cause entanglements, so it is important to have a knife that will allow you to cut yourself or your buddy free.

The many designs of dive knives include large knives and small knives. A small knife positioned where you can reach it easily is better than a large knife that you cannot reach. The most important feature of a dive knife is an effective cutting edge. Good blades are corrosion-resistant and hold a sharp edge; serrated blades cut line more effectively than straight blades.

Some knives are multipurpose tools designed for prying, digging, pounding, and measuring, in addition to cutting. If you use a knife as a diving tool, it is a good idea to also have a small, separate dive knife.

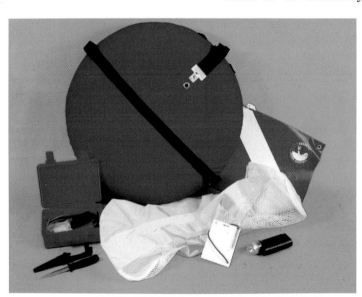

Figure 5.23 Divers must carry a dive knife, and other equipment can also be helpful.

A dive knife comes with a sheath, which has some means to lock the knife in place inside the sheath. Make sure the sheath lock is positive because it is disappointing to lose a knife. You may attach a small knife to your leg, your arm, your console, or your BC. Wear a large knife on the inside of your leg and secure it with straps that stretch to compensate for exposure suit compression.

To prevent corrosion, rinse your dive knife after diving. Inspect the edge for sharpness, remove any rust, and coat the blade with grease.

What is the most important feature of a dive knife?

Accessory Equipment

You are likely to need several small, but important, items of accessory equipment. These items include a gear bag, a dive flag and float, dive lights, dive kits, dive slates, signaling devices, and a diver's first aid kit.

Gear Bags.   You need so much equipment for diving that you also need a means to carry it. Gear bag designs feature multiple compartments, padding, novel ways for carrying or moving, sealed fabric edges, and various fabrics. The bags may be simple or complex. The type for you depends on your needs and how much you want to invest. Be sure to get a bag with webbing handles that completely surround the bag to provide full, durable support. No matter what your budget, you will need a gear bag for your equipment.

Dive Flags and Floats.   In many areas, local law requires use of a dive flag while diving. In the United States, the traditional dive flag is a red flag with a white diagonal stripe. The flag usually is vinyl, mounted on a fiberglass staff, and stiffened with a wire so it will stand out from the staff at all times.

In addition to the red-and-white flag, use the international Alpha flag, a swallow-tailed blue-and-white flag, when diving from a vessel. The Alpha flag is a general dive flag in countries other than the United States.

Unless you are diving from a boat, you need a float to support your dive flag. Some flagstaffs have a float attached to them. There are attachments to secure a dive flag to an inner tube and flag-holding canvas coverings for inner tubes.

Dive Lights.   A dive light can increase your diving enjoyment. Light levels are low underwater, and a light restores color to objects at depth and allows you to peer under ledges and into holes. You will see and enjoy much more when you have and use a dive light.

The many types of dive lights available include large, powerful, rechargeable lights and small lights that use disposable batteries. Consider a small dive light initially. A large light is for night diving, which is an advanced activity. A small light is easy to carry, useful for day dives, and useful as a backup light for night diving. Many of today's small dive lights are bright and compact. Maintain your dive light according to the manufacturer's instructions.

Dive Kits.   Two equipment kits are recommended: a dive kit and a "save-a-dive" kit. The dive kit contains items you use frequently for diving. The save-a-dive kit contains items you may need to salvage a dive. The items you might include in each are listed in the margin sidebar. Because the items in your dive kit are small and get wet, you may wish to keep them in a container by themselves so you can find them easily. Once you get yourself and your equipment to a dive site, you don't want a minor equipment problem to keep you from diving. A broken

Equipment Kits

Dive Kit

- Defogging solution for your mask
- Wet suit shampoo
- Sunscreen
- Lip balm
- Seasickness medication

Save-a-Dive Kit

- Mask strap
- Fin strap
- Snorkel keeper
- Tank valve O-rings
- Quick-release buckle
- Weight keepers
- Regulator mouthpiece
- Crescent wrench
- Screwdrivers
- Cable ties
- Twine
- Duct tape

strap, a missing O-ring, or a torn mouthpiece are examples of problems that can stop you from diving unless you have spare parts. Keep items for a save-a-dive kit in a waterproof box. Do not mix wet items from your dive kit with dry items in your save-a-dive kit.

Dive Slates. You need to record and refer to information around and in the water when you dive. Plastic slates are better than paper because water does not affect the slates. Dive slates include checklist slates, reference slates, log book information-transfer slates, and writing slates. All types are of value. You probably will have several slates when you become an experienced diver. Initially, you should have an equipment checklist, a dive-planning slate, and an underwater writing slate.

Signaling Devices. Long-range signaling devices are invaluable if you become adrift, especially in areas where currents are strong. A whistle is more effective than shouting to gain attention, so you should have a whistle readily available. The sound from a whistle does not require much energy to produce, and it travels well over water.

A small diver's air horn, powered by low-pressure air, works with as little as 50 psi (3.4 ATM) of tank pressure and produces a sound that can be heard up to a mile away. The device is so loud you must point the horn away from yourself to avoid hearing damage.

You can get long, bright, thin, inflatable safety tubes that fit easily into your BC pocket. Inflate a safety tube at the surface to make yourself easier to spot in the water.

You can use a signal mirror to flash sunlight long distances over water. Other forms of signaling devices for divers are flashlights, strobe lights, inflatable balloons, and flares. The greater the chance of being caught in a current, the greater your need for signaling devices.

Diver's First Aid Kit. Diving takes place in remote areas, and because it is a physical activity, someone may be injured. It is a good idea to be prepared for an emergency. You should have a first aid kit at the dive site. The items helpful in a standard first aid kit are listed in the following sidebar. Pack the items in a waterproof container to make a diver's first aid kit. Chapter 6 addresses the use of the first aid items.

What three types of dive slates should a beginning diver have?

Under what diving conditions are signaling devices most likely to be needed?

First Aid Kit

- Rescue breathing mask
- Seasickness medication
- Isopropyl alcohol
- Hydrogen peroxide
- White vinegar
- Baking soda
- Analgesic and antiseptic ointment
- Hot packs
- Eyewash
- Tweezers
- Bandage scissors
- Penlight
- Coins for emergency phone calls
- Emergency contact information for diving emergencies
- Diving first aid book
- Space blanket
- Pen and small notebook

Summary

Diving involves a great deal of equipment. You are beginning to understand the equipment you need to have, how to select it, and how to care for it. You will learn more about equipment from your instructor, from retailers, from magazines, and from other divers. Get good equipment and give it the best care possible. Diving is not enjoyable if you have constant equipment problems.

6 Diving Skills

Diving is a physical activity that requires many skills. To learn these skills, you must repeat them correctly until you can execute them automatically. When you have mastered the skills of diving, your enjoyment can begin because you will be able to devote more attention to things of interest. This chapter introduces you to the basic skills of skin diving and scuba diving.

You will learn most of the diving skills in controlled conditions, and when you have developed the basic skills, you will apply them in open water. (Open water is any body of water representative of dive sites in the local area.) When you can demonstrate the skills of diving in open water, you will be ready to receive your diving certification.

Preparing to Skin Dive

Skin diving is breath-hold diving underwater. This section discusses the skills of skin diving, many of which also apply to scuba diving.

How should you prepare these pieces of equipment prior to a dive?
a. Mask
b. Snorkel
c. Diving vest or BC
d. Weight belt
e. Personal equipment
f. Gear bag

Preparing Equipment

Be ready to go when you come to your first water session. Prepare your mask, snorkel, and fins in advance. Clean your mask lens thoroughly so it will not fog. Adjust the mask strap so it is snug but not tight. Attach the snorkel to the mask strap on the left side, and adjust the snorkel so it is comfortable in your mouth. If your fins have heel straps, adjust them so they are snug but not tight. Complete all adjustments before your first water session.

Inspect your skin diving vest or BC by inflating it, making sure it does not leak, and then deflating it. Put it on, reinflate it, and adjust the straps so the vest or BC will stay in position in the water. You may need to use a strap that runs between your legs and attaches to the front and back of the flotation device to keep the device from riding up when you are in the water. If the flotation device has a CO_2 detonator, inspect the CO_2 cartridge and detonator.

Your instructor will suggest an initial amount of weight for your weight belt. Adjust the length of the belt at the buckle end so that the excess strap at the opposite end does not exceed 6 in. (15 cm). Allow 2 in. (5 cm) for each two-slot weight you thread onto a belt. Distribute the weight on both sides of the belt so you will be balanced in the water. Lock the weights in place with weight retainers.

Mark your personal equipment with your initials so you can identify it. You can use special paint or markers (available at dive stores) or colored tape.

Pack your equipment in a gear bag. Place the items you will don last, such as your fins, on the bottom. Place the items you will don first, such as your exposure suit, on the top.

In what order should you don the following equipment?
a. Mask
b. Snorkel
c. Fins
d. Exposure suit
e. Diving vest or BC
f. Weight belt

Donning Equipment

Don your exposure suit pants or legs first, then your boots, and then the top part of your suit. Donning a snug-fitting wet suit is easier if you wet the inside of your suit with water mixed with mild shampoo or if you wear a spandex suit as an undergarment. Place the ends of the legs of your wet suit over the tops of your boots so water can drain from your suit when you exit from a dive. If the boots are outside the legs of your wet suit, water from the suit will balloon your boots when you get out of the water. If you become warm while donning the exposure suit, cool yourself before proceeding with your preparations. For open-water diving, don a cold-water hood before donning your wet suit jacket so the skirt of the hood will be underneath your jacket.

Don your skin diving vest or BC next. Place a skin diving vest over your head, and then secure the straps. Inflate the vest fully to make sure the adjustment will not be too tight. The straps should be as snug as possible without being uncomfortable or interfering with breathing.

Don your weight belt after the skin diving vest so it will be clear of the vest straps. Grasp the free end (the end without the buckle) of the weight belt in your right hand and grasp the buckle end with your left hand. Pick up the belt, step through it, pull it into position across your back, bend forward so gravity will support the weight of the belt, and then tighten the belt and secure the quick release. Always wear the weight belt with a right-hand release, even if you are left-handed. Do this so that a rescuer will know how to release your belt in an emergency. If you always hold the free end of the belt in your right hand when donning it, you always will have a right-hand quick release.

> **Why is it important to wear a weight belt with a right-hand release?**

Don the remainder of your skin diving equipment—mask, fins, and snorkel—at the water's edge or, if it is calm, in the water. Defog the mask, place it on your forehead, and pull the strap over the back of your head using both hands to position the strap. Position the mask on your face, clearing any hair from beneath the sealing edge of the mask. Reposition the split strap so it lies flat and so the split is above and below the crown of your head. You don your snorkel when you don your mask. Check the adjustment of the snorkel when your mask is in place.

Stabilize yourself when donning fins so that you don't lose your balance and fall. Hold onto your buddy or an object for support, or sit at the water's edge. Hold the side of a fin, bend one leg into a figure "4" position, push the fin onto your foot, and pull the strap or heel pocket into place. Repeat the process for the other fin. Avoid walking with fins. If you must walk a few steps while wearing fins, shuffle your feet while walking backward. If you try to walk forward, you can lose your balance or damage your fins. Figure 6.1 illustrates the process of equipment donning.

Inspecting Equipment

After you have donned your equipment, inspect it for completeness, correct positioning, and adjustment. When you are satisfied with your equipment, inspect your buddy's while he or she inspects yours. Inspect from head to toe. You may be able to see something that your buddy could not see, or vice versa. Develop the habit of inspecting each other's equipment before every dive.

Figure 6.1 Don your skin diving equipment in this order: (a) exposure suit, (b) BC, (c) weights, (d) fins, and (e) mask.

Skin Diving Skills

There are three categories of skills for diving: skin diving skills, scuba diving skills, and problem management skills. This section introduces skin diving skills.

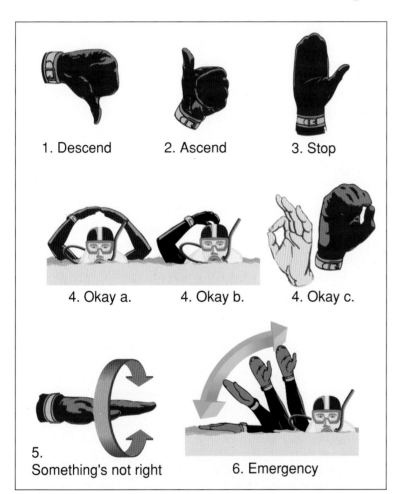

Figure 6.2 Skin diving hand signals.

Skin Diving Hand Signals

You cannot talk with a snorkel in your mouth and your face in the water, so you use hand signals as a primary means of communication. You need to learn and use the hand signals shown in Figure 6.2. You will learn additional hand signals for scuba diving. Display hand signals clearly and deliberately when you send them, and acknowledge all hand signals you receive.

Using a Skin Diving Vest

You inflated and deflated your skin diving vest as part of your diving preparations. You need to learn how to deflate and inflate the vest in the water. To deflate the vest, position your body so the exhaust port is the highest point. Hold the deflation valve open while you sink lower in the water. The water pressure helps force the air from the vest. You may have to hold the collar of the vest down with one hand to remove the air from that area. When you have vented all of the air from the vest, close the valve. Get your buddy to confirm that all of the air is out of your vest.

It is easier to inflate the vest in the water with your face underwater instead of above water. Take a breath of air, duck your face beneath the surface, insert the oral inflator into your mouth, and exhale into the vest. Repeat the bobbing process until you have the desired buoyancy.

If your vest has a CO_2 detonator and you choose to use it to quickly inflate the vest, grasp the activation cord and pull it downward firmly and then pull it from side to side. If your vest has CO_2 inside, avoid inhaling the gas, which is harmful to your lungs in strong concentrations. If you use a CO_2 cartridge to inflate your vest, remove and replace the cartridge at the first opportunity. It is unwise to leave an expended cartridge in the vest because rust particles inside the cartridge may damage your vest.

What position should your body be in to deflate a skin diving vest? To inflate it?

Testing Buoyancy

Your buoyancy should be neutral at the surface. If you are "light," you will have to struggle to descend and remain underwater. If you are "heavy," you will tire quickly at the surface and sink while swimming underwater. Adjust your buoyancy so it is correct.

If you are wearing an exposure suit, you need weights to offset the suit's buoyancy. With all equipment in place, position yourself in chest-deep water. Exhaust all air from your skin diving vest. Take a full breath, hold it, lift your feet from the bottom, and remain motionless while you slowly count to 10. If you sink, remove some weight and try again. When your weighting is correct, you will remain at the surface while holding a full breath and will begin to sink after exhaling. Adjust your weighting until you are able to do this.

| How can you tell if you're weighted correctly? |

Clearing the Mask

If you get water in your mask while skin diving, simply pull the bottom of your mask away from your face slightly when you are above the water and let the water run out. You will learn how to clear water from a mask while underwater when you learn to use scuba equipment.

Using the Snorkel

Stand in the water and lean forward with the snorkel in your mouth. Place your face in the water and inhale gently. If you inhale forcefully at first, you may inhale water. When you are sure the tube is clear, you may breathe more forcefully through your snorkel. When you descend beneath the surface, the snorkel tube may fill with water. As described in chapter 5, self-draining snorkels will drain nearly all of the water from the tube when you surface.

If your snorkel is not the self-draining type, you will have to blast the water from the tube with a strong, sharp exhalation. To do this, blow hard into the snorkel to force the water out. Inhale cautiously after exhaling. If a little water remains in the tube, you can breathe past it if you inhale gently. After you fill your lungs again, expel the remaining water with another forceful exhalation.

| Describe the displacement method of clearing your snorkel. |

If you have a simple snorkel without valves, you can clear the tube while ascending by using the displacement method. Begin by looking up to invert the snorkel; then exhale a small amount of air into the tube. As you ascend, the air expands according to Boyle's law and displaces the water in the tube, which will be clear of water when you reach the surface. The tube is inverted at this point, however, so when you turn it to an upright position, water will flow into the tube unless you exhale while rolling your head forward at the surface. Continuous exhalation prevents water from entering the tube. When you use the displacement method, which is easier than the blast method, you may take a breath the moment you reach the surface. Figure 6.3 shows the displacement method.

a

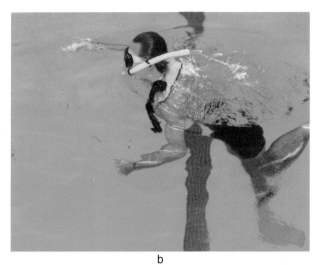

b

Figure 6.3 Displacement method of clearing a snorkel.

Learn to keep the snorkel in your mouth when you are in the water. Avoid the temptation to remove the mouthpiece and shake the water from the snorkel. You do not have to remove the mouthpiece when you can clear your snorkel proficiently. When your hands are occupied, you will not be able to remove and replace the snorkel.

Using Fins

Fins provide large surfaces you can push against the water for propulsion. The strong muscles of your legs can push the fins against the resistance of the water. The blades of the fins need to push the water the way a broom sweeps a floor. A broom will not sweep if you move it up and down, and your fins will not provide propulsion if you move them lengthwise in the water. You must kick them back and forth in wide, sweeping kicks. Small fins allow short, quick kicks, but larger fins require wider, slower kicks. Moving efficiently, not speedily, is your objective when wearing fins.

The most common fin kick is the **flutter kick**. You may do this up-and-down kick facing down, up, or to the side. Your fins need to be underwater to provide propulsion. It is easier to keep your fins submerged at the surface when you are on your back or on your side instead of your stomach. Extend your legs almost fully throughout each stroke and use wide, slow kicks. Keep your hands at your sides or extend them in front. Do not use your hands and arms to swim.

The **scissors kick** is similar to a flutter kick. Use the scissors kick as a resting stroke. Hold a streamlined position with your toes pointed while you glide through the water between kicks. When you come to a stop, repeat the stroke. Extend your legs almost fully throughout the stroke.

A **modified frog kick** (which is different from a swimmer's frog kick) uses different muscles than the flutter or scissors kicks. It is good to be able to change kicks if you become tired or develop leg cramps. Extend your legs almost fully throughout the stroke, and then hold the final position with your feet together, point your toes, and glide. When you come to a stop, repeat the stroke.

flutter kick
A kick done by moving the legs up and down at the hip while bending the knees only slightly

scissors kick
A resting kick done by extending one leg backward and the other forward while lying on the side, then pulling the legs together quickly

modified frog kick
A kick done in the facedown position with the ankles rotated so the tips of the fins are pointed outward, the feet are moved apart, and then the bottoms of the fins are pulled together quickly in a wide, sweeping arc

dolphin kick
A kick done in the face-down position with the legs kept together at all times while force is exerted on the water with a wave-like motion of the body. When the shoulders are raised, the fins are pushed downward; when the shoulders are lowered, the fins are pushed upward.

The **dolphin kick** is also useful for a change of pace. When you see this kick demonstrated, you'll be able to learn it by imitation. If you lose a fin, you can use the dolphin kick to propel yourself. Cross your legs with the leg without a fin behind the one that has a fin. Figure 6.4 shows what the four kicks look like.

Figure 6.4 Divers have many types of kicks to choose from for propelling themselves, including the flutter kick, scissors kick, modified frog kick, and dolphin kick.

Surface Dives

You need to be able to dive down to see the beautiful world beneath the surface. The initiation of a skin dive beneath the surface is a surface dive. The principle of a surface dive is simple: You raise part of your body above the water and point yourself straight down; the weight you have above the water drives you downward. Once you are submerged, you start swimming to continue your descent.

There are several types of surface dives: pike, tuck, and feet-first (see Figure 6.5). You do the pike dive while moving forward at the surface. Bend forward at the waist and make the trunk of your body vertical in the water. Next, quickly lift your legs out of the water to a vertical position. The more of your legs you can lift out of the

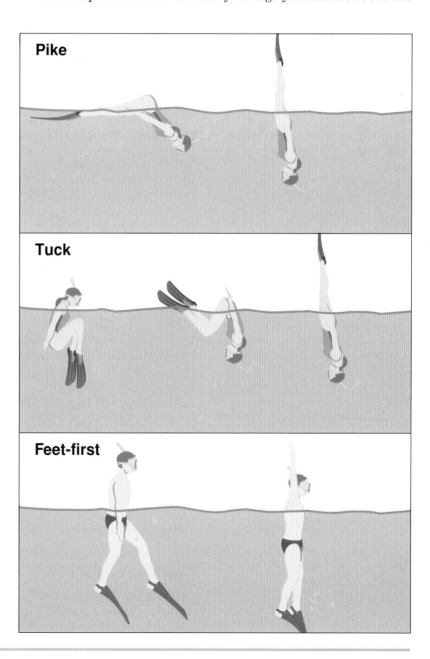

Figure 6.5 You can use a pike dive, tuck dive, or feet-first dive to descend underwater.

water, the further your surface dive will push you under the water. For shallow dives, you can do the pike dive by lifting only one leg.

When you have learned the pike dive, you will be ready for the tuck dive, which is similar. Do the tuck dive from a stationary position. Begin in an upright position in the water, pull your knees to your chest, and sweep backward with your arms to roll yourself forward in the water. When you are inverted, extend yourself fully into a vertical position. You must make this coordinated movement quickly to get your legs above water. Once your legs are extended, the remainder of the dive is the same as the pike dive.

Use a feet-first dive in areas where surface plant growth is dense, because you're less likely to become entangled. Begin in a stationary, upright position and use a strong scissors kick to propel yourself up and out of the water as far as possible. Pull your arms downward to your sides for added lift. When you reach the highest point, point your toes downward and hold your arms to your sides. The weight of your body will push you below the surface. When your downward momentum ends, do a tuck dive to invert yourself, and then continue your descent.

Descents, Underwater Swimming, and Ascents

To prepare to descend, vent all air from your flotation device. Pre-equalize your ears using an ear-clearing maneuver at the surface so that it will be easy to clear them while you descend. Hyperventilate three times, inhale as fully as possible, and don't exhale until you return to the surface.

Initiate your descent with a good surface dive. Equalize the pressure in your ears and mask every couple of feet during your descent. Use wide, slow, powerful kicks to propel yourself to your desired depth, then relax as much as possible.

Swimming underwater sounds simple, but some people have trouble controlling direction. Your head is your rudder. Pull your head back while swimming facedown and you will go up. Bend your head forward and you will go down. Bend your trunk to the left or right to turn. With practice, you can go in any direction you choose without using your hands.

The three rules for ascents are to reach up, look up, and come up slowly. Extend one arm over your head for protection, and look up to avoid obstructions and determine when the surface is near. A slow ascent is better than a rapid ascent because swimming rapidly uses more oxygen. Make one or two revolutions during your ascent to check your surroundings. Figure 6.6 shows a skin diver ascending.

Alternate breath-hold dives with your buddy. Make sure your buddy knows where you are at all times.

Handling Equipment

Occasionally you may need to remove, adjust, and replace skin diving equipment while you are in the water. You should be able to handle your equipment easily with training and practice.

When is it beneficial to use a feet-first dive to descend?

What part of your body controls direction while you're swimming underwater?

Name the three rules for skin diving ascents.

Figure 6.6 Extend your arm for protection when ascending.

Should you be above water or underwater when adjusting the following equipment:
a. Mask
b. Fins
c. Weight belt

To remove, adjust, and replace your mask, begin by inflating your skin diving vest. Because you will make the adjustment above water, use buoyancy to reduce the effort. After you make the adjustment, replace your mask using the four-step procedure for donning the mask described earlier in this chapter.

You may need to adjust a fin strap or remove sand or gravel from your fins while diving. The fins are easier to remove, adjust, and replace than the mask is. You do not need as much buoyancy to work with your fins because you can look into the water and adjust them underwater. In fact, too much air in your skin diving vest can be a nuisance. Keep your face in the water, breathe through your snorkel, and work with one fin at a time.

You may need to tighten, adjust, or replace your weight belt. The weights may slip or the belt may fall off. To tighten or replace your weight belt, you need to get the belt across the small of your back while you are in a facedown position breathing through your snorkel. If you try to replace or tighten the belt in an upright position, you will have a constant fight with gravity. When you are in the correct, facedown position, gravity becomes your ally while you secure the buckle. To get the belt into position across your back, begin in an upright position holding the free end of the weight belt against the outside of your right thigh. Lean back into a horizontal, faceup position momentarily, then roll to your left to a facedown position while continuing to hold the free end of the belt against your right thigh. At this point, the belt will be draped across the backs of your thighs. Clear your snorkel so you can breathe. While holding the free end of the belt in your right hand, reach down with your left hand, grab the buckle end, and pull the belt into position across your back.

Removing Equipment

Your equipment helps you adapt to the underwater environment. Develop the habit of keeping it in place while you're in the water. You may need to defog your mask or make an adjustment, but other than that you should wear your equipment continuously. Avoid the tendency to prop your mask on your forehead when you are at the surface. Mask propping is a sign of distress and a good way to lose your mask and snorkel. If you must remove your mask while in the water, pull it down around your neck where it will be secure.

The removal of fins varies with bottom conditions at dive sites. In some areas you may remove your fins in waist-deep water and wade out of the water. In other areas, you need to wear your fins until you are clear of the water. There are several ways to remove fins. When you prepare to climb a boat ladder, hold the ladder continuously while using the figure "4" position to remove each fin. If the boat has a platform at the rear, swim onto the swim step and remove your fins while in a kneeling position. When you remove fins in waist-deep water or on land, use your buddy for support. On steep beaches, you may choose to crawl from the water. Your buddy can remove your fins while you are on your hands and knees. Your buddy then crawls ahead of you, and you remove your buddy's fins. When you stand up, you exchange fins.

Weight belt removal also varies. When you can walk or climb out of the water, wear your belt. When you remove a weight belt, lower it gently instead of dropping it. You may cause damage or injury if you develop the habit of dropping your weight belt. If you must pull yourself onto a dock or into a small boat, remove your belt first and hand it up.

Keep your skin diving vest in place until you are clear of the water. Remove your skin diving vest, then your wet suit. Remove your wet suit by turning it inside out. Be sure to remove your boots before your wet suit pants. You may need assistance from your buddy when removing a pullover jacket or a jumpsuit.

Preparing to Scuba Dive

> **What is the easiest way to carry your equipment to a dive site?**

Figure 6.7   Proper way to carry equipment.

Nearly all of the skills of skin diving are embodied in scuba diving, but you'll need to learn many additional skills for scuba diving. In this section, you are introduced to the preparatory skills of scuba diving; the next section covers basic and postdive skills. The more familiar you become with the skills by studying them, the better you will be able to develop them when you do them. It is important to learn skills correctly from the outset so that you develop correct habits for your diving safety.

Packing Equipment

It is inconvenient to get ready to dive and discover that something is missing or not right. You can (and should) take steps to prevent equipment inconveniences. Begin by using a checklist when you pack your diving equipment to be sure you have everything you need (see the diving equipment checklist in the appendix). After taking inventory, inspect your equipment as you pack it. If you have not used your equipment for a while, assemble it and test it first. Make sure everything works properly.

Pack your equipment in your gear bag except for your weight belt and tank. When you have to carry your equipment, put your BC on your tank, carry the tank on your back, your gear bag in one hand, and your weight belt in the other hand (see Figure 6.7). Equipment-carrying devices can reduce the work of moving your diving equipment.

Assembling Equipment

Today's backpacks are part of the BC and have one or more bands to secure the scuba cylinder. Many of the bands are made of webbing, which stretches when wet. Soak a fabric tank band in water for a couple of minutes before securing it around a scuba tank. The soaking softens the webbing and allows it to stretch when you tighten the band. A dry fabric belt may allow the tank to slip when the band gets wet and stretches. The tank band must be tight so the tank will not slip from the pack. A tank that slips from a pack can be a hazard.

Orient your backpack with the opening of the tank valve facing the backpack. Stand the tank up with the valve handle facing to your right, slide the tank band over the tank with the tank between you and the pack, and tighten the band so the valve opening points directly toward the pack.

The height of the tank band on the tank varies with the type of backpack. Generally, the top of the pack will be even with the base of the tank valve. After you attach the pack and before you attach the regulator, don the scuba tank and check the height adjustment by slowly tilting your head backward. If your head hits the tank valve, the tank is too high in the pack. Reach over your shoulder for the tank valve. If you cannot touch it, the tank is too low in the pack. Adjust the height as needed. When you become familiar with the correct height adjustment, you will not need to test it before completing the assembly of the scuba unit, but you should check it before entering the water.

Tighten the pack band as much as possible before securing it, and test the tightness by grasping the tank valve with one hand and the top of the pack with the other hand. Try to move the pack up and down on the tank. If there is movement, the band needs to be tighter.

Attach the regulator assembly to the scuba tank. The tank valve should have a valve protector or a piece of tape over the valve opening. Remove the cover or tape (but do not litter with the tape—put the tape in a trash container or in your gear bag). Loosen the regulator yoke screw and remove the dust cover. If your regulator second stages have purge depressors, release the purges. Expel any water or dirt from the valve by opening the tank valve slightly and momentarily before you attach the regulator to the tank.

Your regulator has several hoses. Orient the hose to your primary second stage to the same side of the tank as the handle of the tank valve so that the hose will come over your right shoulder. When you orient the hose this way, the other hoses orient automatically as long as they are untangled and can hang freely.

Carefully seat the inlet opening on the regulator on the valve outlet and turn the yoke screw or DIN fitting until it is snug but not tight. Tighten the fittings with your fingers and thumb. (See Figure 6.8 for an example of a regulator attachment.)

Attach various regulator hoses to the scuba unit. It is easier to attach the low-pressure hose to the BC before you pressurize the hose. Attach your instrument console to the BC, but do not attach your extra second stage yet.

Turn on the air. Hold the SPG with the front of it facing away from you and others so it will not injure anyone if it fails when pressurized. The SPG blowout plug should prevent an explosion from occurring, but orienting the gauge is a good precaution to take. Open the tank valve slowly in a counterclockwise direction. Open the valve all the way; then close it one-quarter turn. You will feel the hoses stiffen under pressure. Listen for leaks in the system. If the regulator free-flows, cover the mouthpiece opening with your

How can you test the height of the tank so your scuba unit fits properly?

What is the proper orientation of your primary second stage hose to the handle of your tank valve?

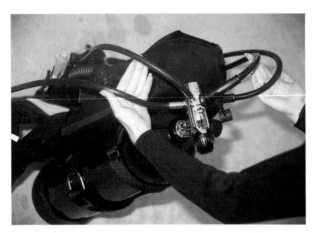

Figure 6.8 Your regulator and hoses should look this way if attached correctly to the cylinder.

How will you know if you haven't opened the tank valve sufficiently?

Under what conditions is it a good idea to don your BC in the water?

thumb to stop the flow. If air leaks from the tank valve seal, turn the air off, remove the regulator, and inspect the seal. You may have to replace the O-ring. Solve all air leakage problems before you use the scuba unit.

Testing the unit is the final step. Use your SPG to make sure the tank is full. Reset instruments in your console as needed. While looking at the SPG, depress the regulator purges momentarily to test the second stages and clear them of any debris; then breathe deeply through each second stage several times. The tank pressure reading should remain constant while you breathe from the regulator. If the pressure reading drops when you inhale, you have not opened the tank valve sufficiently. Do not open a valve partially to check the pressure of a tank. When you have finished testing the regulators, attach the extra second stage to the BC. Depress the low-pressure inflator valve on the BC for 1 or 2 seconds to make sure the valve functions correctly. When you have completed the assembly and testing of the unit, lay it on its side with the regulator and instruments on top.

Equipment assembly procedures are the same for experienced divers and new divers alike. Always assemble and test your scuba equipment before you suit up. Practice will help you recall the assembly procedures.

Donning Equipment

With skin diving equipment, you don the weight belt after the skin diving vest, but with a jacket-type BC, it usually is better to don the weight belt before the scuba unit.

A good way to don a scuba unit out of the water is for your buddy to hold the system and help you into it. Once your arms are through the shoulder straps, bend forward and balance the unit on your back while you secure the waistband. Place the regulator hoses over your shoulder while you fasten the waistband to keep the hoses from being trapped beneath the waistband. Some dive boats have vertical tank racks on seats to allow you to sit while donning the system. But do not sit on the deck or ground to don a scuba tank, because the tanks of other scuba divers may strike you in the head.

Some divers prefer to don the scuba unit in the water—a good practice if you dive from a small boat or have a minor back problem. Put the scuba unit into the water first. To don a jacket-type BC unit the way you would don a coat in the water, inflate it fully, sit on it, put your hands through the armholes, and slide off and into the unit. Or you may don your scuba unit over your head. Maneuver the tank in front of you with the valve facing you and the backpack facing up. Place the regulator in your mouth and keep the primary second stage hose between your arms. (If you place your right arm inside the loop of the hose, it will wrap around your arm when you try to lift the tank over your head.) Place your forearms completely through the armholes just past your elbows, and begin to lift the scuba unit over your head. Rather than lifting the unit, push yourself down in the water and duck beneath the scuba unit. Lower the tank into position on your back. Use your left hand to pull your snorkel clear of your BC as the tank lowers into position. When the tank is in place, lean forward and secure the waistband.

Inspecting Equipment

What implications does the acronym BAG have for scuba divers?

When you have donned your scuba equipment and the remainder of your diving equipment, inspect all your equipment to make sure it is positioned, adjusted, and functioning correctly. Your buddy should do likewise. Then inspect each other's equipment.

There are three areas of equipment inspection: buoyancy, air supply, and general. The acronym *BAG*, which uses the first letter from each area, is a handy memory jogger. Specific checks for each area are listed in the following sidebar.

BAG Method of Inspecting Equipment

Buoyancy (B)

- The weight system is in place.
- The quick release is accessible.
- The weights are free to drop.
- The weight belt has a right-hand release.
- You know how to operate the weight system release.
- The BC is operational.
- The low-pressure inflator functions.
- The deflator valve functions.
- The CO_2 mechanism (if there is one) functions.*

Air supply (A)

- The tank is full and the tank valve is open all but one-quarter turn.
- All regulator hoses are oriented correctly and free for use.
- The primary and secondary second stages function.
- The alternate air source is secured in such a way it will not free-flow, and you can locate it easily.

General (G)

- Your buddy's equipment is complete.
- The equipment is correct from head to toe.
- Remember that you can see things your buddy cannot see.

*To inspect the CO_2 mechanism, unscrew the cartridge and examine it to ensure that it has not been used. While the cartridge is removed, examine the firing pin to make sure it moves freely when you operate the firing arm. Return the firing arm to the unfired position, and replace the cartridge.

Equipment inspections are important. It is easier to solve problems before you enter the water than afterward. It does not take much time to inspect each other's equipment, but the practice can save a lot of time. Make predive inspections a habit.

Basic Scuba Diving Skills

To be a scuba diver (and enjoy diving with minimum risk of injury), you need to learn the proper procedures for skills such as entering and exiting the water, controlling your buoyancy, descending and ascending, monitoring your instruments, and coordinating with a buddy. This section provides a helpful introduction to these skills, but you must learn them by doing. You will learn the skills in pool-like conditions and then apply them in open water.

Entry Techniques

The four basic types of water entries for divers are wading, seated, feet-first, and backroll (see Figure 6.9). You need to learn when to use which type and the procedures for each. The objective of any entry is to get into the water the easiest way possible without injuring yourself or losing any equipment. After you enter the water and are under control, switch from your regulator to your snorkel if you are going to swim or remain at the surface.

You can make open-water entries from the shore or from a boat. Shore entries may be wading entries, or you may enter from a human-made structure, such as a dock, pier, or jetty. There may be surf. Bottom conditions can range from smooth and soft to rough and firm. The bottom may slope gradually or steeply, and there may be holes and drop-offs. There may be plants, animals, and rocks in the entry area. The conditions vary greatly, and so do the entry techniques. A good entry technique for one location will be inappropriate for another. It takes experience and knowledge of the area to determine an effective entry procedure.

There are some general techniques to keep in mind when making wading entries at an open-water site. A wading entry sounds simple, but diving equipment affects your center of gravity, your mobility, and your peripheral vision. You must walk backward when wearing fins.

If there is very little or no surf, you may be able to wade in, don your fins, and begin your dive. Breathe through your regulator, and have your BC inflated partially. Shuffle your feet to detect holes and rocks and to chase away bottom-dwelling creatures. When the water reaches your thighs, lie down in the water and start swimming. In some areas with muddy bottoms, do not wade because you can sink deeply into the mud and lose a fin when you try to extract your foot. Where the bottom is firm and the water is calm, you can wade into the water without your fins and don them in the water. It helps to have information about the bottom conditions of a dive site.

> How should you enter the water when there's a muddy bottom? High surf at the shore?

Figure 6.9 You can enter the water in several ways: wading in, feet-first, from a seated position, or with a backroll.

In most areas where there is surf, don your fins before you enter the water and do not remove them until you are clear of the water after the dive. Time your entry to coincide with small waves (see the discussion on wave sets in chapter 2). Keep all equipment in place and breathe through your regulator. Deflate your BC because you want to duck beneath breaking waves when they are higher than your waist. If you inflate your BC, you will be unable to duck beneath the waves and a large wave could lift and toss you. Hold your mask with one hand at all times; spread your fingers and curl them over the top of the mask so you can see. Keep your knees bent and shuffle sideways into the waves to minimize your profile to the moving water. Stop moving just before a wave hits you, allow the wave to pass, then resume your shuffling until the water is deep enough to swim. Allow incoming waves to pass over you, and move through the surf zone quickly.

To enter the water from a commercial dive boat, you may enter from the side or from a water-level platform at the back of the boat. Have all equipment in place, breathe from your regulator, and hold your mask securely. Have any specialty items, such as a camera, handed to you after you are in the water or retrieve them from an equipment line. When entering from the side of a boat, note the direction of boat movement. Wind will cause an anchored boat to swing from side to side. If you enter the water at the wrong moment, the boat may pass over you after you enter.

You can do a controlled-seated entry from a dock, swimming platform on a boat, or any surface where you can sit close to the water, which may be only a few feet deep or too deep to stand. With all equipment in place, turn and place both hands on one side of yourself on the surface on which you are seated, lift yourself slightly, move your body out over the water, and lower yourself into the water. A controlled-seated entry is a simple, easy, controlled entry.

Use feet-first entries when the distance to the water is too high for a seated entry, such as when entering from a commercial charter boat. There are two types of feet-first entries: giant-stride and feet-together.

Use the giant-stride entry when the distance to the water is about 3 to 5 ft (0.9 to 1.5 m) and you desire to remain at the surface during the entry. Stand at the entry point with all equipment in place and your BC partially inflated. Observe the point of entry, and make sure the area is clear. Hold your mask firmly with one hand, spreading your fingers so you can see. Look straight ahead while stepping out with one leg. The entry is a step, not a hop or a jump. If you step out as far as you can, your trailing leg follows automatically. Keep one leg extended forward and the other leg extended backward until you hit the water; then pull your legs together quickly to stop your downward momentum. As soon as you stabilize at the surface, turn and signal that you are OK, and then move away from the entry point so the next diver may enter.

Use the feet-together entry when the distance to the water is too high for a giant-stride entry and when you are concerned about discomfort from the impact with the water. The procedures

> **Describe the difference between giant-stride and feet-together entries.**

are the same as for the giant-stride entry except that after you step out from the entry point, you bring your legs together before you hit the water. A feet-together entry submerges you. After you bob back to the surface and stabilize, signal the next diver and clear the entry area.

A backroll entry can be done from either a seated or a squatting position. You should use the seated backroll entry from a low, unstable platform, such as a small boat. Use a backroll entry when the distance to the water is too high for a controlled-seated entry and the platform is too unstable for you to stand. To do a seated backroll, sit with all equipment in place and your back to the water. Move your bottom to the very edge of the surface on which you are sitting. Have someone make sure the entry area is clear. Hold your mask with one hand and your mask strap with the other hand. If you do not hold the mask strap, the force of the water may wash it up over your head and your mask may fall off. Lean backward to begin the entry. Hold your knees to your chest as you roll backward to avoid clipping your heels on the edge on which you were seated. You are likely to do a backward, disorienting somersault in the water with this entry. You can reorient yourself when you bob back to the surface.

A squatting backroll is used when there is no suitable surface on which to sit. The thin side of a small, rocking boat is a good example of an unsuitable seat. For a squatting backroll entry, prepare yourself while sitting on an adequate seat immediately adjacent to the entry area. Make sure the entry area is clear, then stand partially, turn your back to the entry area, and literally sit down into the water. Pull your knees to your chest as you enter so you do not catch your heels.

Recovering and Clearing the Regulator

When you are in the water wearing scuba equipment, you need to recover your regulator second stage from behind your right shoulder when you get ready to use it. The second stage will have water inside, so you must clear the water before you breathe. If you start with the regulator in your mouth, you need to place the regulator in the water. The task is more difficult than it sounds because if you place the second stage in the water with the mouthpiece facing up, the regulator free-flows. Place the second stage in the water with the mouthpiece facing downward to prevent free-flow.

There are two ways to recover the regulator second stage from behind your shoulder. The most popular method is the sweep method. Lean to the right side so gravity swings the second stage away from you. Reach back with your right hand until you touch the bottom of your scuba tank, and then extend your arm and sweep it forward in a large arc. The hose will lie across your arm, where you can retrieve the second stage easily.

The second method of recovering the second stage is the over-the-shoulder reach. Reach back toward your regulator first stage with your right hand while lifting the bottom of your scuba tank with your left hand. Grasp the second stage hose where it attaches

If you're diving from a small, rocking boat with narrow edges, what kind of entry should you use?

Why is it important to place the regulator mouthpiece facedown in the water?

to the first stage and follow it down to the second stage end. Some divers find this recovery method difficult or impossible.

Clearing the regulator can be as simple as exhaling into it. As long as the exhaust valve is at the lowest point, the water inside the second stage will be displaced. If the exhaust valve is not at the lowest point when you exhale, only part of the water may be exhausted, and you may inspire some water when you inhale. To avoid choking on inhaled water, find out where the exhaust valve is on your regulator, be sure to make it the lowest point when you clear your regulator, and inhale cautiously after clearing the regulator.

Another method to clear a regulator second stage—the purge method—uses low-pressure air to clear the water from the chamber. If you insert the mouthpiece into your mouth and depress the purge, you may blow water down your throat. There are two ways to prevent this. One way is to depress the purge lightly as you place the bubbling regulator in your mouth, and use back pressure from your lungs to keep water out of your mouth and throat. The other method is to place the regulator in your mouth, block the opening with your tongue, and depress the purge momentarily to clear the chamber. Either method is acceptable. If you are purging the regulator while placing it in your mouth, release the purge the moment the regulator is in place to avoid overinflating your lungs.

Snorkel-Regulator Exchanges

You need to be able to switch between breathing from your snorkel to breathing from your regulator and vice versa. When you prepare to descend for diving, you exchange your snorkel for your regulator; when you surface after a dive, you exchange your regulator for your snorkel. Do both exchanges with your face in the water. Take a breath, exchange one mouthpiece for the other, and clear the new breathing device.

BC Inflation and Deflation

There are three ways to inflate a BC and two ways to deflate one, and you should be familiar with all of these means.

The easiest and most commonly used means of inflation is the low-pressure inflator, which is used to add air to the BC in short bursts. Inflating the BC for several seconds can cause serious buoyancy control problems if the inflator valve sticks. By adding air a little at a time, you will have better control of your buoyancy.

If your low-pressure inflator or your integrated second stage develops a problem while you are diving, you may need to disconnect the low-pressure hose. When you disconnect the hose, the low-pressure inflator no longer functions, so you will have to control buoyancy by orally inflating the BC. The mouthpiece of a BC usually is more elaborate than the mouthpiece of a skin diving vest. To help exclude water from a BC, the mouthpiece has a purge so the water inside may be cleared before you open the

How can you avoid inhaling water when you first begin to use your regulator?

If you use the purge method of clearing your regulator, when should you release the purge?

valve to the BC. To clear the BC mouthpiece and inflate the BC, follow these procedures:

1. Insert the mouthpiece into your mouth.
2. Exhale a small amount of air into the mouthpiece to clear it.
3. Keep the mouthpiece in your mouth.
4. Depress the manual inflator-deflator valve.
5. Exhale into the BC.
6. Repeat the procedure until you achieve the desired buoyancy.

You may use the same bobbing technique at the surface that you learned for the skin diving vest (see page 125), but oral inflation procedures are different underwater. To inflate a BC orally underwater, follow these steps:

1. Grasp the inflator valve with your left hand and your regulator second stage with your right hand.
2. Take a breath.
3. Insert the BC mouthpiece into your mouth.
4. Clear the mouthpiece.
5. Exhale most of the air in your lungs into the BC.
6. Save enough air to clear the regulator, which fills with water when you remove it from your mouth.
7. Repeat the procedure until you achieve the desired buoyancy.

The third method of BC inflation is with a CO_2 detonator, an optional feature many diving professionals consider neither necessary nor desirable. If you choose to equip your BC with this option, take care of the mechanism and know how to operate it.

You can deflate your BC with the manual inflator-deflator valve or with a dump valve. If you do not use a dump valve, you must open the deflator valve at the lower end of the BC hose and hold it higher than the highest point of the BC. It is more convenient to use a dump valve than the deflator valve. Note that you can deflate your BC only when the exhaust port is the highest point. Air will not escape if you try to deflate a BC in a horizontal or inverted position, so you need to be in an upright position to deflate your BC.

What position must your body be in to deflate your BC?

Testing Buoyancy

There are similarities between buoyancy testing for skin diving and buoyancy testing for scuba diving, but there also are some important differences. Buoyancy varies more when you scuba dive than when you skin dive, and the volume of air in your lungs also varies more with scuba diving. You dive deeper, so suit compression affects your buoyancy more. As you use air from your scuba tank, your buoyancy changes. You need to sense buoyancy changes quickly to maintain control of your buoyancy.

Your initial buoyancy test for scuba diving can be the same as for skin diving. Begin by testing your BC at the surface. Inflate it fully, then deflate it. Make sure the low-pressure inflator and all deflator valves function correctly. With your regulator in your mouth and your BC completely deflated, relax and breathe slowly. When your lung volume is high, you should remain at the surface with your eyes just below the interface. If you sink with your lungs full of air, you need to remove some weight. When you exhale completely, you should sink. If you cannot sink after a complete exhalation, you need more weight. Test your buoyancy while you are close to your point of entry, and correct any buoyancy problems before you dive.

As you descend in open water, you may need to add air to your BC to maintain neutral buoyancy. Strive to maintain a neutral state of buoyancy continuously. Add air to your BC in small amounts, and test your buoyancy by stopping all motion and observing what happens. If you are sinking, inhale and add air to your BC. If you are rising in the water, exhale and release air from your BC. With experience you will know when to add air to or vent air from your BC and how much air to add or release.

To evaluate your buoyancy on the bottom, assume a rigid, face-down position with your arms at your sides. If your buoyancy is correct, a slow, full inhalation will raise your shoulders while your fin tips remain on the bottom and a slow, complete exhalation will cause your shoulders to sink. Some people call this buoyancy evaluation **diver's push-ups** (although you do not use your hands). If you do not rise with a full inhalation, add a small amount of air to your BC and try again. Figure 6.10 shows a diver doing diver's push-ups.

> **diver's push-ups**
> **Buoyancy evaluation where, when weighted properly, a full inhalation will raise the shoulders while the fin tips remain on the bottom and an exhalation will cause the shoulders to sink**

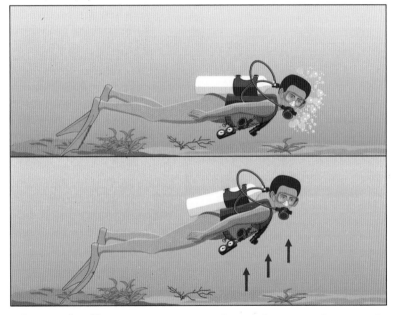

Figure 6.10 Successfully performing diver's push-ups indicates good buoyancy control.

As a scuba diver, you want enough weight to get down at the beginning of a dive and enough weight to allow you to remain in control when you ascend at the end of the dive. The precise weight for scuba diving is the amount you need to hover at a depth of 15 ft (4.6 m) with 300 psi (20 ATM) of air in your tank and no air in your BC. The amount may overweight you slightly at the beginning of a dive. Test your buoyancy at a depth of 15 ft (4.6 m) at the end of a dive to see if you need to make an adjustment for your next dive.

Controlling Buoyancy

No skill identifies a scuba diver's ability as much as buoyancy control. The ability to finely control buoyancy is important for safety, for enjoyment, and for the welfare of the environment. When your buoyancy is out of control, a hazard exists for both you and the environment around you.

With your buoyancy adjusted to the point where you can pivot on your fins on the bottom while inhaling and exhaling, push yourself about 2 ft (0.6 m) off the bottom and remain motionless. You may or may not remain in a horizontal position, but that is not important. Maintain your depth by controlling your average lung volume, but remember to breathe continuously. If you are sinking, keep more air in your lungs. If you begin rising, reduce the amount of air in your lungs. With practice, you will be able to hover motionless just off the bottom.

To demonstrate mastery of hovering, assume a vertical position in the water. Cross your legs at the ankles, grasp a wrist with the opposite hand, and remain motionless. Find an eye-level reference and develop the ability to hover motionless while upright in the water. Pay attention to the buoyancy effects of breathing. Once you master hovering in both horizontal and vertical positions, you will realize several benefits. Your air will last longer, swimming will not tire you as much, you will need fewer buoyancy adjustments, and you will do less damage to the diving environment. Once you can hover, your buoyancy control will continue to improve with practice until you become a highly experienced diver.

Another skill useful for maintaining neutral buoyancy is a BC venting technique called an **open-valve ascent**. When you ascend, air in your BC expands and affects your buoyancy. You must release the expanding air to maintain control of buoyancy. If you vent the air from time to time, your buoyancy will be in a constant state of change: You may not release enough air, or you may release too much. The open-valve ascent is a better alternative. Hold the BC inflator-deflator valve just below the level of your shoulder, point the mouthpiece of the inflator-deflator valve downward, and open the deflator valve. Air will not escape because the opening is lower than the exhaust port of the BC. While you hold the mouthpiece downward and the deflator valve open, raise the inflator-deflator slowly until air just begins to bubble from the mouthpiece. Bubbling occurs when the mouthpiece and the exhaust port on the BC are at the same level. If you hold the inflator-deflator valve at the bubbling level while ascending, the expanding air inside the BC will bubble out through the open valve and your buoyancy will remain constant. If you need to release additional air to control buoyancy, raise the inflator-deflator slightly; if you need to decrease the amount of air you release, lower the assembly slightly.

Using the Dive Flag

You should display the appropriate dive flag or flags when diving. Some areas require you to use a flag, but authorities in all areas encourage use of a dive flag. Follow these conventions when you use a dive flag: Display the flag only when divers are in the water, and surface within 100 ft (30 m) of your flag—the closer the better. The flag does not guarantee your safety from boaters, who are supposed

> **What advantages are there to mastering buoyancy control to the point that you can hover motionless?**

> **open-valve ascent**
> A method for maintaining neutral buoyancy during an ascent by keeping the BC inflator-deflator valve open while holding the valve in a special way

What is the maximum distance you should surface from your flag?

Figure 6.11 Surface as close as possible to a dive flag.

to give the flag a berth of at least 100 ft (30 m), but it does serve as a signal to many boaters who recognize that the flag means divers are in the vicinity. Figure 6.11 shows divers using a dive flag.

If you support your flag with a surface float, you will need to tow your float to the area where you wish to dive. In areas lacking underwater plants, you may be able to tow the float while you dive. In areas with plants, you need to anchor the float to keep it from drifting away, and you must navigate back to the flag at the end of your dive. Tow a surface float behind you when entering through surf, and push it ahead of you when exiting through surf.

Descending

Scuba descents are different than skin diving descents. You'll need to learn several procedures. You usually descend head-first when skin diving, but scuba divers descend feet-first. This is because a feet-first descent allows better control of buoyancy, provides better orientation, allows buddies to maintain contact during descent, helps prevent the swallowing of air, and allows easier equalization of air spaces.

Descending involves several procedures, which seem complex at first but become routine with practice. The process of descending includes preparing to descend, initiating the descent, and completing the descent.

1. Preparing to Descend
   - Check your instruments. Orient yourself at the surface and set a reference on your compass. Be sure your underwater timer and depth gauge are zeroed.
   - Confirm that your buddy is ready to begin.
   - Exchange your snorkel for your regulator.
   - Pressurize your ears slightly to begin the equalization process.
   - Hold your BC deflator valve in your left hand.
   - Give or acknowledge the signal to descend.

2. Initiating the Descent
   - Begin the descent by venting your BC. It is better to do this with the dump valve than to hold the deflator valve above your head. Hold the inflator-deflator valve in your left hand throughout the descent so you can add or release air from your BC at any time. Exhale fully to help get started downward.
   - Breathe shallowly for the first 10 ft (3 m).
   - Equalize your ears about every 2 ft (0.6 m) for the first 15 ft (4.6 m). If you experience equalizing problems, ascend a few feet (about 1 m) to reduce the pressure, equalize again, and redescend. Exhale some air into your mask to prevent a mask squeeze.
   - Keep your fins still while you descend so you do not stir up silt on the bottom.
   - Control your rate of descent by the average amount of air you keep in your lungs. When you begin sinking while

contact descent
A descent made by maintaining contact with a descent line or the slope of the bottom

noncontact descent
Vertical descent without contact with a line or the slope of the bottom

your lungs are full, add a short burst of air to your BC to regain neutral buoyancy.

3. Completing the Descent
   - Remain with your buddy throughout the descent.
   - Avoid contact with the bottom.
   - Hover above the bottom, level off to a swimming position, agree on a direction with your buddy, and begin your dive.

There are two types of descents in open water: contact and noncontact. Whenever possible, do a **contact descent**. A **noncontact descent** is more difficult to control.

Clearing the Mask

Above the surface, water inside a mask will run out if you pull the bottom of the mask away from your face. Water inside a mask underwater also flows out the bottom of the mask if you displace the water with air. It is easy to put air inside the mask—just exhale lightly through your nose. A long, light exhalation is better than a short, forceful one because a strong exhalation blows air past the seal of the mask and does not displace water effectively.

To clear a mask while scuba diving, you need to be able to breathe through your mouth with your nose exposed to water. With concentration and practice, you can master this skill quickly. Try inhaling through your mouth and exhaling through your nose first, and then try inhaling and exhaling through your mouth. If you feel water going up your nose, exhale through your nose immediately to keep the water out.

To clear a mask that has a purge valve, seal the mask against your face, tilt your head downward to make the purge the lowest point in the mask, and exhale through your nose until the mask is clear of water.

To clear a mask without a purge, hold the top of the mask against your forehead, take a breath, and start exhaling slowly. When the level of the water is below your eyes, tilt your head back while continuing to exhale and the remainder of the water will flow out the bottom of the mask. You must be exhaling when you tilt your head back or water will run up your nose. Bubbles from the bottom of the mask indicate that you have cleared all the water from your mask. It may sound like it takes a long time and a lot of air to clear a mask, but with practice you will be able to flood and clear your mask several times after a single inhalation. Clearing requires only a few seconds.

To practice clearing a mask, you must flood it with water. This is not difficult, but a few tips make it easier. If you exhale lightly while tilting the mask forward on your face to break the seal at the top, the mask releases from your face easily, and the air escapes at the highest point. When you reseat your mask to begin clearing it, hold back any strands of hair with one hand while you reseat the mask with the other. Hair under the mask causes leakage. If you are wearing a hood, make sure the hood is clear of the mask before attempting to clear water from the mask.

What factors require
closer proximity to your
buddy?

Buddy Diving

It is important to have a companion while diving. A buddy provides reminders and assistance and sees things that you might not see. Buddies inspect each other's equipment, provide feedback based on observations, and work as a team. Dive buddies should remain close enough to each other that each can immediately assist the other in an emergency. The more turbid the water and the greater the depth, the closer buddies should remain to each other. During your training strive to remain within touching distance of your buddy at all times; learn to keep track of your buddy. It is not difficult to maintain contact with a dive buddy in open water when you follow a few standard procedures.

Agree on a position relative to one another and maintain that position as much as possible. That way, your buddy will know where to look for you, and you will know where to look for your buddy. The best dive team configuration is side by side; the least desirable is for one diver to be behind the other.

Agree on a direction of movement. Both parties should maintain that direction until both agree to proceed in a different direction. When you follow this practice, there are fewer directions to consider if you and your buddy become separated.

Confirm your buddy's position every few seconds. If you scan the areas ahead from side to side while swimming, you should get a glimpse of your buddy each time you turn your head in your buddy's direction.

When visibility is poor, physical contact can keep you and your buddy together. Holding hands is appropriate. Or you can use a **buddy line** to keep in contact with each other.

If you become separated from your buddy underwater, look for your buddy for up to 1 minute. If you are unable to locate your buddy, ascend slightly and turn in a circle while looking for bubbles. The visibility often is better a few feet above the bottom than it is on the bottom. If you do not see your buddy's bubbles, ascend to the surface and wait for your buddy, who also is supposed to follow this procedure. When you have reunited at the surface, descend again and continue your dive. Obviously, it is better to remain together underwater than to surface to reunite.

If you are unable to relocate your buddy underwater and if your buddy does not surface promptly, look at your surroundings to mark your position so you will know the approximate location where your buddy was last seen. If someone is overseeing the diving operations, notify that person that your buddy is missing so a search can be initiated. If you are alone, try to locate bubbles that could indicate your buddy's position.

buddy line
A short piece of line used to keep in contact with a diving partner when visibility is low

Swimming Underwater

When you swim along the bottom, your fins can raise a cloud of silt that harms the environment and reduces visibility. Silting is more of a problem when you are overweighted because the excess weight angles your fins toward the bottom when you swim (see Figure 6.12). The first step in reducing silt is to weight yourself properly.

Figure 6.12 Overweighting causes divers to stir up silt.

What action should you take if you kick something underwater?

compass heading
The direction in which a diver is moving as determined by a compass

compass course
A series of headings that lead to a destination

square course
A series of headings that allows the diver to travel in a square pattern so that the dive ends where it began

In areas where the bottom silt is thick, add air to your BC to make yourself slightly buoyant underwater. The buoyancy forces you to swim at a slight downward angle and keeps your fins' thrust directed upward. Another way to reduce silt is to remain far enough from the bottom to keep from disturbing it. Finally, consider changing your kick if you boil up silt with your kick strokes.

When you kick something while swimming, you must overcome the tendency to want to get away from whatever you kick. Your kicks are strong and can damage the environment or injure another diver. As soon as you feel something with your fin, stop kicking, look back to see what you have hit, and maneuver yourself clear before proceeding.

Navigation

To find your way underwater you can use natural navigation or compass navigation. You can best determine your relative position with a combination of these types.

Natural navigation is the use of your natural surroundings to determine where you are. Light, shadows, plants, formations, water movement, depth, and other natural indicators can help you navigate. As you move, note your surroundings. Ask yourself which way you are going relative to the movement of the water, to sand ripples on the bottom, to the depth contour, and to the angle of the sun. By noting natural aids to navigation, you can find your way underwater.

A dive compass increases the accuracy of navigation. (See Figure 6.13 for an example of a dive compass.) You need to be able to set a **compass heading** and to determine which way you are going relative to the directional reference you have set. Your compass should have a lubber line that you point in the direction of travel. The north-seeking needle or card of the compass establishes a position relative to the lubber line as long as you hold the compass in a level position. Many dive compasses have index marks on a movable bezel. You set the index marks to indicate the heading.

To go in the direction set on the compass, you must hold the compass so the lubber line is directly in line with the centerline of your body. If the lubber line points to one side, you will not be on course even though the north reference is at the correct point on the dial.

There are many types of **compass courses**. One frequently used course is the **square course**. To navigate a square course, set your initial heading and proceed in that direction for a given distance, which may be measured by time, tank pressure, or fin kicks. Stop, turn 90° to the right while continuing to keep the lubber line aligned with the centerline of your body. Note the relative position of north on the compass, and proceed in the new direction the same distance you did on the first leg of the course.

Figure 6.13   A dive compass.

How can you determine if you have good instrument-monitoring skills?

Stop again, and turn another 90° to the right. Note the position of north on the compass, which should be opposite your initial heading. Proceed along the third leg of the course the same distance as before. Stop once more, turn again 90° to the right, note the relative position of north, and follow the new heading back to your starting point.

Divers also frequently follow a **reciprocal course**, an out-and-back course. Set the initial heading on the compass. Then at the midpoint of the dive, turn 180° until north on the compass is directly opposite the original heading, and follow the reciprocal heading back to your starting point.

If you do not know precisely where you are when the end of a dive is near, it may be wise to surface, find a reference for your exit, and set a compass heading that leads directly to the end-of-dive location. Be especially careful if you surface more than 100 ft (30 m) from your dive flag.

A compass provides correct directional reference information when it is not affected by nearby objects. Metal objects, other compasses, and electrical fields within a couple of feet of a compass can cause the compass reading to deviate from its correct reading. Keep metal, magnets, dive lights, and other compasses away from your compass to help ensure accuracy.

Monitoring Your Instruments

Most diving instruments are passive: They do not provide information unless you look at them. Some instruments emit an audible beep (one dive computer talks), but most require observation to provide information. Develop the habit of checking your instrumentation frequently while diving so you can control your depth, dive time, and direction and avoid running out of air. You should be able to accurately estimate your tank pressure at any time during training. If you cannot estimate the pressure within 300 psi (20 ATM) at any time, you need to monitor your submersible pressure gauge (SPG) more frequently.

When you are planning to dive in open water, look at your instruments when you assemble your equipment. Look at your instruments again when you inspect your equipment, again before you descend, and again while you descend. Refer to your compass for directional reference before you begin moving underwater. Monitor your gauges every few minutes while diving, and compare your air pressure with your buddy's several times during a dive. At any given time during a dive, you should be able to estimate accurately your depth, your dive time, your direction, your tank pressure, and your buddy's tank pressure. If you cannot do this, you need to improve your instrument-monitoring skills.

Scuba Diving Hand Signals

Scuba divers use several hand signals that are not used for skin diving. The scuba signals relate to air supply. Learn and use the standard hand signals described in Figure 6.14. Remember to display hand signals clearly and deliberately and also to acknowledge them.

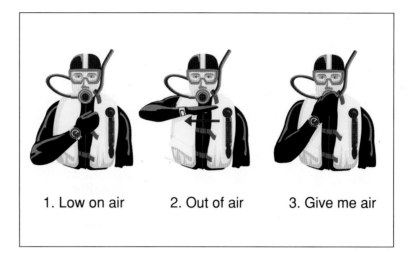

1. Low on air   2. Out of air   3. Give me air

Figure 6.14 Scuba diving hand signals.

Normal Ascents

Scuba ascents are different than skin diving ascents, but there are a few similarities. The procedures become automatic with practice and experience.

To initiate an ascent, one member of a buddy team gives the ascent signal, which the other acknowledges. Always obey the ascent signal. Prepare to ascend by noting your time, depth, and remaining air. Locate and hold your BC inflator-deflator assembly in your left hand. Begin the procedures for the open-valve ascent described on page 143.

Begin ascending slowly with your buddy while breathing continuously. Monitor your depth gauge and keep tabs on your buddy. The maximum rate of ascent is 1 ft/s (.3 m/s) which is quite slow. Some instruments warn you when your rate of ascent is too rapid. You need training, practice, and awareness to avoid exceeding the maximum rate of ascent.

Stop and decompress (outgas) for 1 to 3 minutes at a depth of 15 ft (4.6 m) to help prevent DCS. The procedures for decompression are discussed in chapter 7. As you ascend, look up and around. Extend one hand above your head for protection against overhead obstacles. Make one full rotation to view the surrounding area as you near the surface.

When you reach the surface, make another rotation to view the area, then inflate your BC to establish buoyancy. Exchange your regulator mouthpiece for your snorkel.

Handling Equipment

There will be situations when you need to remove, adjust, and replace scuba equipment while you are in the water. You may need to remove equipment to exit the water onto a boat, to make an adjustment, or to free the equipment from an entanglement. With training and practice, you should be able to handle your equipment easily.

Removing the scuba unit is easy because it is similar to removing a coat. Open the releases, slip your left arm free, swing the scuba tank forward under your right arm, hold the scuba unit with your left hand, and pull your right arm free. It is easier to free your left arm if you insert your hand and wrist through the armhole of the BC first and remove it hand-first than it is to try to pull your arm through first. If you are at the surface in water too deep to stand when you want to remove your scuba unit, remove your weight belt first and place it on a surface float or support station. Replace the scuba unit in the water according to the in-water donning procedures presented on pages 134-135.

Exit Techniques

The technique you'll use to exit the water will depend on the situation. To exit from shallow water in a swimming pool, begin by removing your weight belt, tank, and fins (in that order). Carefully place the equipment on the side of the pool; then climb out by using the ladder or lifting yourself up onto the edge of the pool.

To exit from the deep end of a swimming pool, begin with your BC partially inflated. If you exit using a ladder, grasp the ladder with one hand and remove your fins with the other, maintaining contact with the ladder at all times. Place your fins on the edge of the pool or slide the heel straps over your wrists; then climb the ladder to exit the water. Clear the exit area at once, and take your fins with you.

To exit from deep water without a ladder, begin by carefully placing your weight belt out of the water. Remove the scuba unit and use one hand to trap the regulator hose against the surface onto which you will exit. Place both hands on the exit edge. With the regulator hose trapped under one hand, lower yourself to about chin level in the water while you extend one leg forward and one leg backward. Move upward and pull your legs together forcefully in a strong scissors kick to provide upward momentum. Pull with your arms until you are far enough out of the water to push downward and lift yourself from the water. Immediately after your exit, turn around and pull your scuba unit from the water carefully.

If you're exiting onto a boat that has a ladder, keep your tank on and use the ladder exit technique. Maintain contact with the ladder at all times when you are in the water. If the boat has a platform at the rear, you usually swim onto the platform, remove your fins, and then stand on the platform and board the vessel.

Techniques for wading exits in open water vary with the environment. Usually, you should wear all your equipment until you are clear of the water. Shuffle your feet along the bottom while moving backward.

Surf exits require training and practice. Stop outside the breaking waves and evaluate the surf. Approach the surf zone with your regulator in your mouth and your BC deflated. Hold your mask continually in the surf zone. Follow a breaking wave, and allow additional waves to pass over you until the water is only a couple of feet deep. If the surf is mild, you may stand at that point and back out of the water. If the surf is strong, swim until you can crawl; then crawl clear of the water. (Figure 6.15 demonstrates the different exit techniques.)

Figure 6.15 Exiting the water requires care and forethought, and the method you choose depends on the conditions.

When you are clear of the water, work with your buddy to remove your fins. The buddy system is in effect all the time, not just while you are in the water.

Disassembling Equipment

The first step in disassembling your scuba equipment is to turn off the air by turning the valve in a clockwise direction. Release the pressure in the hoses by depressing the purge on the regulator second stage. Keep the purge depressed until you bleed all the air from the hoses. Next, disconnect all hoses connected to the scuba unit—the low-pressure inflator, the extra second stage, and the SPG. Loosen the yoke screw and remove the regulator from the tank. Dry the first stage dust cover thoroughly and replace it. Loosen the tank band and remove the BC from the scuba tank.

Managing Physiological Problems

If you do everything you are trained to do as a scuba diver, you can avoid problems. But it's not a perfect world. If you fail to pay attention or forget to do something, a problem may occur. Good divers can deal with nearly any problem. This section introduces you to proven ways of dealing with potential diving difficulties. Do not be overly concerned about the problems presented. You can prevent them, but knowing how to deal with them helps reduce your apprehension.

Difficulties affecting your physiology include seasickness, dizziness, stress and panic, overexertion, coughing, and cramping. When you have one of these conditions, your body sends messages that something is wrong. You need to know the messages and the physical actions you can take to help your body overcome physiological difficulties.

Seasickness

It is best to prevent seasickness (see chapter 4) because taking medication after you are seasick is usually ineffective. If you do get seasick, you are likely to vomit. Vomiting underwater can be dangerous due to involuntary gasping that can cause you to choke. Only you can determine your degree of nausea. If you throw up or feel you are on the verge of doing so, do not dive. If you feel queasy, getting into the water may help you overcome the feeling. Some divers who feel slightly nauseated find that they feel better if they get into the water quickly and dive. After the first dive, they are fine for the remainder of the day.

Surface if you feel nauseated while diving. If you must vomit underwater, do not vomit through your regulator. Hold the second stage against one corner of your mouth and depress the purge fully

Why is vomiting underwater dangerous?

while you vomit. You should get air instead of water if you gasp. When you have finished throwing up, place the second stage in your mouth, clear it, and resume breathing. The purge method should be a last resort.

If you are seasick and have to throw up while aboard a boat, do it over the rail on the side of the vessel opposite the wind. Do not use the rest room, or head, as it is called on a boat. The best remedy is to get to land, rest until you feel better, take seasickness medication, and return to the vessel. If you are ill from motion sickness, there is land nearby, and the dive boat has a dinghy, request to be taken to shore for a while so you can overcome your illness.

Dizziness

The absence of visual clues in a weightless environment can cause temporary dizziness. Visual references can help you prevent disorientation (see chapter 4). Injury, temperature changes, and pressure changes affecting the inner ear also can cause a whirling feeling called vertigo, which may be more difficult to overcome than dizziness caused by disorientation.

To cope with either dizziness or vertigo, first seek a fixed visual reference. If possible, make physical contact with something solid for a point of reference. If there is nothing to see or to grasp, close your eyes and hug yourself. In most cases, dizziness will pass in a minute or two. If you then move slowly and keep your head still, you should be able to surface. A good buddy will recognize your difficulty and assist you.

What three steps can you take to overcome dizziness underwater?

Stress and Panic

When you face a situation you feel is beyond your ability to manage, you experience stress, which affects your physiology. Stress affects your breathing, circulation, and awareness. Unless you exercise control over your thoughts and body, stress can lead to panic—a sudden, uncontrolled, unreasoning, inappropriate, fearful reaction to a real or an imagined danger. Avoid panic. It is the diver's worst enemy.

Stress has a cycle. A problem (real or imagined) triggers a fight-or-flight physiological reaction. Your breathing becomes faster and shallower. If the trend continues, you develop a feeling of air starvation that adds to the anxiety you have, further affecting breathing, which influences how you feel and how you think. Unless you interrupt the cycle, it can continue until you panic. (See Figure 6.16.)

Describe the stress cycle and explain how to control it.

You can control stress, but first you must be aware of it. You must recognize when your breathing is incorrect and intervene. Stop all activity and breathe deeply. Analyze the situation and determine the best action to take. When your breathing is under control, take action to deal with the problem. You can break the stress cycle.

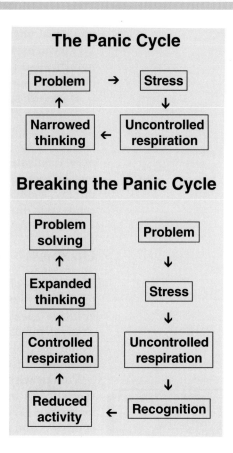

Figure 6.16 The panic cycle and how to break it.

Overexertion

If you work too hard while scuba diving, the equipment may not be able to supply enough air to meet your respiratory needs. You'll experience a sudden feeling of suffocation, and you may suspect your equipment has malfunctioned. It is unlikely that scuba equipment will suddenly malfunction in a way that restricts airflow. More likely than not, overexertion is causing the feeling that you cannot get enough air. You manage overexertion similarly to the way you manage stress. Stop all physical activity and breathe deeply; you should overcome your respiratory problem within a minute or two.

Coughing

When water strikes your larynx, a reflex coughing action tries to clear the foreign matter from your airway. When you cough while in water, you may inhale additional water, which can complicate the situation. You need to overcome the reflex as quickly as possible. The best way is to swallow hard three times in rapid succession. If you must cough, try to do so through a regulator so you will inhale air rather than water if you gasp. You can lose buoyancy as you expel air when coughing, so you may need to establish positive buoyancy if you cough excessively.

Cramps

When your muscles get cold or when circulation to your muscles is inadequate, cramping may occur. A *cramp* is a sudden, strong, involuntary, persistent, painful contraction of a muscle that lacks circulation. Divers tend to get cramps in the lower legs and the feet. To remove a cramp, stretch the affected muscle and rub it to increase circulation. Pounding a cramped muscle is ineffective and causes tissue damage. If you experience a cramp in your leg or foot in the water, you may be able to release it by grasping the tip of your fin and pulling it toward you. Buddies can and should assist one another with cramp removal. Figure 6.17 shows a diver releasing a cramp.

How can you remove a cramp?

Figure 6.17 Grabbing your fin and pulling the tip toward you can release a cramp.

Managing Physical Problems

Potential physical diving difficulties include entanglement; loss of buoyancy control; loss of air supply; and a distressed, injured, or incapacitated buddy. As with physiological problems, you can overcome these problems, but you should be able to avoid them. It is much better to prevent problems than to deal with them.

Entanglement

In the water you probably will encounter fishing line, nets, wire, string, and rope, and these items may entangle you. Underwater plants can also entangle divers in some areas. Streamlining your equipment to minimize places where things can get caught helps reduce the chance of entanglement. Being aware also helps. When you encounter something that can entangle you, swim around it, or push it beneath you and swim over it. Avoid swimming beneath things that could cause entanglement. The area of your tank valve and regulator first stage is one of the easiest places to become entangled and also one of the most difficult areas to free from entanglement.

If you become entangled underwater, stop. Then try to examine the problem without turning because turning often compounds the problem. If you can reach the entanglement, free yourself. If not, signal to your buddy to help you get free. If you can see what you are doing, you may use your dive knife to cut yourself free. Trying to cut yourself free from something in the area of your tank valve would be an obvious mistake. If your tank is entangled, you can't reach the entanglements, and your buddy is not nearby to lend assistance, remove your scuba unit, free it from entanglement, and then put it back on.

> **What is the safest way to free your tank from entanglement if you can't reach the entanglement and if your buddy isn't nearby?**

Loss of Buoyancy Control

You could lose control of buoyancy underwater if you lose weights, if a low-pressure inflator on your BC or dry suit sticks, or if the CO_2 cartridge on your BC accidentally detonates. You can take steps to prevent loss of buoyancy control. Check your weight system from time to time while diving to make sure it is secure. Inspect your low-pressure inflators before each use, and have them serviced at the first sign of unusual operation.

If your weights fall off underwater, immediately maneuver yourself into an inverted position, swim down forcefully, and retrieve the weights. If you are successful, you will be able to avoid an uncontrolled ascent; if you are unsuccessful, you will float to the surface. Your rate of ascent will depend on how buoyant you are without your weights, the type of exposure suit you are wearing, the amount of air in your BC at the time, the depth, and the amount of surface area you can expose to the direction of motion. You learned about resistance to movement, or drag, in chapter 3. The greater the cross-sectional area of an object moving in a given direction, the greater the resistance to movement in that direction. If you lose control of buoyancy and your ascent is uncontrolled, you can slow your rate of ascent by **flaring**, which is the method recommended to slow a buoyant ascent. Figure 6.18 shows a diver in the flaring position.

> **flaring**
> **A method of slowing an uncontrolled ascent by arching the back, extending the arms and legs, and positioning the fins so they are parallel to the surface**

Unless you care for your BC inflator carefully and have it serviced annually, the inflator valve will stick eventually. If your low-pressure inflator valve sticks in the open position, the first action you should take is to hold your BC vent open. Modern BCs vent air faster than the low-pressure inflator admits air. If the inflator valve remains stuck, disconnect the low-pressure hose. If you are unable to vent enough air to control your buoyancy and an uncontrolled ascent results, flare to slow your rate of ascent.

CO_2 compresses more than air. If your BC has a CO_2 detonator and it misfires underwater, the resulting buoyancy will depend on the pressure (depth), the water temperature, and the size of the

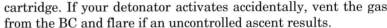

Figure 6.18 Flaring is an appropriate way to slow a buoyant ascent.

cartridge. If your detonator activates accidentally, vent the gas from the BC and flare if an uncontrolled ascent results.

Loss of Air Supply

You are unlikely to have air supply difficulties if you have your regulator serviced annually, if you maintain your regulator properly, and if you monitor your SPG. Potential problems are a regulator that free-flows, low air pressure, and no air to breathe. There are ways to deal with each of these difficulties.

Sand, dirt, and freezing can cause regulator free-flow. If free-flow occurs, your best course of action is to switch to your extra second stage. You also could use your buddy's extra second stage. If there is no source of air except the regulator that is free-flowing, you can breathe from it by pressing your lips lightly against the mouthpiece, taking the air you need, and allowing the excess air to escape. Look down while you breathe from the regulator to keep the escaping air from causing your mask to leak.

You are supposed to end a dive with at least 300 psi (20 ATM) of air in your tank. If you are inattentive and breathe nearly all of the air from your cylinder while diving, it will become difficult to get air from your regulator. Divers often refer to this situation as being "out of air," but, in reality, they are out of air only at the depth at which breathing is difficult. As you ascend, the lower ambient pressure allows you to obtain additional air from your tank. When breathing becomes difficult and your tank is nearly empty, use your buddy's alternate air source (AAS) or ascend while continuing to breathe shallowly through your regulator.

In the rare event that you should completely lose your primary source of air while underwater, you have five ascent options. The order of preference for ascent options is shown in Figure 6.19.

Emergency Ascent Option Hierarchy

5. Buddy breathe.

4. Make a buoyant emergency ascent (BEA)
if the depth is 50 ft (15 m) or greater.

3. Make an emergency swimming ascent (ESA)
if depth is less than 50 ft (15 m).

2. Breathe from buddy's alternate air source (AAS).

1. Breathe from a backup scuba unit.

Figure 6.19 Loss-of-air-supply flowchart.

An extra second stage—assisted ascent—an octopus-assisted ascent—closely approximates a normal ascent. You ascend while breathing from your buddy's extra second stage. When you require air underwater, get your buddy's attention and give the signals for "out of air" and "give me air," if possible. If your buddy's extra second stage and primary second stage are similar, your buddy will hand you, or you may take, the extra second stage. If your buddy has an extra second stage integrated into the BC low-pressure inflator, he or she will hand you the primary second stage and breathe from the integrated second stage. If you are unable to gain your buddy's attention, take his or her extra second stage, begin breathing, and then signal your buddy that you have no air. After you establish a breathing rhythm, hold on to each other and ascend normally.

An emergency swimming ascent (ESA) is a scuba ascent you do using only the air in your lungs. The ascent rate of an ESA is faster than a normal ascent but not rapid. Retain your regulator in your mouth and try to breathe from it from time to time. Do not hold your breath, or you risk a lung overexpansion injury. If you exhale too much air, you will have a strong urge to breathe. The key to a successful ESA is to exhale enough air so your lungs remain at a comfortable volume. When you do an ESA correctly, you can ascend 50 ft (15 m) easily without an overwhelming desire for air. If the depth is 50 ft (15 m) or more, establish buoyancy by discarding your weights to initiate a buoyant emergency ascent (BEA). Swim for the first portion of the ascent, but allow yourself to drift up when buoyancy can replace swimming. Flare during the last 15 ft (4.6 m) of a BEA, and keep your lungs at a comfortable—but not maximum—volume.

Buddy breathing is the least desirable loss-of-air option; it jeopardizes the safety of two people. You and your buddy should practice buddy breathing at the surface before beginning a dive if

Explain the difference between an ESA and a BEA.

buddy breathing
The sharing of a single regulator second stage by two divers

buddy breathing is a loss-of-air option for the dive. Buddy breathing attempted by two divers who are not proficient with the skill can result in disaster, but proficient buddy breathers can make a loss-of-air situation a mere nuisance.

Initiate buddy breathing with the "out of air" signal followed by the signal for "give me air." Your buddy holds the regulator second stage in the right hand and grasps your shoulder strap with the left hand. Your buddy extends the second stage toward you and holds it in such a way that you have access to the purge. You grasp the wrist (not the regulator) of the donor with your left hand and your buddy's shoulder strap with your right hand. Guide the second stage into your mouth and push your lips against the mouthpiece to make a seal instead of inserting the mouthpiece into your mouth. By not putting the mouthpiece into your mouth, you can exchange the regulator quickly and reduce mask leakage caused by facial movements. Take several quick breaths initially; then pass the regulator back to your buddy. Exhale a small amount of air continuously when you are not breathing from the regulator. The exhalation helps prevent a lung overexpansion injury during ascent. After the initial contact, you and your buddy should each take two breaths before passing the regulator. Do not inhale fully when buddy breathing, because full breaths cause buoyancy problems or a lung injury. A medium inhalation is adequate because you receive air every few seconds. (See Figure 6.20.)

> **Why shouldn't you put your buddy's regulator in your mouth when buddy breathing?**

Figure 6.20 Buddy breathing requires good skills and cooperation.

As soon as you and your buddy establish a breathing rhythm, you should swim to the surface, holding on to each other throughout the ascent. Blow bubbles continuously when the regulator is not in your mouth. Remember to control your buoyancy.

Skills for loss-of-air situations require proficiency, so they must be learned well and renewed periodically. Discuss the procedures for a loss-of-air situation with your buddy and agree on the options you will use. You should both be familiar with the signals, positions, and techniques.

Assisting Your Buddy

You have read about many ways in which you may assist your buddy and how your buddy can assist you, so you should realize the importance of the buddy system while diving.

In addition to helping your buddy handle entanglements, cramps, equipment problems, and loss-of-air situations, you may need to provide assistance if your buddy is incapacitated from exhaustion, illness, or injury.

A buddy who becomes excited at the surface needs assistance in regaining control. Help such a buddy establish buoyancy, calm down, and breathe slowly and deeply. When the situation is under control, you may be able to help your buddy resolve the difficulty that caused the excitement.

If your buddy becomes exhausted at the surface, provide assistance with the bicep push or the fin push. Both pushes are illustrated in Figure 6.21. Use the bicep push when your buddy can help and the fin push when your buddy is too exhausted to help at all. Monitor your buddy and offer encouragement as you provide assistance.

Figure 6.21 The bicep push and fin push are ways to assist an exhausted buddy.

Managing Emergencies

Diving accidents occur when divers do not exercise good judgment or when they fail to follow recommended practices. If you do what you are supposed to do, the chances of your being the victim of a diving accident are extremely small. But you may have to render aid to someone else who violates safety rules. This section identifies the aid you should be capable of providing.

Training and Preparation

Three types of emergency preparedness training are recommended for all divers: first aid, cardiopulmonary resuscitation (CPR), and diving rescue techniques. You can get first aid and CPR training from various public service organizations. You'll learn some diving rescue techniques in your entry-level course, but you should complete a rescue specialty course.

Emergency preparedness includes having emergency equipment and information available. Emergency equipment desirable at a dive site includes

- a diving first aid kit,
- an oxygen delivery system,
- a blanket (if appropriate), and
- drinking water.

You may not have all of the emergency equipment yourself, but you can determine if it is available aboard a boat or as part of an organized dive.

Have a means of communication—a telephone, cellular phone, CB radio, or marine radio—to summon assistance. Have contact information for local emergency medical assistance and for the emergency treatment of divers at the dive site. Have phone numbers and radio frequencies for local emergency support services. Examples of numbers to have include those for the U.S. Coast Guard, paramedics, hospital, ambulance, sheriff's office, recompression facility, and the International Diver's Alert Network (IDAN). IDAN has a 24-hour emergency number to assist with coordinating the response to diving accidents. You should be an IDAN member and know the IDAN emergency number, which is (919) 684-8111.

> List the phone numbers you should have available in case of an emergency.

Rescues

An unconscious diver underwater will drown unless rescued immediately. Illness, drugs, and blows to the head can cause loss of consciousness. If you discover an unconscious diver underwater, make the diver buoyant and get him or her to the surface immediately. You need not concern yourself about expanding air if the diver is not breathing because an unconscious person exhales automatically regardless of head position. Do not be concerned about the diver's decompression status; he or she can be treated for bends but will die after 4 minutes without air. Do not jeopardize your safety when attempting to rescue another diver.

A nonbreathing diver needs air quickly and must get it at the surface. This is where your CPR and diving rescue techniques training are invaluable. Open the person's airway. Often this is all an unconscious person needs to be able to breathe. To open the airway, tilt the head back. Turn the person's head to the side to drain water from the mouth and throat. Vomiting is common, so be prepared for it. Clear vomitus from the mouth and throat at once, or the person may inhale it.

How often should a
person who's not
breathing get a breath
from the rescuer?

A person who is not breathing requires rescue breathing and medical assistance. Call for help. While keeping the person's airway open, lightly pinch his or her nostrils to seal them. Seal your mouth over the other person's and fill his or her lungs with air. It is easier to ventilate a person in the water if you turn his or her head toward you slightly. Give the person a breath every 5 seconds while swimming to safety. Watch for vomiting. If water flows into the victim's mouth, turn the person's head to the side and drain the water before continuing rescue breathing. The preferred method of in-water artificial respiration is with a rescue breathing mask, which you can carry in the pocket of your BC. Figure 6.22 shows a person administering rescue breathing using such a mask.

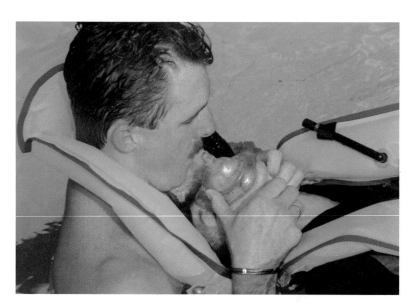

Figure 6.22 Rescue breathing with a breathing mask.

You probably will not be able to detect a pulse in the water, so don't bother trying. You cannot administer CPR in the water; you must remove the victim from the water, and position him or her on a firm surface.

First Aid

There are some aspects of diving first aid that standard first aid courses do not teach. This section addresses the basics of those aspects, but you need additional study and training—which you can get in rescue specialty and oxygen administration courses.

We have addressed the most important aspects—breathing and circulation—of diving first aid. Nothing is more important than attending to basic life support. The next priority for first aid treatment of any serious diving injury is treatment for shock. Lay the injured diver on the back or side, keep the person warm (but avoid overheating), and administer sips of water if he or she is conscious. When you suspect an air embolism, DCS, or near drowning, have the person breathe oxygen in the highest possible concentration. Keep any diver who has been unconscious in the water or who has symptoms of DCS lying down until he or she can be evaluated at a medical facility. Monitor the injured diver continuously.

You should be able to recognize signs and symptoms that indicate a serious diving illness. In addition to unconsciousness, the following symptoms indicate an injury that requires the prompt administration of oxygen and medical treatment:

- Sudden, extreme weakness
- Numbness
- A "pins and needles" sensation
- Paralysis
- Unequal pupils
- Inability to do simple motor skills

There are venomous marine animals in different parts of the world. A few venomous animals can inflict life-threatening punctures or stings (see chapter 2). The wounds can cause pain, weakness, nausea, shock, mental confusion, paralysis, convulsions, depression or arrest of breathing, and even cardiac arrest. Fortunately, such wounds are rare.

First aid for venomous puncture wounds involves removing all foreign matter from the wound, applying hot packs to the injured area for a half hour, and keeping the injured area below the level of the heart. Obtain medical attention.

First aid for a venomous sting includes killing any stinging cells that are in contact with the skin, removing any residue, cleansing the area, applying an analgesic ointment for pain relief, and obtaining medical attention. Vinegar is a good solution to apply to stings to neutralize stinging cells initially.

You may not recall the first aid procedures in the event of an accident, so it is a good idea to have a diving first aid book on hand to help you identify an injury and administer the appropriate first aid.

| **What solution helps stop stinging?** |

Managing Accidents

If a serious diving accident occurs, and no supervisory personnel are available to take charge, you must manage the situation to the best of your ability. Summon help, but do not leave a seriously injured diver unattended. Enlist the aid of others. Try to locate the injured diver's identification and medical information. Write down what happened, the person's dive profile, his or her symptoms, times, and so forth. Pin the information in a conspicuous place, and send it with the injured diver to the medical facility. Accompany the patient to the medical facility, if possible.

Summary

The skills of diving range from simple skin diving procedures to complex scuba skills to problem management. You need to learn the skills correctly the first time, practice them until you can do them easily, and renew them frequently to keep yourself proficient. You also need to be trained and prepared to handle a diving emergency.

7 Dive Planning

First you learn the theory of diving, then the skills, and then you apply what you have learned. Your training objective is to qualify to dive without supervision; this involves planning your underwater excursions.

In this chapter you'll learn about all phases of dive planning—advance planning, short-term planning, on-site planning, and postdive planning. You'll also learn how to obtain area orientations and how to do dive profile planning. An essential part of dive planning is to schedule your time and depth to help avoid DCS.

Dive-Planning Factors and Phases

A well-planned dive helps increase enjoyment and satisfaction and decreases the risk of injury. A poorly planned dive can be disappointing, embarrassing, and discomforting. After you read this chapter, you will understand the significance of the expression "Plan your dive, then dive your plan."

Dive-Planning Factors

Many factors affect your plans for a dive or a dive trip. Keep the considerations that follow in mind when you are looking ahead to a dive outing.

Health and fitness are important. Illnesses, required medications, and recent operations probably disqualify you for diving. If your health is not normal, consult a diving physician. If there is any doubt, do not dive until you are in good health. Try to prevent motion sickness if you are prone to it.

The climate is a big factor affecting dive planning. If you dive close to where you live, dive planning is easier than if you intend to dive thousands of miles away. A difference in climate usually means a big difference in diving conditions, which means a difference in your equipment requirements.

When you travel many hours to a diving destination, the distance affects your planning. Allow a day to rest and recover from travel before you dive. After 2 or more days of repetitive diving, wait 1 full day before flying home.

Weather affects diving conditions significantly. Storms and sudden changes in the weather can make diving dangerous. Know the weather forecast, and reschedule your dive if the weather forecaster predicts poor weather. Know the expected wind speed, air temperature, and water conditions.

Seasonal changes affect water movement, water visibility, air and water temperatures, entry and exit areas, and the presence of certain types of animals. You should know what to expect at a dive site at different times of the year. It helps to know the visibility, water temperatures, tides, surf, surge, currents, bottom composition, silt conditions, plants, and animals.

You need to be physically and mentally fit for diving. Fitness for diving implies that you

- are well rested,
- are well nourished,
- have the physical strength and stamina to meet the requirements of the environment and the activity,
- are qualified for the activity,
- are not apprehensive about your plans,
- are not goaded into doing something you are not prepared to do, and
- do not allow pride to affect good judgment.

Your objective for the dive affects your planning. Different diving activities require different plans and equipment. For example, the planning of an underwater photography dive is not the same as the planning of a dive where you intend to hunt for game.

You must know and observe laws, regulations, and customs. Some areas have laws that require use of a dive flag. Obey fish and game regulations. Some diving professionals discourage the taking of any living thing in an area. You need to know the behavior expected of you. It is better to know the expectations in advance than to be embarrassed at the dive site.

Etiquette is important. Will early diving activities be offensive to home owners adjacent to the dive site? Will the parking of vehicles at a site irritate people? Be considerate of others who may be in the area where you intend to dive. Consider the impact of noise, the changing of clothes, and dive site access; also consider how your activities affect those fishing nearby. Then make your plans reflect good etiquette.

Advance Planning and Preparation

The first phase of dive planning is the determination of why, who, where, when, how, and what.

? **WHY**—Determine the objective of the dive. What do you want to do? Take photos? Explore? Look for artifacts?

? **WHO**—Determine with whom you want to dive. Select a buddy who is interested in your dive objective.

? **WHERE**—Determine a primary and an alternate site.

? **WHEN**—Determine the best time to dive. The water usually is calmer in the morning in most areas than it is in the afternoon. Tidal currents and height may affect when you dive.

? **HOW**—Decide how to reach the dive site. Who will drive? What are the directions?

? **WHAT**—Determine what equipment you'll need for the dive. Who will bring the float and flag? How many tanks do you need? Are there any special needs for the intended activity?

Advance preparation may include

- making reservations,
- paying deposits,
- buying or renting equipment,
- having equipment serviced or repaired,
- getting tanks filled,
- obtaining a fishing license or permit,
- buying film for photography, and
- obtaining emergency contact information.

Your preparations usually include a trip to your local dive facility. Inspect your equipment before you go. You may discover a needed repair that requires some time to complete. Identify your equipment needs early.

Short-Term Planning and Preparation

The day and evening before you intend to go diving, you need to do two things. First, find out the weather forecast and current water conditions so you can determine if conditions will be acceptable for your diving activities. Call your dive buddy to discuss and confirm your plans. Last-minute revisions, such as going to the alternate site, may be necessary. If you anticipate poor diving or weather conditions, reschedule the dive.

The second step of short-term preparation is packing your diving equipment and your personal items. (See the appendix for an equipment checklist.) Write down your dive plans and schedule, and leave the information with a friend. Instruct your friend to notify the authorities if you fail to return by a certain time.

On-Site Planning and Preparation

When you and your buddy arrive at the dive site, determine if the conditions are acceptable for diving. If not, go to an alternate site. If the conditions at the alternate site also are unacceptable, abort the dive.

An important step in assessing a dive site is estimating the current. Look for telltale signs such as kelp bent over from water movement, a wake around the anchor line or behind an anchored boat, or objects drifting on the surface.

Determine the velocity of moving water by measuring how long it takes a floating object to move a known distance, such as the length of your boat. When an object moves 100 ft (30 m) in 1 minute, its speed is approximately one knot (1.15 mph or 1.85 km/hr). When a current exceeds about 1/3 knot (0.38 mph or 0.6 km/hr), you must pay heed to it because you can only sustain a speed of about 3/4 knot (0.86 mph or 1.4 km/hr). Plan the dive so that the current assists you to your exit point at the end of the dive. Figure 7.1 shows a table that can help you estimate current velocity.

If the diving conditions are favorable, determine the diving area. Select the entry and exit areas, and discuss the entry and exit procedures. Agree on the course to be followed during the dive. Agree on time, minimum air pressure, and landmarks for changes in direction. You and your buddy should know in advance approximately where you will be at any time during the dive.

An important part of your planning is the discussion and agreement about buddy system procedures. Decide who is in charge of the team, where you will position yourselves relative to each other, how you will move (steadily or start-and-stop), and what reunion procedures you will follow in the event of separation. Remember communication is much easier on land than it is underwater, so take advantage of the opportunity you have to communicate and coordinate while preparing for a dive.

Why is it important to leave your dive plans with a friend?

How can you determine the velocity of moving water?

List seven things you should discuss with your buddy before you enter the water.

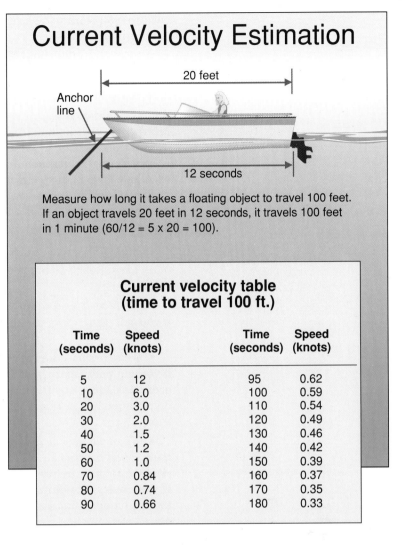

Current Velocity Estimation

20 feet

Anchor line

12 seconds

Measure how long it takes a floating object to travel 100 feet. If an object travels 20 feet in 12 seconds, it travels 100 feet in 1 minute (60/12 = 5 x 20 = 100).

Current velocity table (time to travel 100 ft.)

Time (seconds)	Speed (knots)	Time (seconds)	Speed (knots)
5	12	95	0.62
10	6.0	100	0.59
20	3.0	110	0.54
30	2.0	120	0.49
40	1.5	130	0.46
50	1.2	140	0.42
60	1.0	150	0.39
70	0.84	160	0.37
80	0.74	170	0.35
90	0.66	180	0.33

Figure 7.1 You can estimate the velocity of a current if you time how long it takes a floating object to move the length of your boat.

Plan for emergencies. Agree on air-sharing procedures. Discuss what to do in the event of a serious diving emergency. Know where, how, and whom to call for help. Make sure you both have access to a first aid kit and other emergency equipment. A few minutes spent coordinating procedures before an emergency can save precious seconds should an accident occur.

Scuba diving requires dive profile planning. You and your buddy need to agree on the maximum time and depth for your dive. You must limit time and depth to avoid DCS. We will discuss dive profile planning right after area orientations, which is another important subject.

Area Orientations

Area orientations have been referred to throughout this book, so by now you should understand the importance of learning about a dive site before diving there. Because orientations are vital, and because you want to be a responsible diver, you need to learn how to obtain orientations.

Area orientations may be formal or informal. A formal orientation is one provided as a service by a diving professional. The professional will tell you what to look for and what to look out for in the area and will lead you on a dive. A professional dive guide will provide guidance and suggestions and will point out items of interest as well as hazards. When you have completed a formal orientation, ask the professional to sign and stamp your log book. A continuing education dive course in a new area is another excellent form of formal orientation.

Formal orientations are ideal, but if you cannot arrange one, consider some or all of the following options for an informal orientation:

• *Obtain and read books, articles, and brochures about diving in an area.* Learn as much about an area as you can before you go there.

• *Write to dive stores in the region where you intend to dive.* Ask if you can participate in a dive class session for your orientation to the area.

• *Write to dive clubs in the region where you intend to dive.* Ask if you can participate in a club-sponsored dive when you are in the area. Ask for contact information for several club members who dive regularly and who may be willing to allow you to go diving with them.

• *When you arrive in a new area, find local dive sites and visit them when divers are likely to be there.* Ask the divers about the sites while they are preparing to dive or after they exit from a dive. If you have your equipment ready, you may be able to accompany them on a dive, but make sure they have experience diving at the site.

• *Purchase a space on a diving charter boat.* When you board the vessel, tell the crew you are new to the area. Ask for advice about diving procedures and ask to be introduced to an experienced diver who can provide additional information.

When you dive with local divers, allow them to go first. Do as they say and do as they do. Procedures vary from region to region. A procedure you use in your area may be inappropriate for a different area. For example, in your normal diving environment it may be fine to enter the water from a boat in a current without holding on to a line. But if you tried to do so in an area you aren't used to diving in, you might be swept away at once. Be humble, listen to others, and follow their example to avoid embarrassment.

Dive Profile Planning

There are time limits for how long you may remain at various depths. These limits are determined by the amount of nitrogen

residual nitrogen
Nitrogen remaining in a diver's system from a dive made within the past 12 hours

repetitive dive
Any dive made within 6 to 24 hours (number of hours depends on the dive tables used) of a previous dive

precautionary decompression stop
A 2- to 5-minute delay in ascent at 15 ft (4.6 m) made at the end of every dive to minimize the risk of DCS

absorbed by your body. You may absorb the nitrogen during one dive or during a series of dives, and it takes time to eliminate nitrogen from your body. If you dive again before the excess nitrogen has had time to outgas, you add to the nitrogen already in your body and reach critical nitrogen levels faster than if you did not have excess nitrogen in you before the dive. You need to be aware of the effects of **residual nitrogen** when you make **repetitive dives**. Figure 7.2 shows how the amount of nitrogen in the body builds with repetitive dives. A **precautionary decompression stop** during ascent reduces DCS risk.

Decompression experts use complex mathematical calculations and field testing to establish time limits for various depths for single and repetitive dives. The experts put the time limits (and each diving organization has its own) on tables and calculators and program them into dive computers. You need to know how to use dive planning devices so you can plan your dive profile to minimize your risk of DCS. The table on page 178 shows the maximum number of minutes the major diver training organizations recommend for specific depths.

No dive-planning device can guarantee you will not develop DCS. Dive tables, calculators, and computers provide information

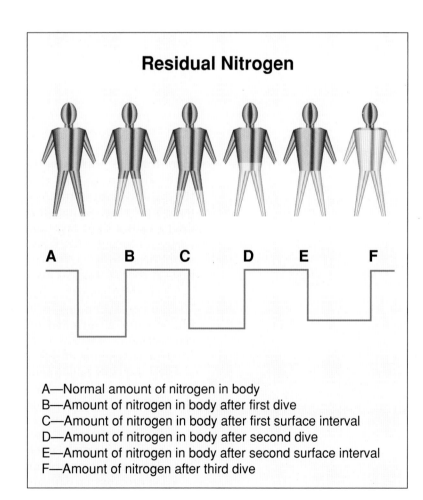

Residual Nitrogen

A—Normal amount of nitrogen in body
B—Amount of nitrogen in body after first dive
C—Amount of nitrogen in body after first surface interval
D—Amount of nitrogen in body after second dive
E—Amount of nitrogen in body after second surface interval
F—Amount of nitrogen after third dive

Figure 7.2 If you make a repetitive dive before allowing the excess nitrogen to leave your body, the nitrogen continues to accumulate.

Dive Time Limits of Various Diver-Training Organizations (in minutes)

	USN	YMCA	NAUI	PADI 1	PADI 2	SSI	DCIEM
30 FSW	–	–	–	–	205	205	300
40 FSW	200	150	130	140	130	130	150
50 FSW	100	80	80	80	70	70	75
60 FSW	60	50	55	55	50	50	50
70 FSW	50	40	45	40	40	40	35
80 FSW	40	30	35	30	30	30	25
90 FSW	30	20	25	25	25	25	20
100 FSW	25	20	22	20	20	20	15
110 FSW	20	13	15	16	15	15	12
120 FSW	15	10	12	13	10	10	10
130 FSW	10	5	8	10	5	5	8
140 FSW	10	5	–	8	–	–	7

Note. FSW = feet of salt water (depth). All other numbers are time limits in minutes. USN = United States Navy; YMCA = YMCA Scuba Program; NAUI = National Association of Underwater Instructors; PADI 1 = Professional Association of Diving Instructors (Dive table); PADI 2 = PADI Recreational Dive Planner (Circular calculator); SSI = Scuba Schools International; DCIEM = Canadian Defence and Civil Institute of Environmental Medicine.

based on statistics acquired through testing. The statistical probability that a diver who adheres to the profile limits of a device will develop DCS is small. The devices assume that you are in good health, you do not get cold during the dive, you do not exert strenuously, and you ascend at the correct rate.

If you dive to the maximum time limits of any dive-planning device, you increase the likelihood of DCS. The shorter your exposure to pressure, the less the chance you'll develop the bends.

Using Dive Tables

More than 30 years ago, the U.S. Navy (USN) developed tables for dive planning. The recreational diving community adopted the military tables and has used modified versions successfully for many years. Although the tables were designed for military diving rather than recreational diving, many decompression experts still consider the USN dive tables—with reduced maximum dive times—to be appropriate tables for recreational use. Variations of the USN tables are used widely today.

The USN tables use compartments with half times of 5 minutes, 10 minutes, 20 minutes, 40 minutes, 80 minutes, and 120 minutes. The amount of nitrogen remaining in the 120-minute (2-hour) compartment determines the group designations of the tables. Because outgassing of a compartment takes 6 half times, you can see why the USN tables define a repetitive dive as any dive within 12 hours (6 × 2 hours) of a previous dive.

The USN dive tables consist of four sets of tables:

- No-Decompression Timetable
- Surface Interval Timetable
- Residual Nitrogen Timetable
- Decompression Timetables

> Why do USN tables consider dives made within 12 hours of each other repetitive dives?

Modifications to the Dive Tables

Diving organizations and manufacturers have modified the USN dive tables to make them more appropriate for recreational diving. The following are some of the typical differences between the USN dive tables and modified USN dive tables:

• *Reduced time limits*. Dive-planning devices today include maximum time limits that are less than the no-decompression limits of the USN dive tables.

• *Reduced depth limits*. The USN dive tables provide dive planning information for depths to 190 ft (58 m). The recommended maximum depth limit for recreational diving is 130 ft (39.6 m). New divers should limit diving to depths of about 60 ft (18 m). Advanced divers qualify to dive to approximately 100 ft (30 m). Divers completing a deep diving specialty course qualify to dive to 130 ft (39.6 m). Depth in water is similar to speed on land. When you qualify for a driver's license, you may drive at speeds up to 65 mph (104.6 km/hr). With experience, you probably will drive faster—but not much faster because it is dangerous. Driving at very fast speeds is hazardous and requires special training, special equipment, and controlled situations to minimize the risk of serious injury or death. Deep diving (beyond 100 ft or 30 m) is similar to race car driving in many respects. Deep diving is a professional endeavor that unqualified recreational divers should not attempt.

• *Revised SITs*. In 1983 a USN study reported a number of errors in the Surface Interval Timetable. The errors usually do not affect the type of diving that recreational divers do, but some modified versions of the tables include the corrections.

• *Combined tables*. Modified versions of the USN dive tables often incorporate information to make the tables easier to use. Table 3 may include the AMDT for repetitive dives along with the RNT. Table 1 often includes required decompression information to eliminate a separate decompression timetable.

> **surface interval time (SIT)**
> **The time spent at the surface between repetitive dives**

Comparison of Dive Table Terms

USN Tables	Modified USN Tables
Bottom time	Actual dive time (ADT)
No-decompression limit	Maximum dive time (MDT)
Equivalent bottom time	Equivalent dive time (EDT)
Surface interval time	Surface interval time (SIT)
Residual nitrogen time	Residual nitrogen time (RNT)
	Adjusted MDT (AMDT)

> **Commit the dive table rules to memory.**

Dive Table Use

After you learn to use the modified USN dive tables in this book (see p. 175), you will be able to use most dive tables because the procedures

maximum dive time (MDT)

The maximum time a diver may spend underwater for the deepest depth reached during a dive

decompression stop

A delay in ascent at a given depth to permit the elimination of excess nitrogen

letter group designation

The letter on a dive table that corresponds to the amount of nitrogen in a diver's body

residual nitrogen time (RNT)

The time in minutes, converted from a letter group designation, that is equivalent to the nitrogen remaining in the body from a previous dive

actual dive time (ADT)

The amount of time a diver spends underwater

equivalent dive time (EDT)

The sum of the ADT and the RNT; ADT + RNT = EDT

are similar. An overview of these modified USN tables makes it easier to understand how to solve a specific dive-planning problem. (See last page of book for dive table purchasing information.)

Table 1 provides three items of information: the **maximum dive time** (MDT) without required **decompression stops** for various depths, a **letter group designation** for various dive profiles, and the time duration for emergency decompression stops.

Table 2 provides letter group information based on your surface interval time (SIT). You begin a surface interval with one letter group designation; as you outgas nitrogen, you acquire lower letter group designations.

Table 3 provides adjusted (reduced) dive time limits based on the amount of nitrogen in your body from a previous dive or dives.

Table 4 converts a letter group designation at the end of a surface interval to an amount of time at a planned depth. You add **residual nitrogen time** (RNT) to your **actual dive time** (ADT), or underwater time, to determine your **equivalent dive time** (EDT) for a repetitive dive. Use the equivalent time, which represents the total amount of nitrogen in your system, to return to Table 1 for a new end-of-dive letter group designation.

Now you're ready to learn how to plan dives using all four tables. The horizontal listings are rows, and the vertical listings are columns.

Rules for using the dive tables are simple and easy to remember.

Dive Table Rules

• When you consult the tables, use the deepest depth you attained during a dive. If you spend part of the dive at one depth and the remainder of the dive at a shallower depth, treat the dive as if you spent all the time at the deepest depth.

• Enter the tables at a depth that is exactly equal to, or is the next depth greater than, the maximum depth of your dive. The USN tables have 10-ft (3-m) increments. If the depth of your dive is 50 ft (15 m), use the 50-ft (15-m) listing. If the depth of your dive is 51 ft (15.5 m), you must use the 60-ft (18-m) listing.

• If the depths shallower than 40 ft (12 m) are not on the version of the tables you use, calculate all dives shallower than 40 ft (12 m) as 40-ft (12-m) dives.

• From the times listed for a specific depth, select the time that is exactly equal to, or is the next greater than, the time of your dive. If you dive to 60 ft (18 m) for 22 minutes, use the 25-minute listing on the tables because there is no 22-minute listing for that depth.

• When time at the surface is less than 10 minutes, add the times of the dives together and use the deepest depth of the dives when you consult the tables. Do not include the surface time as part of your dive time. Although the USN tables indicate a minimum surface interval time of 10 minutes, the minimum recommended time between recreational dives is 1 hour.

HKP Dive Table Instructions

1. Begin first dive at Table 1. Use exact or next greater number for all depths and times. Find end-of-dive letter group at bottom of Table 1.
2. Find end-of-surface-interval letter group at left of Table 2. Use exact or next greater time. Use the letter group to refer to Tables 3 and 4.
3. Actual dive time of a repetitive dive must not exceed the times indicated by Table 3 coordinates.
4. Add residual nitrogen time (RNT) from Table 4 coordinates to actual dive time (ADT) to obtain equivalent dive time (EDT). ADT + RNT = EDT.
5. Use EDT to return to Table 1.

Table 1—MDT and EDT Table

Time (minute)

Ft	M	A	B	C	D	E	F	G	H	I	J	K	L
30	9	15	30	45	60	75	95	120	145	170	205	250	310/5
40	12	15	25	25	30	40	50	70	80	100	110	130	150/5
50	15	→	10	15	25	30	40	50	60	70	80		100/5
60	18		10	15	15	25	30	40	50	60/5	60/5	70	80/7
70	21	→	5	10	15	20	25	30	35	40	50/5	60/8	70/14
80	24		5	10	15	20	25	30	35	40/5	50/10	60/17	
90	27	→	5	10	12	15	20	25	30/5	40/7	40/15	50/18	
100	30		5	7	10	15	20/5	25/5	30/5				
110	33	→	5	10	13	15/5	20/5	30/7					
120	36		5	10	12	15/5	25/6	30/14					
130	39	→	5	8	10/5	15/5	25/10						

Table 2—SIT Table

	A	B	C	D	E	F	G	H	I	J	K	L
↓ L												0:26
↓ K											0:28	0:45
↓ J										0:31	0:49	1:04
↓ I									0:33	0:54	1:11	1:25
↓ H								0:36	0:59	1:19	1:35	1:49
↓ G							0:40	1:06	1:29	1:47	2:03	2:19
↓ F						0:45	1:15	1:41	2:02	2:20	2:38	2:53
↓ E					0:54	1:29	1:59	2:23	2:44	3:04	3:21	3:36
↓ D				1:09	1:57	2:28	2:58	3:20	3:43	4:02	4:19	4:35
↓ C			1:39	2:38	3:24	3:57	4:25	4:49	5:12	5:40	5:48	6:02
↓ B		3:20	4:48	5:48	6:34	7:05	7:35	7:59	8:21	8:50	8:58	9:12
↓ A	12:00	12:00	12:00	12:00	12:00	12:00	12:00	12:00	12:00	12:00	12:00	12:00

Table 3—AMDT Table

ADT + RNT = EDT Return to Table 1

Repetitive dives should not exceed 80 ft (24 m).

M	Ft	A	B	C	D	E	F	G	H	I	J	K	L
9	30										39	229	↑
	40									120	130	138	↑
	50								110				↑
	60	14	15	18	21	24	27	30	33	36	39		↑
	70	29	24										↑
	80	43	14	6	3	3	5	2	2	3	2	5	↑
141		57	24	6	3	3							↓
162		69	33	14	9	7			2	5	2		↓
180		81	42	20	14	12	5	2	5	9	6	2	↓
196		93	51	26	20	17	9	6	9	13	10	5	↓
211		105	59	33	25	22	14	10	14	18	13	9	↓
225		113	67	39	31	27	18	13	18	22	17	12	↓
238		123	74	45	36	31	22	17	22	31			↓

Table 4—RNT Table

Ft	M	A	B	C	D	E	F	G	H	I	J	K	
30	9	12	25	39	54	70	88	109	130	160	190	229	→
40	12	7	17	25	37	49	61	73	87	101	116	138	→
50	15	6	13	21	29	38	47	56	66	76	87	99	→
60	18	5	11	17	24	30	36	44	52	61	70	79	→
70	21	4	9	15	20	26	31	37	43	50	57	64	→
80	24	4	8	13	18	23	28	32	38	43	48	54	→
90	27	3	7	11	16	20	24	29	33	38	43	47	→
100	30	3	7	10	14	18	22	26	30	34	38	43	→
110	33	3	6	10	13	16	20	24					→
120	36	3	6	9	12	15	18	21					→
130	39	3	6	8	11	13	16	19					→

HUMAN KINETICS PUBLISHERS

Box 5076, Champaign, IL 61825-5076
1-800-747-4457

ABBREVIATIONS

ADT–Actual Dive Time
MDT–Maximum Dive Time
EDT–Equivalent Dive Time
SIT–Surface Interval Time
AMDT–Adjusted Maximum Dive Time
RNT–Residual Nitrogen Time

WARNING: NO DIVE TABLE CAN GUARANTEE AVOIDANCE OF DECOMPRESSION SICKNESS. USE THE TABLES CONSERVATIVELY.

Use Table 1 to determine the maximum dive time (MDT) for a dive. Enter the table on the row corresponding to the depth you plan to dive, and proceed to the right to determine the MDT for the depth. The numbers in bold print indicate MDTs.

To use Table 1 to obtain a letter group designation following a dive, enter the table on the row corresponding to the maximum depth of your dive, and proceed to the right to the first time you do not exceed. Proceed downward along that column and obtain a letter group designation for the dive. For example, a dive to 50 ft (15 m) for 30 minutes assigns you to letter group E. A dive to 45 ft (14 m) for 28 minutes also places you in letter group E. (Remember, when you exceed a number, you must use the next larger number.)

Example 1
MDT and EDT Table

Ft	M	Time (minute)											
30	9	15	30	45	60	75	95	120	145	170	205	250	310/5
40	12	5	15	25	30	40	50	70	80	100	110	130	150/5
50	15	→	10	15	25	30	40	50	60		80		100/5
60	18		10	15	20	25	30	40	50		60/5		80/7
70	21	→	5	10	15	20	30	35	40		50/5	60/8	70/14
80	24		5	10	15	20	25	30	35	40/5		50/10	60/17
90	27	→	5	10	12	15	20	25	30/5		40/7		50/18
100	30		5	7	10	15	20		25/5			40/15	
110	33	→		5	10	13	15	20/5			30/7		
120	36			5	10	12	15/5			25/6	30/14		
130	39	→		5	8	10/5					25/10		

		↓	↓	↓	↓	↓	↓	↓	↓	↓	↓	↓
		A	B	C	D	E	F	G	H	I	'	
←	L											
	K											
←	J											
	I											
←	H											
	G											
←	F											
	E											
←	D											

Use the Surface Interval Timetable, Table 2, to determine a letter group designation following a surface interval time. Enter the table using the letter group designation you obtained from Table 1. Move downward along the column until you find the first time (expressed as hours:minutes; e.g., 1:26 is 1 hour 26 minutes) that equals or exceeds your surface interval. Remember that whenever you exceed a number on the tables, you use the next larger number. Follow the column to the left and obtain the new letter group designation. For example, if your letter group was E at the beginning of a 1-hour 58-minute surface interval, your letter designation would be group C at the end of the surface interval. The designation would be letter group C for a surface interval from 1:58 to 3:24.

Example 2
SIT Table

		A	B	C	D	E	F	G	H	I	J	K	L
←	L												0:26
	K											0:28	0:45
←	J										0:31	0:49	1:04
	I									0:33	0:54	1:11	1:25
←	H								0:36	0:59	1:19	1:35	1:49
	G							0:40	1:06	1:29	1:47	2:03	2:19
←	F						0:45	1:15	1:41	2:02	2:20	2:38	2:53
	E					0:54	1:29	1:59	2:23	2:44	3:04	3:21	3:36
←	D				1:09	1:57	2:28	2:58	3:20	3:43	4:02	4:19	4:35
	C			1:39	2:38	3:24	3:57	4:25	4:49	5:12	5:40	5:48	6:02
←	B		3:20	4:48	5:48	6:34	7:05	7:35	7:59	8:21	8:50	8:58	9:12
	A	12:00	12:00	12:00	12:00	12:00	12:00	12:00	12:00	12:00	12:00	12:00	12:00

> **adjusted maximum dive time (AMDT)**
> **The amount of time a diver may spend at depth, considering the RNT and the SIT;**
> **AMDT = MDT – RNT**

Use Table 3 to determine your **adjusted maximum dive time** (AMDT) for a repetitive dive. Residual nitrogen in your body reduces your maximum dive time from Table 1. Table 3 provides the reduced time limits. For example, if your letter group is C from a previous dive or dives and you plan to dive to 70 ft (21 m), your dive time must not exceed 25 minutes.

Example 3
AMDT Table

M	9	12	15	18	21	24	27	30	33	36	39
Ft	30	40	50	60	70	80	90	100	110	120	130

Upper portion:

depth	M							
60	18	5						
70	21	4	9					
80	24	4	8	13	18			
90	27	3	7	11	16	20		
100	30	3	7	10	14	18	22	
110	33	3	6	10	13	16	20	24
120	36	3	6	9	12	15	18	21
130	39	3	6	8	11	13	16	19

Return to Table 1

Repetitive dives should not exceed 80 ft (24 m).

RNT portion (Ft: 30, 40, 50, 60, 70, 80, 90, 100, 110, 120, 130):

30	40	50	60	70	80	90	100	110	120	130	grp
21											L ←
60	14										K
90	29	4									J ←
120	43	14									I
141	57	24	6	3	3						H ←
162	69	33	14	9	7						G
180	81	42	20	14	12	5	2				F ←
196	93	51	26	20	17	9	6	2			E
211	105	59	33	25	22	14	10	5	3		D ←
225	113	67	39	31	27	18	13	9	6	2	C
238	123	74	45	36	31	22	17	12	9	5	B ←

Use the Residual Nitrogen Timetable, Table 4, to convert your letter group designation into a time in minutes that is equivalent to the nitrogen remaining in your body from a previous dive. The amount of time varies depending on the depth of the dive you plan to make. To determine your RNT, find the column corresponding to the depth you plan to dive and the row that corresponds to your letter group following your surface interval. The numbers at the coordinates indicate your RNT. For example, if your letter group was C at the end of the surface interval and you were planning to dive to a depth of 70 ft (21 m), your RNT would be 15 minutes.

Example 4
RNT Table

Ft	M	A	B	C	D	E	F	G	H	I	J	K	
30	9	12	25	39	54	70	88	109	130	160	190	229	→
40	12	7	17	25	37	49	61	73	87	101	116	138	
50	15	6	13	21	29	38	47	56	66	76	87	99	→
60	18	5	11	17	24	30	36	44	52	61	70	79	
70	21	4	9	15	20	26	31	37	43	50	57	64	→
80	24	4	8	13	18	23	28	32	38	43	48	54	
90	27	3	7	11	16	20	24	29	33	38	43	47	→
100	30	3	7	10	14	18	22	26	30	34	38	43	
110	33	3	6	10	13	16	20	24					→
120	36	3	6	9	12	15	18	21	ADT + RNT = EDT				
130	39	3	6	8	11	13	16	19	Return to Table 1				→
M	9	12	15	18	21	24	27	30	33	36	39		
Ft	30	40	50	60	70	80	90	100	110	120	1??		
	21							Repetitive dive?				
	60	14						should not ?				

Add your RNT to the ADT of your repetitive dive to establish the EDT. Using the EDT, reenter Table 1 and obtain a new letter group designation. For example, if your RNT is 15 minutes and your ADT is 20 minutes for a dive to 70 ft (21 m), your EDT is 35 minutes (20 + 15), and your end-of-dive letter group is G.

Example 5
MDT & EDT Table

Ft	M	Time (minute)											
30	9	15	30	45	60	75	95	120	145	170	205	250	310/5
40	12	5	15	25	30	40	50	70	80	100	110	130	150/5
50	15	→	10	15	25	30	40	50	60	70	80		100/5
60	18		10	15	20	25	30	40	50		60/5		80/7
70	21	→	5	10	15	20	30	35	40		50/5	60/8	70/14
80	24		5	10	15	20	25	30	35	40/5		50/10	60/17
90	27	→	5	10	12	15	20	25	30/5		40/7		50/18
100	30		5	7	10	15	20		25/5			40/15	
110	33	→		5	10	13	15	20/5			30/7		
120	36			5	10	12	15/5			25/6	30/14		
130	39	→		5	8	10/5					25/10		
		↓	↓	↓	↓	↓	↓	↓	↓	↓	↓	↓	
		A	B	C	D	E	F	G	H	I	J		
←	L												
	K												
	I												

emergency decompression
A required delay in ascent a diver must take if the ADT or EDT exceeds the MDT for a dive

limiting line
The point at which the recommended duration of a precautionary decompression stop increases beyond 3 minutes

dive profile
A visual representation of a dive made by plotting time and depth

To determine the time for **emergency decompression** for a dive in excess of the MDT, enter Table 1 just as you did to obtain a letter group designation for a dive that did not require decompression. If the ADT or EDT of your dive exceeds the MDT for the depth, decompress at a depth of 15 ft (4.6 m) for the number of minutes indicated to the right of the slash for the bottom time. (The point at which the recommended duration of a precautionary decompression stop exceeds 3 minutes is the **limiting line**.) For example, if your EDT for a dive to 70 ft (21 m) exceeds 40 minutes but is not more than 50 minutes, you must decompress for at least 5 minutes. Following a dive requiring emergency decompression, refrain from further diving for at least 24 hours. Plan your dive profiles so you do not exceed the MDTs.

Dive Profile Terms and Rules

There are several types of **dive profiles**. Figure 7.3 shows a diagram of a standard dive profile. A square profile describes a

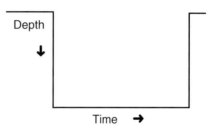

Figure 7.3 Standard dive profile.

dive to a constant depth for a given period of time. It is depicted graphically as a profile with square corners. A multilevel or step profile is a dive that progresses from deep to shallow during a given period of time. When you make a dive in a series of steps, you may refer to it as a **step dive**. A sawtooth profile is a dive that progresses from deep to shallow and back to deep. You should avoid this type of dive, which is depicted graphically as a sawtooth. The fourth profile is the bounce profile. It is a dive with a short ADT, such as a dive to free a fouled anchor. You also should avoid this profile, which is, appropriately enough, depicted graphically as a spike. Bounce-profile dives are sometimes called **spike dives**. Figure 7.4 shows how the four profiles are depicted graphically.

step dive
A dive that progresses from deep to shallow during a given period of time

spike dive
A dive where a diver descends to a depth and ascends again quickly

All dive-planning devices assume you dive according to certain procedures. For example, a dive-planning device assumes you do not exceed a maximum rate of ascent. The USN (or modified USN) dive tables assume a maximum rate of 60 ft (18 m) per minute. Do not exceed this ascent rate. The tables assume you ascend at the correct rate. If you ascend faster, you may get DCS, especially during repetitive dives.

What is the maximum rate at which a diver should ascend?

Why should your first dive of the day be your deepest dive?

Because you absorb nitrogen as pressure increases and it takes time for you to eliminate it, you should always make your deepest dive the first dive of the day; then make each successive dive to a progressively shallower depth. If you make a shallow dive followed by a deeper dive, residual nitrogen from the shallow dive will

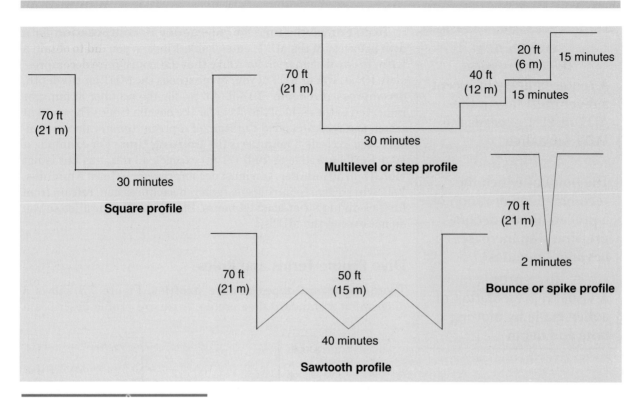

Figure 7.4 Types of dive profiles.

reduce the time you may stay at the deeper depth. When making a multilevel dive, go to the deepest depth first, and ascend to shallower depths as the dive progresses.

Short exposures at depths in excess of 80 ft (24 m) affect certain tissues in the body. Subjecting these tissues to repetitive dives in excess of that depth may result in DCS. Do not make repetitive dives in excess of 80 ft (24 m).

Dive Profile Diagramming

Diagram your dive profiles when planning and recording your dives. Include planned and actual depths, MDTs, ADTs, letter group designations, and SITs. For repetitive dives, include RNTs and EDTs. A simple method for diagramming dive table problems is to use a worksheet like the one shown in Figure 7.5.

Try the following exercise, which combines diagramming with the dive table procedures you have learned. Use the blank diagramming worksheet in Figure 7.5. If you have any difficulties, refer to the preceding section regarding use of each of the tables. Assume all dive times include 3 minutes of precautionary decompression. Calculate and diagram the following series of dives (the answers to the diagramming problem are in the next paragraph and in Figure 7.6):

- The first dive is to 78 ft (24 m) with an ADT of 20 minutes followed by an SIT of 1-1/2 hours.
- The second dive is to 55 ft (16.8 m) with an ADT of 25 minutes followed by a surface interval of 2 hours.
- The third dive is to 40 ft (12 m) with an ADT of 25 minutes.

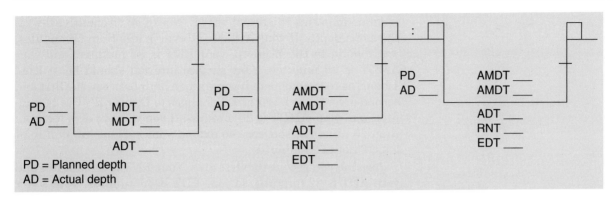

Figure 7.5 Make photocopies of this worksheet to use as you plan your dives.

Solution: The letter group following the first dive is E. Following the surface interval, the letter group changes to D. The RNT for a D diver at 60 ft (18 m) is 24 minutes. The EDT (ADT + RNT) for the second dive is 49 minutes (25 + 24). The letter group following the second dive is H. Following the second surface interval, the letter group changes to E. The RNT for an E diver at 40 ft (12 m) is 49 minutes. The EDT for the third dive is 74 minutes (25 + 49). The letter group following the third dive is H.

The following tips help make dive profile diagramming easier:

- Begin by entering the maximum allowable time (MDT for the first dive and AMDT for repetitive dives) for the planned depth. ADT must not exceed the maximum allowable time.
- Enter a letter group at every upper corner of a profile except the first corner.
- Add ADT and RNT to obtain EDT for every repetitive dive. Use the recall word *ARE* to help remember that you are to add ADT and RNT to obtain EDT.

Planning Time and Depth Limits

Now combine the dive table procedures to plan a series of dives. Use the blank diagram shown in Figure 7.5. Assume the depth of the first dive—the deepest dive—is 60 ft (18 m). The MDT, according to Table 1, is 50 minutes. Assume an ADT of 22 minutes (including precautionary decompression) for the dive. Your letter group des-

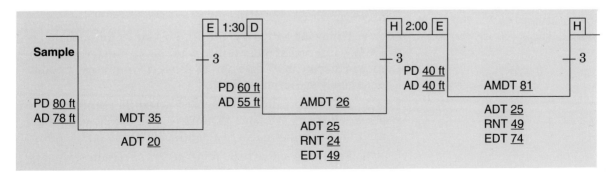

Figure 7.6 An example of how to complete the diagramming worksheet.

ignation following the first dive is E. Now plan a repetitive dive to the same depth. If your surface interval is less than 55 minutes, you remain in the E group, your RNT is 30 minutes, and your AMDT is 20 minutes. Your surface interval should be at least 1 hour, as recommended. If you wait an hour between the first and second dives, your letter group changes to D, your RNT is 24 minutes, and your AMDT is 26 minutes. If you want to dive for more than 26 minutes, you need to extend your surface interval to at least 3 hours 25 minutes.

Assume you repeat the first dive. Your RNT is 24 minutes and your ADT is 22 minutes, so your EDT is 46 minutes. Your letter group following the second dive is H.

Assume the dive site is so good that you wish to make a third dive to 60 ft (18 m). Refer to Table 3 to plan the dive because Table 3 provides the maximum allowable times for various letter group designations. There is no allowable time at 60 ft (18 m) for a diver with a group H designation. Only 6 minutes are allowed for a diver with a group G designation. Proceed up the column. If you want to dive to 60 ft (18 m) again for more than 20 minutes, you need to attain letter group D, which allows 26 minutes of diving without required decompression. When you know the group you need to attain and your starting group, you can plan your surface interval. The Surface Interval Timetable tells you that you must wait at least 2 hours 24 minutes to move from group H into group D.

Use the tables to help you plan dives to avoid emergency decompression. There are three options for planning repetitive dives that will not require emergency decompression. If your RNT prevents you from making a desired dive, you may (a) reduce the duration of the dive, (b) reduce the depth of the dive, or (c) increase the surface interval preceding the dive.

Test what you have learned by answering the following questions. Diagram the problems. Include precautionary decompression time in all dive times. Compare your answers with those following the questions.

Learn this principle: For repetitive dive planning, the minimum SIT for a required group is 1 minute more than the time for a preceding group. For example, the minimum SIT for a group F diver to reach group C is 2:29.

What three things can you do to make a repetitive dive without emergency decompression possible?

Dive-Planning Problems

1. Following a dive to 71 ft (21.6 m) for 27 minutes and a surface interval of 60 minutes, what is the maximum depth to which you may dive for at least 15 minutes without emergency decompression?

2. Following a dive to 77 ft (23.5 m) for 24 minutes and a surface interval of 1 hour 45 minutes, what is the maximum allowable time for a dive to a depth of 50 ft (15 m)?

3. Following a dive to 60 ft (18 m) for 21 minutes, what is the minimum surface interval that will allow a dive of the same duration to the same depth without emergency decompression?

Solutions to Dive-Planning Problems

1. The letter group following the first dive is G. The letter group changes to F after the surface interval. Refer to Table 3. Group F allows 9 minutes for 70 ft (21 m), 14 minutes for 60 ft (18 m), and 33 minutes for 50 ft (15 m). The maximum depth to which you may dive for at least 15 minutes without emergency decompression is 50 ft (15 m).

2. The letter group following the first dive is F. The letter group changes to D after the surface interval. The maximum allowable time without emergency decompression for a group D diver at 50 ft (15 m) is 51 minutes.

3. The letter group following the first dive is E. You must have a letter group designation of D for a repetitive dive of 21 minutes without emergency decompression (refer to Table 3). Changing from group E to group D requires a minimum surface interval of 55 minutes.

Special Procedures

Unusual circumstances may arise that require special procedures. The following are examples of such circumstances:

- A cold or strenuous dive
- Variations in the rate of ascent
- Multilevel dives
- Omitted decompression
- Diving after required decompression
- Altitude after diving
- Precautionary decompression causes ADT or EDT to exceed the maximum time limits.
- The RNT for a repetitive dive exceeds the ADT of the previous dive.

> Memorize the procedures for handling unusual circumstances.

When you have finished studying this section, you should be able to describe the procedures for using the modified USN dive tables for dive profile planning for each of these situations.

When a dive is particularly cold or strenuous, use the next greater time for the dive. If the dive is cold *and* strenuous, use the next greater time and depth.

If you ascend faster than 60 ft (18 m) per minute, extend your precautionary decompression stop by at least 2 minutes. The faster you ascend, the more you should increase the stop time.

Consider dives to multiple levels to be square profile dives with all the time of the dive at the deepest depth of the dive. Do not attempt to extrapolate the dive tables.

If you need to decompress but fail to do so, use the following procedure for omitted decompression. If you have no symptoms of DCS following the dive, remain out of the water, breathe oxygen in the highest concentration possible, rest, drink water, and be alert for symptoms of DCS. Wait 24 hours before diving again. If you suspect DCS, proceed at once to a hyperbaric facility for a medical examination. The USN has a procedure for in-water decompression, but diving medical experts agree this procedure is inappropriate.

If precautionary decompression causes your ADT or EDT to exceed the maximum time limits, determine your letter group designation with the MDT limit.

After a dive that requires decompression, wait at least 24 hours before diving again.

If the RNT for a repetitive dive exceeds the ADT of the previous dive, use the RNT for planning the repetitive dive.

Ascending to altitude after diving increases the likelihood of DCS due to the further reduction in pressure. Driving into the mountains or flying after diving can cause DCS that would not occur if you remained at sea level until you eliminated the excess nitrogen.

The International Divers Alert Network (IDAN) recommends waiting a minimum of 12 hours before ascending to altitude in a commercial jet airliner (up to 8,000 ft or 2,438 m). If you make multiple dives for several days or make dives that require decompression stops, wait for an extended surface interval beyond 12 hours before flight. The greater the interval before the flight, the less likely it is that DCS will occur.

IDAN does not have a recommendation for flying or driving at lower altitudes. The most extensively tested tables for altitudes are the Swiss dive tables, which use a compartment with a much longer half time than the USN tables. A recent approach to altitude delays after diving makes the USN dive tables' surface intervals equivalent to those of the Swiss tables. Converted USN minimum surface intervals in the following Altitude Delay Timetable specify the minimum time to attain permissible nitrogen levels for various altitudes.

Altitude Delay Timetable

Altitude	ABC	D	E	F	G	H	I	J	K	L	Group*
2,000	0:00	0:00	0:00	0:00	0:00	0:00	0:00	0:00	0:00	2:26	K
3,000	0:00	0:00	0:00	0:00	0:00	0:00	0:00	0:00	2:37	4:08	J
4,000	0:00	0:00	0:00	0:00	0:00	0:00	0:00	2:53	4:30	5:51	I
5,000	0:00	0:00	0:00	0:00	0:00	0:00	3:04	4:57	6:29	7:44	H
6,000	0:00	0:00	0:00	0:00	0:00	3:20	5:24	7:12	8:38	9:54	G
7,000	0:00	0:00	0:00	0:00	3:41	6:02	8:06	9:43	11:10	12:36	F
8,000	0:00	0:00	0:00	4:08	6:50	9:11	11:04	12:41	14:19	15:40	E
9,000	0:00	0:00	4:57	8:06	10:48	12:58	14:51	16:39	18:11	23:09	D
10,000	0:00	6:18	10:37	13:25	15:56	18:05	20:10	21:18	23:24	24:50	C

Column group "Starting repetitive group" spans ABC through L.

Note. Times represent the minimum recommended time delay before ascending to listed altitude and are USN surface interval times with a delay factor of 5.4. Altitude is in feet. Times are in hours:minutes; for example, 5:24 is 5 hours 24 minutes.

*Recommended minimum repetitive groups for indicated elevations.

How long must you wait
to ascend to an altitude of
9,000 ft if your starting
repetitive group is G?

Altitude is any elevation above 1,000 ft (300 m). The Altitude Delay Timetable provides recommended time delays for altitudes up to 10,000 ft (3,000 m). To use the Altitude Delay Timetable, enter the table horizontally on the top line and find your starting repetitive group. Next, find the altitude to which you wish to ascend. If you exceed a number, use the next greater one. The time at the coordinates of the desired altitude and your starting repetitive group indicate the minimum time delay recommended before ascending to the altitude selected. Note that for about half the table no delay (0:00) is required.

Profile Contingency Planning

When you plan a dive profile, plan for contingencies. You should know what to do if you unintentionally exceed your planned depth or time, or both. A simple matrix, such as that depicted in Figure 7.7, is helpful. Prepare a contingency matrix before your dives and carry it with you while diving.

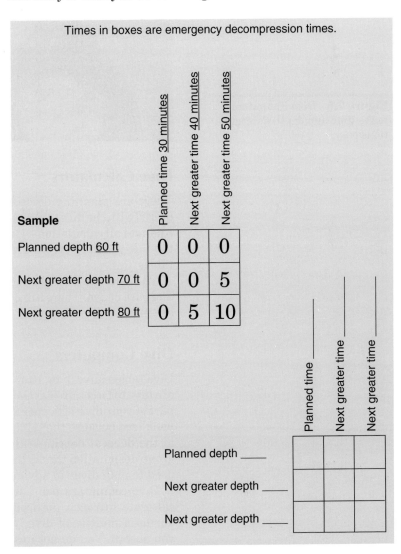

Times in boxes are emergency decompression times.

Sample

	Planned time 30 minutes	Next greater time 40 minutes	Next greater time 50 minutes
Planned depth 60 ft	0	0	0
Next greater depth 70 ft	0	0	5
Next greater depth 80 ft	0	5	10

	Planned time	Next greater time	Next greater time
Planned depth ____			
Next greater depth ____			
Next greater depth ____			

Figure 7.7 A contingency matrix helps you plan ahead for unexpected events.

Using Dive Calculators and Computers

The benefits of a dive computer outweigh the potential problems. Learn how to use dive tables and dive calculators so you will know how to plan a dive if you do not have a dive computer, but plan to obtain a dive computer as soon as you can. Figure 7.8 shows a photo of a dive computer.

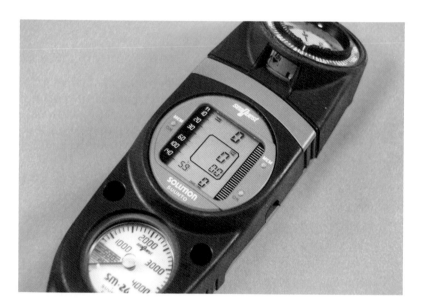

Figure 7.8 Dive computers make time and depth determinations easy.

Dive Calculators

There are planning devices that eliminate the mathematics required with the dive tables. Circle-shaped calculators automatically compute all calculations. Guides on the calculators help eliminate the line-jumping errors divers frequently make when using dive tables.

The calculator for the modified USN tables features simplicity and ease of use. There are only a few instructions for use, and they are printed directly on the calculator.

Dive Computers

Dive tables have 5- or 10-ft increments and require all of the time of a dive to be counted at the maximum depth of the dive. If the first part of your dive is deeper than the remainder of the dive, you are penalized because the tables consider the entire dive to take place at the deepest depth. At the end of the dive you receive a letter group designation that is higher than you deserve. Dive tables are used to plan dives in advance.

Dive computers use 1-ft increments for profile planning and calculate nitrogen absorption continuously. As you vary depth during a multilevel dive, you are charged only for the nitrogen you absorb. You do not incur the maximum-depth penalty of the dive tables, so your RNT is less following a multilevel dive with a dive computer compared to the same dive planned with dive tables. The penalty avoidance is the primary advantage of a dive computer as a dive-planning device. Dive computers provide advance planning information, but you also can carry them with you when you dive, and they provide information about your decompression status continuously.

Regardless of the type of computer you use, you should understand some basic principles.

Dive Computers: Advantages & Disadvantages

Advantages

- You avoid the maximum-depth penalty of the dive tables.
- Dive profile information is accurate.
- Dive computers may provide a stored record of the dive profile.
- Using dive computers eliminates the errors made with manual dive planners.
- Additional features, such as an ascent rate indicator, are available.

Disadvantages

- Dive computers are electronic instruments that can fail.
- Dive computers are expensive to purchase and service.
- Each diver must have a separate computer.
- The mathematical model varies from one type of computer to another, so some confusion results when each diver forming a buddy team uses a different type of computer.
- Not all dive-planning information displayed by a computer may be accepted at face value. You must learn and apply the dive computer guidelines included in this section.

First, be sure to read the instruction manual that comes with your computer. Wait 24 hours after diving with dive tables before using a dive computer. Do not exceed the ascent rate specified by the manufacturer, and do a 5-minute precautionary stop at a depth of 15 to 20 ft (4.6 to 6 m) at the end of every dive. If you exceed the rate of ascent specified for your computer, extend the duration of your precautionary stop by at least the amount of time it should have taken you to ascend to the stop depth. Do not make repetitive dives in excess of 80 ft (24 m). Keep your dive computer activated until its outgassing is complete. If your computer fails at any time during a dive at a depth in excess of 30 ft (10 m), terminate the dive immediately with precautionary decompression. If your computer fails or if you switch it off accidentally, discontinue diving for 24 hours.

If you exceed the maximum time limit for a dive, the computer will display a ceiling. You may ascend no shallower than the ceiling depth. As you decompress, the ceiling will become shallower until it indicates you may surface. When you have a ceiling, you are undergoing emergency decompression, a situation you should avoid. Wait 24 hours before diving again following any dive with a ceiling.

The concept of backup planning with dive tables is good for square profiles, but table planning for multilevel computer dives is not feasible.

Dive Profile Planning Recommendations

Whichever planning device you use, you should follow these recommendations to minimize the risk of DCS. Limit multiple-day, multilevel dives because repetitive multiple-depth profiles make you more susceptible to DCS. After 3 consecutive days of repetitive diving, wait a full day before diving again. Avoid repetitive dives with short surface intervals. Use all dive-planning devices conservatively. Exercise good judgment and common sense.

Planning for the Unexpected

contingency plan
A plan for handling unusual events

After you complete your plans, you need to implement them. The first rule of dive planning is "plan your dive, then dive your plan." When on a dive, you and your buddy should make every effort to do as you had agreed to do before the dive. When circumstances force changes in your plans, it helps to have **contingency plans**. Here are some examples of possible procedure contingencies for a dive. You should have a contingency plan for what to do if you do any of the following:

- Surface downcurrent from a boat when you had planned to surface in front of it
- Are unable to reach or use the exit point you had selected on shore
- End the dive a long distance from your exit location
- Exceed the MDT for a dive
- Experience a failure of your dive computer while diving
- Ascend directly to the surface without precautionary decompression

Postdive Planning

After a dive you and your buddy should reflect on the experience. How closely did the actual dive match the dive that you had planned? If there were deviations from the plan, what caused them? Could you have prevented the deviations with a different plan or approach? What changes can you make to improve the next dive? Some problems may require research, or you may need to ask the advice of a diving professional. The experience of the dive should affect your plans for future dives. Your dives with your buddy should progress more smoothly each time you dive together, and each time you visit a dive site, your dive procedures should improve. A review of each dive with your buddy and a discussion about future diving are valuable parts of dive planning. Even if you have a new dive buddy for a dive, you should plan your dives together and discuss the experience afterward. Predive discussions with a new buddy take longer than they do with a regular dive partner.

Summary

The saying "If you fail to plan, you plan to fail" is true for scuba divers. All phases of dive planning are important and help ensure enjoyable and successful underwater experiences. Follow the recommended steps of planning, get area orientations when appropriate, have contingency plans, and discuss your dives with your buddy.

8 Diving Opportunities

As a qualified scuba diver, you can do many things. You can learn more, dive in different areas, be recognized for expertise, help others, or earn money, to name just a few. Opportunities abound.

Continuing Education

A good diver never stops learning. You cannot learn everything you need to know about diving during a single course of instruction. After you complete your entry-level course, you can enroll in intermediate or advanced scuba courses. These courses allow you to gain additional experience under supervision, help you develop important skills (such as navigation), and introduce you to special interest areas of diving (see Figure 8.1). When you have identified the diving specialty you would like to pursue, complete a specialty course for that topic. A specialty course helps you begin enjoying the special interest area from the outset and helps you avoid mistakes and injury. Specialty areas of interest to new divers include the following:

> Are there any diving specialties that interest you? Find out if a course on the specialty is held in your area.

- Underwater photography
- Underwater hunting and collecting
- Underwater environment
- Diving rescue techniques
- Night diving
- Boat diving
- Dry suit diving
- Drift diving
- Cavern diving
- Altitude diving

The following specialty courses are of interest to experienced scuba divers with advanced training:

- Wreck diving
- Ice diving
- Cave diving
- Deep diving
- River diving
- Search and recovery

Figure 8.1 Underwater photography is an enjoyable diving activity.

Courses are only one way to learn about diving. You can also attend diving seminars, workshops, and conferences. Check the calendar section of diving publications to learn of events scheduled for your area. Diving changes constantly, so you need to keep updating your knowledge of diving medicine, diving equipment, and diving procedures. Continuing education programs give you the opportunity to learn from professionals who are involved in diving continually.

You can learn more by reading books, magazines, and newspapers about scuba diving. Subscribe to a scuba periodical and read all you can about diving. The appendix contains a listing of scuba periodicals.

If you have a computer and a modem, you can use computer bulletin boards that have sections for scuba divers. The scuba bulletin boards feature libraries, conferences, and topic discussions; they are "living" publications in which you may participate.

Another good way to continue your diving education is to join a dive club. Dive clubs offer many benefits to divers, including education. A talk on an interesting subject usually is part of a local club's monthly meeting.

Continuing your diving education is important for your safety and enjoyment. When you have increased your knowledge about diving, you may become interested in helping others to learn.

Local Opportunities

You do not need to live in a coastal area to dive regularly or to get involved in diving. You can dive nearly anywhere you can find water, and there are dive stores, dive clubs, and diving events in noncoastal areas.

Get involved in diving in your area right away. Seek out all the diving-related businesses and groups in your area—dive clubs, dive stores, dive boats, diving events, and diving publications. Join a dive club, attend the meetings, and participate in club dives. Use the scuba bulletin board of a computer network to make contact with other divers in the area. Complete continuing education courses. Attend local diving seminars, workshops, conferences, and shows, and talk to other divers when you attend diving events. Seize every opportunity to learn and every opportunity to dive with those who are more experienced than you.

Dive Travel

An aspect of diving most divers enjoy is dive travel. Many divers save all year for an annual dive trip to an exotic destination, and there are thousands of beautiful and exciting diving destinations around the world to choose from (see Figure 8.2). If you are a diver, you will probably travel somewhere to dive, so you need to know how to arrange dive travel, how to prepare to travel, and how to enjoy your trip.

Some travel agencies specialize in dive trips. These agencies can provide valuable information, so it is a good idea to book your

Figure 8.2 Scuba diving can take you to some exotic destinations.

> What benefits can a live-aboard dive boat provide that a shore-based trip can't? What advantages does a shore-based trip have?

trip through one of them; these businesses are familiar with your needs.

You might want to consider a dive package that includes accommodations and diving. Dive resorts advertise these packages in diving publications and often offer packages for bargain prices at dive shows. There are many toll-free numbers you can call to obtain information about dive packages. To ensure the best value for your money, compare several packages before you book a trip. If a brochure from a dive resort is out of date, check with the resort for current offers.

When planning a dive trip, you need to decide where you would like to dive and whether you want to dive from a live-aboard dive boat or from a shore-based dive resort. A live-aboard trip allows you to dive in a variety of locations, including remote areas that only a few divers visit. The vessel moves from place to place in the mornings, evenings, and at night. A live-aboard dive trip can be a wonderful experience if diving is the only objective of your trip and you are not affected by motion sickness (see Figure 8.3).

Consider a shore-based dive trip if you do not care for confinement and you want to participate in activities other than diving. Many beautiful islands and resorts offer a great deal to do in addition to diving (see Figure 8.4). Nondiving members of your group or family usually can find many sources of enjoyment at a land-based diving destination.

Many diving magazine articles and diving location publications are available to help you decide where to dive, although choosing from all the fantastic destinations available can be difficult. Recommendations from other divers, trips sponsored by your dive club or dive store, and travel presentations can help you decide.

When you have decided on the region for your dive trip, get as much information as possible about diving in the area. Obtain and review brochures, books, articles, and anything else you can get on the region. Ask around to find out who has been where you

Figure 8.3 Vacationing on a live-aboard boat immerses you in scuba diving.

plan to go, and talk to them. The more you know in advance, the more enjoyable you can make your experience.

After you've selected your diving destination, you should make your reservations well in advance, confirm all financial arrangements in writing, and get clarification regarding cancellations, refunds, and so forth.

Research and plan your dive trip by learning the water temperature for the time of year when you will be diving and obtaining appropriate exposure protection. Remember that too much insulation is better than too little. Also make sure all your equipment is in good working order.

Plan to avoid sunburn. Sunlight in tropical areas is more intense than in other climates. Use a sunscreen and a lip balm with a sunscreen ingredient, and unless you are well tanned, keep yourself covered at all times—even while in the water. You cannot

Figure 8.4 Dive resorts accommodate any need a vacationing diver may have.

develop a tan in a few days, so it is silly to try if you do not have one. A sunburn can ruin an expensive vacation, and it is painful to don an exposure suit when you are burned. It takes only a few minutes for an untanned person to get burned in the tropics. So be careful!

Obtain all required documentation well in advance. Obtaining passports and visas can take months. Be sure to find out if the country you'll be traveling to requires immunizations.

Learn what to expect when you arrive at your destination. Know the frequency and voltage of the electricity, and take converters if you are taking electrical appliances that operate on a different voltage. Know the monetary exchange rate. Consider taking a small pocket calculator to help compute the conversion of money.

If you have an expensive camera, video equipment, or jewelry, take your property to a customs office before you leave the country and have it documented to avoid being charged duty on the items when you return home.

Do not procrastinate in making preparations. Procrastination can cause a cancellation of your trip, a forfeiture of your deposit, and a great deal of frustration.

Limit what you take when you pack for your trip. You do not need much clothing for a dive trip unless you plan to attend formal events. A few sets of shorts and T-shirts, some bathing suits, and a couple of sets of nice clothes for dinner should suffice. Experienced dive travelers travel light when it comes to clothing and personal effects.

Diving destinations provide tanks and weights, so you do not need to take those items with you (see Figure 8.5). There may be weight limitations for your baggage, so keep this in mind when you pack. Excess baggage costs can be very high. To guard against theft, avoid advertising expensive diving, photography, and video equipment. Use inconspicuous containers to ship your equipment, and it will be less likely to disappear. Insure luggage that contains expensive equipment.

Figure 8.5 It's not necessary to transport tanks because most diving destinations provide them.

Be prepared for travel illnesses. It is easier to obtain medications for nausea, diarrhea, and colds before a trip than it is if you become ill in a foreign land.

Flying is the most common transportation method for dive travel (see Figure 8.6). Air travel usually produces jet lag and dehydration. A viral illness a couple of days after reaching your destination is common because many virus germs are concentrated inside the cabins of airliners. Following are some tips and suggestions concerning air travel.

Figure 8.6 You will probably fly to most diving destinations.

First, schedule your flight to arrive the day before you start diving. It is unwise to plan to dive the same day you arrive. Drink a full glass of water every hour during your flight to help you avoid dehydration. Stay away from alcohol, milk, and drinks containing sugar. The humidity in an aircraft is about 8%, so you will become dehydrated unless you drink plenty of fluids. Avoid eating heavy meals and salty foods when flying. Light foods cause less dehydration than fatty foods. Consider ordering a special meal of salad and fruit.

As soon as possible after reaching your destination, get some exercise and drink plenty of liquids. Limit your consumption of alcohol, which causes dehydration. Getting intoxicated at the outset of a diving vacation is one of the worst things you can do because that increases your chances of getting DCS.

Wash your hands frequently when traveling. If you rub your eyes or your nose, germs from your hands can get into your eyes and nose and lead to viral infections.

Baggage compartments on airliners are unpressurized, and the reduced atmospheric pressure can damage your gauges. Either take your gauges inside the airplane in your carry-on luggage or store them in airtight containers.

Confirm your return air reservations as soon as you arrive at your destination, especially if you travel to another country. If you fail to do this, you are likely to lose the reservations. It is frustrat-

For how many days is it
safe to dive repetitively
before you take a break?

ing to arrive at the airport to go home and discover that your tickets are not valid.

Your first dive of the trip should be an orientation dive. In addition to learning about diving in the area, use the dive to check your buoyancy and make any needed adjustments. Work out any equipment problems during a dive in shallow, still, calm water. Avoid deep dives or moving water until you have acclimated to the area.

After 3 days of repetitive diving, refrain from diving for 1 day so your system can outgas. Go shopping or take a land tour for a refreshing change of pace. Allow 1 day between your final scuba dive and your scheduled flight home. The nondiving day before flying helps prevent DCS caused by altitude and gives you the opportunity to rinse, dry, and pack your diving equipment. Snorkeling is a good last-minute activity, and your mask, snorkel, and fins dry quickly for last-minute packing.

Dive travel can be fun, exciting, and memorable when you plan it well. Avoid unpleasant, frustrating, and disappointing experiences by researching your destination and preparing properly. Good diving to you.

Another Opportunity

There is another opportunity for you as a diver, the opportunity to make a positive contribution to the diving community. You can do this by conducting yourself in a responsible manner at all times and encouraging other divers to act responsibly. Help establish a good image of diving, get involved in issues that pertain to the diving environment, and help educate people who do not dive. Whether your contribution is small and personal or vast and international, you can and should make a difference. Decide now that your involvement in the wonderful sport of scuba diving will be positive.

Appendix

Lists and Checklists

Diver-Training Organizations

International Diving Educators Association (IDEA)
Box 17374
Jacksonville, FL 32245

Multinational Diving Educators Association (MDEA)
Box 52433
Marathon Shores, FL 33052

National Association for Cave Diving
Box 14492
Gainesville, FL 32604

National Association of Scuba Diving Schools (NASDS)
Box 17067
Long Beach, CA 90807

National Association of Underwater Instructors (NAUI)
Box 14650
Montclair, CA 91763

National Speleological Society Cave Diving Section
Box 950
Branford, FL 32008-0950

National YMCA Scuba Program
Oakbrook Square
6083-A Oakbrook Parkway
Norcross, GA 30092

Professional Association of Diving Instructors (PADI)
Box 15550
Santa Ana, CA 92705

Professional Diving Instructors Corporation (PDIC)
1015 River Street
Scranton, PA 18505

Scuba Schools International (SSI)
2619 Canton Court
Fort Collins, CO 80525

Environmental Organizations

Center for Marine Conservation
1725 DeSales Street Northwest
Washington, DC 20036

Cousteau Society
930 West 21 Street
Norfolk, VA 23320

CEDAM
Fox Road
Croton-on-Hudson, NY 10520

Greenpeace
Box 3720
Washington, DC 20007

NOAA Sanctuary and Reserves
Ocean and Coastal Resource
  Management
Universal Building Room 714
1825 Connecticut Avenue
  Northwest
Washington, DC 20235

Oceanic Society
1536 16th Street Northwest
Washington, DC 20036

Project Reefkeeper
16345 West Dixie Highway
Suite 1121
Miami, FL 33160

Sea Shepard
Box 7000-S
Redondo Beach, CA 90277

Wildlife Conservation International
Bronx Zoo
New York, NY 10460

Scuba Periodicals

DAN Alert Diver
Box 3823
Duke University Medical
    Center
Durham, NC 27710

Discover Diving Magazine
Box 83727
San Diego, CA 92138

Dive Training Magazine
405 Main Street
Parkville, MO 64152

Diver Magazine
Box 984
Point Roberts, WA 98281-
    9084

Pacific Diver Magazine
Box 6218
Huntington Beach, CA 92615

Rodale's Scuba Diving Maga-
    zine
6600 Abercorn Street #208
Savannah, GA 31405

Scuba Times
Box 6268
Pensacola, FL 32503

Skin Diver Magazine
8490 Sunset Boulevard
Los Angeles, CA 90069

Sources
NAUI
Box 14650
Montclair, CA 91763

Underwater USA
3185 Lackawanna Avenue
Bloomsburg, PA 17815

Responsible Diver Code

A certified scuba diver has many responsibilities. As a responsible diver you should do the following:

- Avoid diving when you are ill, intoxicated, or hung over.
- Avoid diving when you become chilled and are shivering.
- Keep your air spaces equalized.
- Avoid forceful attempts to equalize pressure in your ears.
- Avoid breath-holding when you are breathing compressed air.
- Avoid overexertion while you are in and under the water.
- Drink fluids before and between dives to avoid dehydration.
- Avoid depths that can lead to nitrogen narcosis and DCS.
- Use complete equipment that fits you well.
- Be thoroughly familiar with the equipment you use.
- Inspect your equipment before use.
- Always clean and maintain your equipment as recommended.
- Have your regulator, including the extra second stage, serviced annually.
- Have your scuba tank visually inspected annually and hydrostatically tested every 5 years.
- Wear appropriate exposure protection for the water temperature.
- Use visual correction if your eyesight is poor.
- Inspect your equipment before and after donning it for use.
- Use a dive flag. Surface within 100 ft (30 m) of the flag and accept the danger of boats if you do not surface close to your flag.
- Weight yourself correctly. Avoid overweighting.
- Descend feet-first in a controlled manner.
- Maintain neutral buoyancy underwater.
- Always dive with a buddy and maintain buddy contact.
- Monitor your instruments. Be aware of time, depth, location, and air supply.
- Prevent, recognize, and be able to deal with typical problems that may occur while diving.
- Be trained and prepared for emergency situations.
- Ascend properly. Look up and around. Have one arm above your head. Do precautionary decompression at the end of every dive.
- Keep your skills current. Complete refresher scuba training following 6 months or more of inactivity.
- Continue to learn about the environment.
- Accept the risk of injury from aquatic animals when you enter the underwater environment.
- Learn to recognize and avoid potentially hazardous aquatic animals.
- Refrain from feeding or touching aquatic animals.
- Do everything possible to preserve the diving environment.
- Do everything possible to educate others and help them learn to preserve the aquatic environment.

ONLY FOOLS STRETCH THE RULES

- Minimize your impact on the environment.
- Abide by fish and game regulations. If you take game, do so in a responsible manner.
- Obtain an environmental orientation when diving in a new area.
- Complete specialty training before diving in specialized environments, such as caverns, caves, and wrecks.
- Refrain from diving when diving conditions are hazardous.
- Plan your dives to avoid swimming against a current at the surface.
- Be physically and mentally fit to dive.
- Delay diving for a day after flying, and delay flying for a day after diving.
- Determine the weather and water conditions in advance of a dive.
- Obey laws and regulations. Conduct yourself in a responsible manner.
- Determine the why, who, where, when, how, and what of a dive.
- Leave your dive plans with someone who can contact the authorities if you do not return by a certain time.
- Abort a dive if the conditions are unfavorable.
- Plan the dive with your buddy and agree on the plan.
- Plan for emergencies.
- Plan your dive profile to minimize the risk of DCS.
- Schedule your diving activities to avoid an accumulation of nitrogen that could cause DCS.
- Use all dive-planning devices conservatively.
- Plan for contingencies.

Diving Equipment Checklist

_____ Mask, snorkel, and snorkel keeper

_____ Fins and boots

_____ Scuba tank (filled)

_____ Buoyancy compensator

_____ Exposure suit, hood, and gloves

_____ Weight system

_____ Regulator with pressure gauge

_____ Alternate air source

_____ Instruments to monitor depth, time, and direction

_____ Signaling devices (whistle, mirror, safety tube)

_____ Dive knife

_____ Float, dive flag, and anchor

_____ Dive tables

_____ Dive light

_____ Slate and pencil

_____ Marker buoy

_____ Collecting bag

_____ Gear bag

_____ Spare equipment

    _____ Scuba tank(s)

    _____ Weights

    _____ Straps

    _____ O-rings

    _____ Snorkel keeper

_____ Secondary equipment

    _____ First aid kit

    _____ Emergency phone numbers and radio frequencies

    _____ Log book

    _____ Swimsuit

    _____ Towel

    _____ Jacket

    _____ Hat or visor

    _____ Sunglasses

    _____ Dive kit

    _____ Save-a-dive kit

    _____ Drinking water

Bibliography

Auerbach, P. (1987). *A medical guide to hazardous marine life*. Jacksonville, FL: Progressive Printing.

Barnhart, R., & Steinmetz, S. (1986). *Dictionary of science*. Maplewood, NJ: Hammond.

Bascom, W. (1964). *Waves and beaches*. Garden City, NY: Anchor Books.

Bove, A., & Davis, J. (1990). *Diving medicine*. Philadelphia: W.B. Saunders.

Divers Alert Network. (1989). *Medical requirements for scuba divers*. Durham, NC: Author.

Edmonds, C., Lowry, C., & Pennefather, J. (1981). *Diving and subaquatic medicine*. Mosman, NSW, Australia: Diving Medical Centre.

Foley, B. (1989). *Physical exam form for scuba divers*. Denver: Recreational Scuba Training Council.

Freeman, I. (1990). *Physics made simple*. New York: Doubleday.

Groves, D., & Hunt, L. (1980). *Ocean world encyclopedia*. McGraw.

Lambert, D., & McConnel, A. (1985). *Seas and oceans*.

Lee, P., Lidov, M., & Tyberg, T. (1986). *The sourcebook of medical science*. New York: Torstar.

Lehrman, R. (1990). *Physics the easy way*. Hauppauge, NY: Barron's Educational Series.

Lippmann, J. (1992). *The essentials of deeper sport diving*. Locust Valley, NY: Aqua Quest.

Maloney, E. (1983). *Chapman piloting seamanship & small boat handling*. New York: Hearst Marine Books.

Miller, J. (Ed.) (1979). *NOAA diving manual* (2nd Ed.). Washington, DC: U.S. Government Printing Office, U.S. Department of Commerce.

National Association of Underwater Instructors (NAUI). (1991). *Advanced diving technology and techniques*. Montclair, CA: Author.

Professional Association of Diving Instructors (PADI). (1988). *The encyclopedia of recreational diving*. Santa Ana, CA: Author.

Sebel, P., Stoddart, D., Waldhorn, R., Waldmann, C., & Whitfield, P. (1985). *Respiration: The breath of life*. New York: Torstar.

Skin Diver. Various equipment articles from 1991 and 1992 issues. Los Angeles: Peterson.

Taylor, E. (Ed.) (1985). *Dorland's illustrated medical dictionary*. Philadelphia: W.B. Saunders.

Whitfield, P., & Stoddart, D. (1984). *Hearing, taste and smell: Pathways of perception*. New York: Torstar.

Index

Page numbers in *italics* refer to figures and tables.

DIVE PLANNING JUST GOT EASIER

HUMAN KINETICS PUBLISHERS

Box 5076, Champaign, IL 61825-5076
1-800-747-4457

ABBREVIATIONS
ADT–Actual Dive Time
MDT–Maximum Dive Time
EDT–Equivalent Dive Time
SIT–Surface Interval Time
AMDT–Adjusted Maximum Dive Time
RNT–Residual Nitrogen Time

WARNING:
NO DIVE TABLE CAN GUARANTEE AVOIDANCE OF DECOMPRESSION SICKNESS. USE THE TABLES CONSERVATIVELY.

© 1993 Dennis K. Graver
ISBN 0-87322-532-5

HKP Dive Tables
1993 • Plastic • 4" x 5-3/4" • Item MGRA0532
ISBN 0-87322-532-5 • $5.95 ($8.95 Canadian)

Special discount terms are available for bulk purchases. Contact the special sales manager for details.

See page 175 for actual size of tables.

The HKP Dive Tables card makes dive planning easy!

This handy card features bigger numbers than other tables and brighter colors to make dive planning calculations a breeze. Vital dive planning information has been separated into four easy-to-use tables for maximum dive time, surface interval time, adjusted maximum dive time, and residual nitrogen time.

Plus, the HKP Dive Tables card measures only 4" x 5-3/4"—the perfect size to fit into the pocket of your buoyancy compensator!

Other features:
- Easy-to-understand instructions printed on the tables
- Special UV coating to keep colors from fading quickly in the sun
- Strong, durable plastic that withstands exposure in the diving environment and is scratch-resistant
- Current time limits to reduce the likelihood of decompression sickness
- U.S. and metric units

Table 4—RNT Table

Ft	M	A	B	C	D	E
30	9	12	25	39	54	70
40	12	7	17	25	37	49
50	15	6	13	21	29	38
60	18	5	11	17	24	30
70	21	4	9	15	20	26
80	24	4	8	13	18	23
90	27	3	7	11	16	20
100	30	3	7	10	14	18
110	33	3	6	10	13	16
120	36	3	6	9	12	15
130	39	3	6	8	11	13

M	9	12	15	18	21	24
Ft	30	40	50	60	70	80

Table 3—A

21						
60	14					
90	29	4				
120	43	14				
141	57	24	6	3	3	
162	69	33	14	9	7	
180	81	42	20	14	12	
196	93	51	26	20	17	
211	105	59	33	25	22	
225	113	67	39	31	27	
238	123	74	45	36	31	

Front

HKP Dive Table Instructions
1. Begin first dive at Table 1. Use exact or next greater number for all depths and times. Find end-of-dive letter group at bottom of Table 1.
2. Find end-of-surface-interval letter group at left of Table 2. Use exact or next greater time. Use the letter group to refer to Tables 3 and 4.
3. Actual dive time of a repetitive dive must not exceed the times indicated by Table 3 coordinates.
4. Add residual nitrogen time (RNT) from Table 4 coordinates to actual dive time (ADT) to obtain equivalent dive time (EDT). ADT + RNT = EDT.
5. Use EDT to return to Table 1.

Table 1—MDT and EDT Table

Ft	M	Time (minute)											
30	9	15	30	45	60	75	95	120	145	170	205	250	310/5
40	12	5	15	25	30	40	50	70	80	100	110	130	150/5
50	15	→	10	15	25	30	40	50	60	70	80		100/5
60	18		10	15	20	25	30	40	50		60/5		80/7
70	21		5	10	15	20	30	35	40		50/5	60/8	70/14
80	24		5	10	15	20	25	30	35	40/5		50/10	60/17
90	27	→	5	10	12	15	20	25	30/5		40/7		50/18
100	30		5	7	10	15	20		25/5			40/15	
110	33	→		5	10	13	15	20/5			30/7		
120	36			5	10	12	15/5			25/6	30/14		
130	39	→		5	8	10/5				25/10			

Table 2—SIT Table

		A	B	C	D	E	F	G	H	I	J	K	L
←	L												0:26
	K											0:28	0:45
←	J										0:31	0:49	1:04
	I									0:33	0:54	1:11	1:25
←	H								0:36	0:59	1:19	1:35	1:49
	G							0:40	1:06	1:29	1:47	2:03	2:19
←	F						0:45	1:15	1:41	2:02	2:20	2:38	2:53
	E					0:54	1:29	1:59	2:23	2:44	3:04	3:21	3:36
←	D				1:09	1:57	2:28	2:58	3:20	3:43	4:02	4:19	4:35
	C			1:39	2:38	3:24	3:57	4:25	4:49	5:12	5:40	5:48	6:02
←	B		3:20	4:48	5:48	6:34	7:05	7:35	7:59	8:21	8:50	8:58	9:12
	A	12:00	12:00	12:00	12:00	12:00	12:00	12:00	12:00	12:00	12:00	12:00	12:00

Back

Prices subject to change.

To request more information or to place your order, U.S. customers call **TOLL FREE 1-800-747-4457**. Customers outside the U.S. place your order using the appropriate telephone number/address shown in the front of this book.

Human Kinetics
The Premier Publisher for Sports & Fitness
http://www.humankinetics.com/